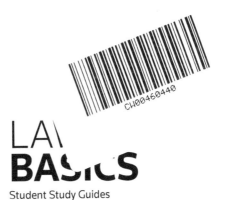

LAW BASICS

Student Study Guides

PROPERTY

THIRD EDITION

LAW
BASICS
Student Study Guides

PROPERTY

THIRD EDITION

By

Daniel J. Carr, LL.B. (Hons), M.Sc., Ph.D.
Lecturer in Private Law, University of Edinburgh

W. GREEN

THOMSON REUTERS

First edition written by David Brand and published 2009

Second edition written by Daniel J. Carr and published 2014

Third edition written by Daniel J. Carr and published 2018

Published in 2018 by Thomson Reuters,
trading as W. Green, 21 Alva Street, Edinburgh EH2 4PS.
Thomson Reuters is registered in England & Wales,
Company No.1679046.
Registered office and address for service:
5 Canada Square, Canary Wharf, London, E14 5AQ.
For further information on our products and services, visit
http://www.sweetandmaxwell.co.uk/wgreen

Computerset by W. Green
Printed and bound by CPI Group (UK) Ltd, Croydon, CR0 4YY

No natural forests were destroyed to make this product;
Only farmed timber was used and replanted

A CIP catalogue record for this book is available from the
British Library

ISBN 978-0-414-06510-9

Orders by email to: trluki.orders@thomsonreuters.com
General enquiries should be directed to wgreen.enquiries@thomson.com

Thomson Reuters, the Thomson Reuters Logo and W. GREEN are
trademarks of Thomson Reuters.

CONTENTS

Page

Table of Cases .... *vii*

1. Introduction: Context and Concepts 1
2. Ownership and Possession 11
3. Original Acquisition 25
4. Derivative Acquisition 37
5. Real Burdens 63
6. Servitudes 79
7. Leases 89
8. Tenements 107
9. Land Ownership 117

Bibliography and Further Reading *135*
Index *137*

TABLE OF CASES

Page

@SIPP Pension Trustees v Insight Travel Services Ltd [2015] CSIH 91; 2016 S.C. 243; 2016 S.L.T. 131 ....7.19

Aberdeen City Council v Wanchoo [2008] CSIH 6; 2008 S.C. 278; 2008 S.L.T. 106 ......6.12

Aberdeen Varieties Ltd v James F Donald (Aberdeen Cinemas) Ltd, 1940 S.C. (H.L.) 52; 1940 S.L.T. 374 HL 5.12, 5.16

Advice Centre for Mortgages Ltd v McNicoll, 2006 S.L.T. 591; 2006 S.C.L.R. 602 OH....7.18

Alvis v Harrison, 1991 S.L.T. 64; (1991) 62 P. & C.R. 10 HL 6.15

AMA (New Town) Ltd v Law [2013] CSIH 61; 2013 S.C. 608; 2013 S.L.T. 959 ....4.23

Anderson v Brattisanni's, 1978 S.L.T. (Notes) 42 IH (1 Div) 9.06, 9.08

Andert Ltd v J&J Johnson, 1987 S.L.T. 268 OH 7.03

Angus v National Coal Board, 1955 S.C. 175; 1955 S.L.T. 245 IH (2 Div) 9.02

Archivent Sales & Developments Ltd v Strathclyde RC, 1985 S.L.T. 154; 27 B.L.R. 98 OH 4.14

Arthur v Aird, 1907 S.C. 1170; (1907) 15 S.L.T. 209 IH (2 Div) 9.29, 9.34

ASA International Ltd v Kashmiri Properties (Ireland) Ltd [2016] CSIH 70; 2017 S.C. 107; 2016 G.W.D. 27-493 IH 6.09, 6.10

Aviemore Highland Resort Ltd v Cairngorms National Park Authority, 2009 S.L.T. (Sh Ct) 97; 2009 G.W.D. 24-388 ....9.22

Aviva Investors Pensions Ltd v McDonald's Restaurants Ltd, 2014 G.W.D. 7-146 OH 7.38

AWG Business Centres Ltd v Regus Caledonia Ltd [2017] CSIH 22; 2017 G.W.D. 9-131 IH (1 Div) 7.19

Bailey's Executors v Upper Crathes Fishing Ltd, 1987 S.L.T. 405 OH 2.25

Bain v Brand (1875-76) L.R. 1 App. Cas. 762; (1876) 3 R. (H.L.) 16 HL 3.15

Bain v Morrison (1871) 8 S.L.R. 539 ....6.13

Barker v Lewis, 2008 S.L.T. (Sh Ct) 17; 2008 G.W.D. 9-167 Sh Pr 5.19

Barkley v Scott (1893) 1 S.L.T. 191; (1894) 10 Sh. Ct. Rep. 23 ....2.22

Baron of Bachuil v Paine [2012] CSOH 161; 2012 G.W.D. 35-707 ....6.12

Bernstein, Lord v Skyviews and General Ltd [1978] Q.B. 479; [1977] 3 W.L.R. 136; [1977] 2 All E.R. 902 QBD 2.08, 2.09

Beveridge v Marshall, November 18, 1808 FC 6.17

Black Loch Angling Club v Tarmac Ltd, 2012 S.C.L.R. 501 ....9.38

Boatland Properties v Abdul, 2014 S.C.L.R. 792 ....8.07

Bocardo SA v Star Energy UK Onshore Ltd [2010] UKSC 35; [2011] 1 A.C. 380; [2010] 3 W.L.R. 654 ....2.09

Boskabelle Ltd v Laird [2006] CSOH 173; 2006 S.L.T. 1079; 2006 G.W.D. 36-734 ....3.25

Botanic Gardens Picture House Ltd v Adamson, 1924 S.C. 549; 1924 S.L.T. 418 IH (1 Div) 5.16

Bradford Corp v Pickles [1895] A.C. 587 HL 9.37

Brand's Trustees v Brand's Trustees. See Bain v Brand

Brown v Baty, 1957 S.C. 351; 1957 S.L.T. 336 OH 9.06

Brown v Lee Constructions Ltd, 1977 S.L.T. (Notes) 61 OH 2.08

Burnett's Trustee v Grainger [2004] UKHL 8; 2004 S.C. (H.L.) 19; 2004 S.L.T. 513 ....4.34

Caledonian Railway Co v Turcan [1898] A.C. 256; (1898) 25 R. (H.L.) 7 HL 9.17

Caledonian Railway Co v Walmsley, 1907 S.C. 1047; (1907) 15 S.L.T. 119 IH (2 Div) 9.09

Campbell v Muir, 1908 S.C. 387; (1908) 15 S.L.T. 737 IH (1 Div) 9.37

Canmore Housing Association Ltd v Bairnsfather (t/a BR Autos), 2004 S.L.T. 673; 2005 S.C.L.R. 185; 2004 G.W.D. 16-352 OH 9.37

Cantors Properties (Scotland) Ltd v Swears & Wells Ltd, 1978 S.C. 310; 1980 S.L.T. 165 IH (1 Div) 7.25

Carmichael v Simpson, 1932 S.L.T. (Sh Ct) 16 ....2.21

Cayzer v Hamilton (No.2), 1996 S.L.T. (Lands Tr) 21 Land Ct 7.20

Central RC v Ferns, 1979 S.C. 136; 1980 S.L.T. 126 OH 6.14

Ceres School Board v Macfarlane (1895) 23 R. 279; (1895) 3 S.L.T. 198 IH (1 Div) 4.34

Chalmers Property Investment Co Ltd v Robson. See Robson v Chalmers Property Investment Co Ltd

Chalmers v Diageo Scotland Ltd [2017] CSOH 36; [2017] L.L.R. 256; 2017 G.W.D. 9-126 ....9.38

Chevron Petroleum (UK) Ltd v Post Office, 1986 S.C. 291; 1987 S.L.T. 588 OH 7.20
Chief Constable of Strathclyde v Sharp, 2002 S.L.T. (Sh Ct) 95; 2002 G.W.D. 11-340
    Sh Pr...4.14
Christie v Smith, 1949 S.C. 572; 1950 S.L.T. 31; 1949 S.L.T. (Notes) 51 IH (2 Div)......3.21
Cinema Bingo Club v Ward, 1976 S.L.T. (Sh Ct) 90...7.42
Clarke v Grantham, 2009 G.W.D. 38-645 Lands Tr 5.19
Clydesdale Bank Plc v Davidson, 1998 S.C. (H.L.) 51; 1998 S.L.T. 522 HL 7.04
Cochrane v Ewart (1861) 4 Macq. 117 ....6.10
Cochrane v Stevenson (1891) 18 R. 1208 IH (1 Div)..3.21
Commercial Union Assurance Co Ltd v Watt & Cumine (A Firm), 1964 S.C. 84; 1964
    S.L.T. 62 IH (1 Div)..7.42
Compugraphics International Ltd v Nikolic [2011] CSIH 34; 2011 S.C. 744; 2011 S.L.T.
    955 ....6.06
Cook v Cadman, 2014 S.L.T. (Lands Tr) 13; 2014 G.W.D. 3-66 Lands Tr 5.36
Co-operative Insurance Society Ltd v Halfords Ltd (No.1), 1998 S.L.T. 90; 1997 S.C.L.R.
    719; 1997 G.W.D. 17-798 OH 7.21
Co-operative Wholesale Society v Ushers Brewery, 1975 S.L.T. (Lands Tr.) 9 Lands Tr 5.12
Cope v X, 2013 S.L.T. (Lands Tr) 20; 2013 G.W.D. 3-100 ....6.18
Coventry (t/a RDC Promotions) v Lawrence [2014] UKSC 13; [2014] 2 W.L.R. 433;
    [2014] 2 All E.R. 622...9.38
Creelman v Argyll and Bute Council, 2009 S.L.T. (Sh Ct) 165; 2009 G.W.D. 34-583 .....9.19
Crown Estate Commissioners v Fairlie Yacht Slip Ltd, 1979 S.C. 156 IH (1 Div)......9.27, 9.29
Crown Estate Commissioners, Petitioners [2010] CSOH 70; 2010 S.L.T. 741; 2011
    S.C.L.R. 1 ....9.27
Cunningham v Cameron [2013] CSOH 193; 2014 G.W.D. 3-69..9.38
Deans v Woolfson, 1922 S.C. 221; 1922 S.L.T. 165 IH (2 Div)..2.22
Dicksons & Laings v The Burgh of Hawick and the Provost, Magistrates, and Town-
    Council thereof (1885) 13 R. 163 IH (2 Div) 2.07
Drury v McGarvie, 1993 S.C. 95; 1993 S.L.T. 987 IH (1 Div) 6.17
Duke of Buccleuch v Magistrates of Edinburgh (1865) 3 M. 528 ....9.07
Dunlea v Cashwell [2017] SAC (Civ) 12; 2017 S.C.L.R. 675; 2017 G.W.D. 13-207.......6.13
Dunlop v Robertson (1803) Hume 515 ....9.04
Earl Zetland v Hislop (1882) 7 App. Cas. 427; (1882) 9 R. (H.L.) 40 HL 5.13
EDI Central Ltd v National Car Parks Ltd [2010] CSOH 141; 2011 S.L.T. 75; 2010 G.W.D.
    37-754..7.32
Fadallah v Pollak [2013] EWHC 3159 (QB) 4.14
Ferguson v Gunby, 2015 S.L.T. (Lands Tr) 200; 2015 G.W.D. 15-265 Lands Tr.............5.19
Fergusson v Campbell, 1913 S.L.T. 241 OH...6.11
Fleeman v Lyon, 2009 G.W.D. 32-539 Lands Tr...5.35
Forbes v Fife Council, 2009 S.L.T. (Sh Ct) 71; 2009 G.W.D. 22-361 ....9.19
Forbes v Livingston (1827) 6 S. 167, IH (1 Div) 2.07
Franklin v Lawson, 2013 S.L.T. (Lands Tr) 81; 2013 G.W.D. 21-414 Lands Tr......5.19, 5.24
Fraser v Cox, 1938 S.C. 506; 1938 S.L.T. 374 IH (1 Div)..6.10
Fry's Metals Ltd v Durastic Ltd, 1991 S.L.T. 689 OH 7.25
Garson v McLeish, 2010 S.L.T. (Sh Ct) 131; 2010 G.W.D. 5-88 ....6.15
Garvie v Wallace, 2013 G.W.D. 38-734...8.07
Geoffrey (Tailor) Highland Crafts Ltd v GL Attractions Ltd, 2010 G.W.D. 8-142 ....7.19
Giblin v Murdoch, 1979 S.L.T. (Sh Ct) 5...5.12
Gilfin Property Holdings Ltd v Beech, 2013 S.L.T. (Lands Tr) 17; 2013 G.W.D. 14-301
    Lands Tr...8.07
Girl's School Co Ltd v Buchanan, 1958 S.L.T. (Notes) 2 IH (2 Div) 5.26
Glebe Sugar Refining Co v Paterson (1902) 2 F. 615...7.23
Gloag v Perth and Kinross Council, 2007 S.C.L.R. 530...9.19
Golden Sea Produce Ltd v Scottish Nuclear Plc, 1992 S.L.T. 942 OH 7.20
Grant v George Heriot's Trust (1906) 8 F. 647; (1905) 13 S.L.T.986 IH (1 Div) 5.13
Gray v Edinburgh University, 1962 S.C. 157; 1962 S.L.T. 173 IH (2 Div)...........................7.06
Gray v MacNeil's Executor [2017] SAC (Civ) 9; 2017 S.L.T. (Sh Ct) 83; 2017 S.C.L.R.
    666 ....7.02
Greenbelt Property Ltd v Riggens, 2010 G.W.D. 28-586 Lands Tr...5.29
Greig v Middleton, 2009 G.W.D. 22-365..6.12

Gunn v National Coal Board, 1982 S.L.T. 526 OH 7.25
Gyle Shopping Centre General Partners Ltd v Marks and Spencer Plc [2014] CSOH 59;
   2014 G.W.D. 18-352..7.17
Halkerston v Wedderburn (1781) Mor. 10495 ....9.06
Harris v Abbey National Plc, 1997 S.C.L.R. 359; 1996 Hous. L.R. 100..........................2.30
Harton Homes Ltd v Durk, 2012 S.C.L.R. 554; 2012 G.W.D. 25-528..............................6.10
Hay's Trustees v Young (1877) 4 R. 398...9.11
Hayman & Son v McLintock; sub nom. Hayman & Son v M'lintock & Others, 1907 S.C.
   936; (1907) 15 S.L.T. 63 IH (1 Div)..4.12
Highland & Universal Properties Ltd v Safeway Properties Ltd (No.2), 2000 S.C. 297;
   2000 S.L.T. 414; [2000] 3 E.G.L.R. 110 IH (1 Div)...7.27
Hill of Rubislaw (Q Seven) Ltd v Rubislaw Quarry Aberdeen Ltd [2013] CSOH 131;
   2013 G.W.D. 27-545..5.11
Hill of Rubislaw (Q Seven) Ltd v Rubislaw Quarry Aberdeen Ltd [2014] CSIH 105;
   2015 S.C. 339; 2014 G.W.D. 40-723...5.11, 5.12
Hill v McLaren (1879) 6 R. 1363 IH (2 Div)..6.15
Hogg v Armstrong and Mowat (1874) 1 Guth. Sh Cas. 438..2.30
Holms v Ashford Estates Ltd [2009] CSIH 28; 2009 S.L.T. 389; 2009 S.C.L.R. 428......6.05
Howie v Kirkcudbright CC, 1963 S.L.T. (Sh Ct) 60; (1963) 79 Sh Ct. Rep. 204.............6.07
Huber v Ross, 1912 S.C. 898; 1912 1 S.L.T. 399 IH (1 Div) 7.20
Humphreys v Crabbe [2016] CSIH 82; 2017 S.C.L.R. 699; 2016 G.W.D. 35-634......8.02, 8.06
Hunter v Tindale, 2012 S.L.T. (Sh Ct) 2; 2011 G.W.D. 25-570 Sh Pr 8.06
Inglis v Paul (1829) 7 S. 469 IH (1 Div)...7.38
Inglis v Robertson; sub nom. Irvine v Inglis; Irvine & Robertson v Baxter & Inglis [1898]
   A.C. 616; (1898) 6 S.L.T. 130; (1898) 25 R. (HL) 70 HL 4.1
International Banking Corp v Ferguson Shaw & Sons, 1910 S.C. 182; 1909 2 S.L.T. 377
   IH (2 Div)...3.30
Inverclyde Council v McCloskey (t/a Prince of Wales Bar), 2015 S.L.T. (Sh Ct) 57; 2015
   Hous. L.R. 14; 2015 G.W.D. 6-126 ....7.30
Inveresk Plc v Tullis Russell Papermakers Ltd [2010] UKSC 19; 2010 S.C. (U.K.S.C.) 106;
   2010 S.L.T. 941..7.32
Irvine Knitters Ltd v North Ayrshire Co-operative Society Ltd, 1978 S.C. 109; 1978 S.L.T.
   105 IH (1 Div)..6.15
JA Pye (Oxford) Ltd v Graham [2002] UKHL 30; [2003] 1 A.C. 419; [2002] 3 W.L.R.
   221..2.30
Johnson, Thomas and Thomas (A Firm) v Smith 2016 G.W.D. 25-456 ....6.05, 6.06
Joint Liquidators of the Scottish Coal Co Ltd, Noters [2013] CSIH 108; 2014 S.L.T. 259;
   2014 G.W.D. 248 ....3.06
Jones v Gray [2011] CSOH 204; 2012 G.W.D. 2-18 ....6.12
Kennedy v Glenbelle Ltd, 1996 S.C. 95; 1996 S.L.T. 1186; 1996 S.C.L.R. 411 IH
   (1 Div) 9.38
Kettlewell v Turning Point Scotland, 2011 S.L.T. (Sh Ct) 143; 2011 G.W.D. 26-582 ......5.19
Kildrummy (Jersey) Ltd v IRC [1990] S.T.C. 657; 1991 S.C. 1 IH (I Div) 7.04
King v Advocate General for Scotland [2009] CSOH 169; 2010 G.W.D. 1-15.................9.38
Kodak Processing Companies Ltd v Shoredale Ltd [2009] CSIH 71; 2010 S.C. 113; 2009
   S.L.T. 1151..7.30
L Batley Pet Products Ltd v North Lanarkshire Council [2014] UKSC 27; [2014] 3 All E.R.
   64; [2014] Bus. L.R. 615 SC 7.19
Leonard v Lindsay & Benzie (1886) 13 R. 958 IH (2 Div) 9.06
Lewis v Hunter, 2017 G.W.D. 19-308, LC..7.31
Little Cumbrae Estate Ltd v Island of Little Cumbrae Ltd [2007] CSIH 35; 2007 S.C. 525;
   2007 S.L.T. 631..7.25
Loch Lomond and Trossachs National Park Authority v Anstalt [2017] SAC (Civ) 11; 2017
   S.L.T. (Sh Ct) 138; 2017 G.W.D. 13-206 ....9.20, 9.22
Lord Advocate v Aberdeen University, 1963 S.C. 533; 1963 S.L.T. 361 IH (2 Div) 3.07
Lord Advocate v Glengarnock Iron & Steel Co Ltd, 1909 1 S.L.T. 15 IH (2 Div)............9.11
Lord Advocate v Young (1887) L.R. 12 App. Cas. 544; (1887) 14 R. (H.L.) 53 HL 2.29
Lousada & Co Ltd v JE Lesser (Properties) Ltd, 1990 S.C. 178; 1990 S.L.T. 823
   IH (2 Div)..7.38
Mack v Glasgow City Council [2006] CSIH 18; 2006 S.C. 543; 2006 S.L.T. 5 ....7.25

Mackay v Bain, 2013 S.L.T. (Lands Tr) 37; 2013 G.W.D. 15-319 ....6.18
Mackenzie v MacLean (George Malcolm), 1981 S.L.T. (Sh Ct) 40 ....3.06
Macneil v Bradonwood Ltd, 2013 S.L.T. (Lands Tr) 41; 2013 G.W.D. 18-372
    Lands Tr 5.36
Mactaggart & Co v Harrower (1906) 8 F. 1101; (1906) 14 S.L.T. 277 IH (2 Div)............5.32
Mann v Houston, 1957 S.L.T. 89 IH (1 Div) 7.07
Maris v Banchory Squash Racquets Club Ltd [2007] CSIH 30; 2007 S.C. 501; 2007
    S.L.T. 447...7.31
Mars Pension Trustees Ltd v County Properties & Developments Ltd, 1999 S.C. 267;
    2000 S.L.T. 581; 1999 S.C.L.R. 117 IH (Ex Div) 7.19
McAdam v Urquhart, 2005 1 J.C. 28; 2004 S.L.T. 790; 2004 S.C.C.R. 506 HCJ............9.09
McDonald v Provan (Of Scotland Street) Ltd, 1960 S.L.T. 231 OH 3.29
McLellan v J & D Pierce (Contracts) Ltd [2015] CSIH 80; 2015 G.W.D. 37-594............9.08
McManus v City Link Development Co Ltd [2015] CSOH 178; [2016] Env. L.R. D1;
    2016 G.W.D. 6-126...7.23, 7.24, 7.25
Mearns v Glasgow City Council, 2002 S.L.T. (Sh Ct) 49; 2001 Hous. L.R. 130; 2001
    G.W.D. 28-1140 Sh Pr 7.24
Mechan v Watson, 1907 S.C. 25; (1906) 14 S.L.T. 397 IH (1 Div)................................7.24
Mendelssohn v The Wee Pub Co Ltd, 1991 G.W.D. 26-1518..6.06
Millar v McRobbie, 1949 S.C. 1; 1949 S.L.T. 2; 1948 S.L.T. (Notes) 82 IH (1 Div) 7.13
Miln v Mudie (1828) 6 S. 967 IH (2 Div)..9.06
Moncrieff v Jamieson [2007] UKHL 42; [2007] 1 W.L.R. 2620;
    [2008] 4 All E.R.752..6.06, 6.10
Moor Row Ltd v DWF LLP [2017] CSOH 63; 2017 G.W.D. 14-213 ....7.27, 7.28
More v Boyle, 1967 S.L.T. (Sh Ct) 38 ....9.37
Morris v Bicket (1864) 2 M. 1082 IH (2 Div) 9.29
Munro v Finlayson, 2015 S.L.T. (Sh Ct) 123; 2015 G.W.D. 9-167 ....9.08
Murray v Medley, 1973 S.L.T. (Sh Ct) 75...6.11
Neill v Scobbie, 1993 G.W.D. 13-887 ....6.06
Neilson v Mossend Iron Co (1886) L.R. 11 App. Cas. 298; (1886) 13 R. (H.L.)
    50 HL 7.42
O'Donnell v McDonald [2007] CSIH 74; 2008 S.C. 189; 2007 S.L.T. 1227..................7.42
Optical Express (Gyle) Ltd v Marks & Spencer Plc, 2000 S.L.T. 644; 2000 G.W.D. 7-264
    OH..7.17
Parker v British Airways Board [1982] Q.B. 1004; [1982] 2 W.L.R. 503 CA (Civ Div)......2.30
Paterson v McPherson (1916) 33 Sh Ct. Rep. 237 ....9.11
Patrick v Napier (1867) 5 M. 683 IH (1 Div)...6.04
Patterson v Drouet, 2013 G.W.D. 3-99 Lands Tr 8.07
Peires v Bickerton's Aerodromes Ltd [2017] EWCA Civ 273; [2017] 1 W.L.R. 2865;[2017]
    2 Lloyd's Rep. 330 CA (Civ Div) 2.08
Phillips v Lavery, 1962 S.L.T. (Sh Ct) 57; (1962) 78 Sh Ct. Rep. 52......................5.12
Pollacchi v Campbell, 2014 S.L.T. (Lands Tr) 55; 2014 G.W.D. 15-275 ....6.18
Pollock v Drogo Developments Ltd [2017] CSOH 64; 2017 G.W.D. 14-221 ....6.15
Prangnell-O'Neill v Lady Skiffington, 1984 S.L.T. 282 IH (2 Div)................................4.14
Procurator Fiscal, Peterhead v Elrick (Lyn) 2017 S.L.T. (Sh Ct) 157; 2017 S.C.L. 1072......2.24
Procurator Fiscal, Peterhead v Elrick (Lyn) 2017 S.L.T. (Sh Ct) 67; 2017 G.W.D. 12-179....2.24
PS Properties (2) Ltd v Callaway Homes Ltd [2007] CSOH 162....................................8.07
Rafique v Amin, 1997 S.L.T. 1385; 1997 G.W.D. 3-118 IH (2 Div) 2.22, 8.03
Randifuird v Crombie (1623) Mor. 15256 ....7.20
Rattray v Tayport Patent Slip Co (1868) 5 S.L.R. 219..6.13, 6.16
Redfearn v Somervail (1830) 1 Dow 50 ....4.20
Renfrew DC v AB Leisure (Renfrew) Ltd, 1988 S.L.T. 635; 1988 S.C.L.R. 512 IH
    (2 Div) 7.38
Renfrew DC v Gray, 1987 S.L.T. (Sh Ct) 70 Sh Pr...7.32
RHM Bakeries (Scotland) Ltd v Strathclyde RC, 1985 S.C. (H.L.) 17;
    1985 S.L.T. 214 HL..9.38
Robson v Chalmers Property Investment Co Ltd, 2008 S.L.T. 1069 HL 6.14
Rodger (Builders) Ltd v Fawdry, 1950 S.C. 483; 1950 S.L.T. 345 IH (2 Div)................4.09
Romano v Standard Commercial Property Securities Ltd [2008] CSOH 105; 2008 S.L.T.
    859; 2008 G.W.D. 26-419..6.06

Russel Properties (Europe) Ltd v Dundas Heritable Ltd [2012] CSOH 175; 2012 G.W.D.
  38-749 ....5.24
Scotmore Developments Ltd v Anderton, 1996 S.C. 368; 1996 S.L.T. 1304 IH (2 Div) 7.38
Scott v Muir, 2012 S.L.T. (Sh Ct) 179; 2012 Hous. L.R. 20; 2012 G.W.D. 5-94 ....7.30
Scottish Environment Protection Agency v Joint Liquidators of the Scottish Coal Co Ltd.
  See Joint Liquidators of the Scottish Coal Co Ltd, Noters
Scottish Ministers v Trustees of the Drummond Trust, 2001 S.L.T. 665; 2001 S.C.L.R. 495;
  2001 G.W.D. 12-444 OH 7.38
Scottish Parliamentary Corporate Body v Sovereign Indigenous Peoples of Scotland [2016]
  CSOH 65; 2016 S.L.T. 761; 2016 Hous. L.R. 48 ....9.09
Scottish Widows Fund v Buist (1876) 3 R. 1078 ....4.20
Sea Breeze Properties Ltd v Bio-Medical Systems Ltd, 1998 S.L.T. 319; 1997 G.W.D. 8-
  341 OH 7.42
Seaforth Trustees v Macaulay (1844) 7 D. 180 IH (2 Div) 7.20
Sharp v Thomson; sub nom. Sharp v Woolwich Building Society; Sharp v Joint Receivers
  of Albyn Construction Ltd, 1997 S.C. (H.L.) 66; 1997 S.L.T. 636; 1997 S.C.L.R.
  328 HL 4.34
Sheltered Housing Management Ltd v Bon Accord Bonding Co Ltd [2010] CSIH 42; 2010
  S.C. 516; 2010 S.L.T. 662 ....5.13
Shetland Islands Council v BP Petroleum Development Ltd, 1990 S.L.T. 82; 1989
  S.C.L.R. 48 OH 7.07
Signet Group Plc v C&J Clark Retail Properties Ltd, 1996 S.C. 444; 1996 S.L.T. 1325;
  1996 S.C.L.R. 1020 IH (Ex Div) 7.42
Sinclair Lockhart's Trustees v Central Land Board, 1951 S.C. 258; 1951 S.L.T. 121; (1949-
  51) 1 P. & C.R. 320 IH (1 Div) 9.17
Smith v Crombie [2012] CSOH 52; 2012 G.W.D. 16-331 ....9.06, 9.0
Smith v Grayton Estates Ltd, 1960 S.C. 349; 1961 S.L.T. 38; 1960 S.L.T. (Notes) 81 IH
  (1 Div) 7.42
Snowie v Stirling Council, 2008 S.L.T. (Sh Ct) 61; 2008 Hous. L.R. 46; 2008 G.W.D.
  13-244 ....9.19
SP Distribution Ltd v Rafique, 2010 S.L.T. (Sh Ct) 8; 2009 S.C.L.R. 891 ....6.15
Star Energy Weald Basin Ltd v Bocardo SA. See Bocardo SA v Star Energy UK Onshore Ltd
Stewart v Bulloch (1881) 8 R. 381 IH (1 Div) 9.33
Stewart, &c. v Duke of Montrose (1860) 22 D. 755 IH (1 Div) 5.11
Tailors of Aberdeen v Coutts (1870) 1 Rob. App. 296 ....5.11
Thomson v Great North of Scotland Railway Co (1899) 2 F. (J.) 22; (1899) 7 S.L.T. 282
  HCJ 9.09
Thomson's Executor, Applicant 2016 G.W.D. 27-494 Lands Tr 5.24, 5.26
Trade Development Bank v Critall Windows Ltd. See Trade Development Bank v David W
  Haig (Bellshill) Ltd
Trade Development Bank v David W Haig (Bellshill) Ltd, 1983 S.L.T. 510 IH (1 Div) 4.09
Tuley v Highland Council, 2009 S.C. 456; 2009 S.L.T. 616; 2009 S.C.L.R. 783
  IH (Ex Div) 9.22
United Investment Co Ltd v Charlie Reid Travel Ltd, 2016 G.W.D. 1-13, Lands Tr 6.18
Valentine v Kennedy, 1985 S.C.C.R. 89 ....3.03
Waelde v Ulloa, 2016 G.W.D. 11-221 ....8.06
Webster v Lord Advocate, 1985 S.C. 173; 1985 S.L.T. 361 IH (2 Div) 9.38
William Tracey Ltd v SP Transmission Plc [2016] CSOH 14; 2016 S.L.T. 678;
  2016 G.W.D. 3-67 ....9.07
Winans v Macrae (1885) 12 R. 1051 ....9.11
Wing v Henry Tse & Co Ltd, 2009 G.W.D. 11-175 ....7.30
Wolfson v Forrester, 1910 S.C. 675; 1910 1 S.L.T. 318 IH (1 Div) 7.24
Wylie and Lochhead v Mitchell (1870) 8 M. 552 III (1 Div) 3.28
Young v Markey 2014 S.L.T. (Lands Tr) 61; 2014 G.W.D. 13-237 ....6.18
Yule v Tobert 2016, G.W.D. 1-11 Lands Tr 6.18

1. INTRODUCTION: CONCEPTS AND CONTEXT

INTRODUCTION

Eminent philosophers have long contested the philosophical justifications **1.01** underpinning the concept of property. These justifications are likely to remain contested, and many learned books will be written about them. This is not such a book. The following pages seek to provide an introduction to the *law* of property in Scotland. The *law* of property in Scotland, at its most basic level, regulates the manner in which persons interact with objects. The law's regulation of these interactions is given effect by way of rights, and the obligations or duties that correspond to those rights. Property law can, therefore, be reduced to the interaction of three concepts: things, persons, and rights.

CONCEPTS

Things, persons and rights

Things
The word "thing" may not appear, at first glance, to be a technical legal **1.02** term—but it is. Thing is the word that the law uses to describe an object that can be the subject of rights. Things are the objects over which property law rights can be exercised: they are the subjects of property rights. The following are examples of things because they can be the subjects of property rights: a pen, a hat, a horse, a car, a train, an oil rig, a farm, and so on. Occasionally the Latin word "*res*" (which simply means "thing") is used, particularly in older sources. Sometimes things are described as "property", which is fine so far as it goes. But "property" can be a slippery word because of a tendency to use it in different conceptual senses, so it must be read with care. "Property" can refer to an object that is the subject of a right; but "property" can also be used to refer to a right over an object, in particular, it is often used to refer to the right of ownership. An owner of a pen who states "this is my property" is referring to two concepts: the thing (the pen) and the right that they have over that thing (ownership of the pen). Thus, things are the subject matter of property law: the regulation of what can be done in relation to things by persons is property law's function.

Persons
Persons are entities that the law recognises can hold and exercise rights and **1.03** be subject to duties. A person can take actions that are legally significant.

Editor's Note: "They" and "their" have been used as singular pronouns throughout this book, in accordance with W. Green's policy on gender neutral language.

The law recognises natural persons and legal or juristic persons. Natural persons are human beings and, in the modern world, all human beings are natural persons for the purposes of the law. Whether a person has capacity is a different question, and not all human beings have full capacity. Legal (sometimes called juristic) persons are entities that the law recognises as being capable of holding and exercising rights, or owing duties. Examples of legal persons include companies and, in Scotland, partnerships. Such organisations are more than the sum of their parts: they have a distinct and independent existence. A company can carry out legally significant actions, such as entering a contract. Yet, natural persons must carry out a company's physical actions, even though the company is a distinct entity. A company can buy a car, but only a human can physically sign the contract and drive it out of the showroom. Persons—natural and legal—wish to make use of things, or, sometimes, to stop others from making use of things. Property law governs such uses of things by rights.

Rights

1.04   Property law is concerned with rights that relate to the interactions between persons and things. A right is an entitlement in favour of a person that can be enforced in a court of law. Rights are the currency of all law, and therefore there are many different types of rights. A fundamental distinction is drawn between "personal rights" on the one hand, and "real rights" on the other.

Personal rights

1.05   Personal rights arise as part of the law of obligations, the main branches of which are the laws of contract, delict and unjustified enrichment. A personal right is a right held by one person against another person. The right is only enforceable against that person. Say A and B enter a contract whereby A will lend B money, and B will repay the loan in six months. Two personal rights (at least) have been created by this contract: B has a personal right against A to receive the money, and A has a personal right against B to be repaid the amount which has been loaned to B. Contracts normally generate mutually enforceable personal rights, though sometimes they create a right in favour of a third party: known at common law as *jus quaesitum tertio* ("JQT"), but the common law JQT will be replaced by statute: Contract (Third Party Rights) (Scotland) Act 2017 ss.1, 11. Delict and unjustified enrichment bestow unilateral personal rights on one person if a triggering event occurs. If C accidentally pays money into D's bank, then the law of unjustified enrichment gives C a personal right to recover the money from D; D receives no personal right against C by virtue of receiving the accidental payment alone. Likewise, if E negligently injures F, the law of delict gives F a personal right to seek damages from E; injuring F does not bestow a personal right on E. In each case a personal right is only enforceable against another person. Real rights are different.

Real rights

A real right is a right that a person has in a thing. Because the right is in the **1.06**
thing itself it is sometimes said that it is good against the world. How so?
Since the right is in the thing itself it affects any person who interacts with
that thing, and so, because that is potentially anyone, it can be said to be
good against the world. Of course, the whole world will not interact with
a thing, but anyone who does interact with it must respect the real right
contained within. Real rights ensure that rules governing the use of a thing
will bind any person who comes into contact with that thing. There are also
different types of real right. The primary real right is the right of ownership.
All real rights other than ownership are subordinate real rights. Subordinate
real rights give a person a right in a thing that is owned by another person.
If the ownership of a thing is transferred from one person to another, any
subordinate real rights in the thing will survive the transfer of ownership.
A real right binds the new owner because it is a right in the thing, rather than
a right against a person. This is important because it means a real right
allows a person to maintain a relationship with a thing that is durable.

For example, if A is the owner of a piece of land they have the primary **1.07**
real right in that land. It might be that A wishes to give other people rights
to interact with that land too. Let us say that A gives B a personal right to
pick flowers on the land, and then gives C a real right to walk across the
land. As long as A remains the owner of the land both B and C can exercise
their respective rights, but they are different types of right. If A decides to
sell the land to D the difference becomes apparent. Although D is now the
owner of the land, they have to continue to allow C to walk across the
land—C has a real right in the land itself that D must respect. The transfer
does not terminate the real right. On the other hand, B's right to pick
flowers will not bind D because that right is a personal right, and not a real
right in the land itself. B had a personal right against A, which does not
bind D. B's right to pick flowers might, depending on its terms, still bind
A; however, that will not allow B to enter that land, which is now owned
by D, to pick flowers. B would only have a personal right to sue A for
breaching the personal right, which is no concern of D. Therefore, only a
real right binds new owners, or, as they are sometimes termed, singular
successors. Real rights also have powerful effects in situations involving
insolvency. A creditor with a real right often has an advantage over those
creditors with an (unsecured) personal right, because a real right is against
a thing rather than the insolvent person.

Fixed list of real rights (*numerus clausus*)

Because real rights can have powerful effects that bind third parties, the **1.08**
law adopts a policy to limit such effects. The *numerus clausus*, or fixed list
principle, limits the type of real rights that can be created. Only real rights
of the type recognised on the fixed list can have real effect and bind third
parties. The idea is that because real rights have these powerful third party
effects, only certain types known to the law should be allowed, because
that means that third parties can anticipate the sort of property rights they

might be subjected to. The principle is a general one, and applies to Scots law. Ownership as the greatest of the real rights is included, as are subordinate real rights recognised by Scots law, such as rights in security, (proper) liferents, servitudes, and leases.

Classification of things

1.09 Things are the subjects of property law and there are many different types. Although there are overarching principles of property law that apply to all things, there are also instances where different rules apply to different types of things. Therefore, the law has developed a classification of things that divides them into categories that are subject to different rules. The main classifications are as follows.

Heritable and moveable property

1.10 Heritable property is the term used to classify property (a thing) that is land and rights connected with land. It is called heritable property for historical reasons relating to the law succession—that is, it relates to "inheritance". Land is sometimes described as "immoveable" property instead of heritable property, but it means the same thing today. Moveable property is any thing that is not classed as heritable property, and therefore is any thing which is not land or connected to land—it is a residual category of classification.

1.11   There are a number of other types of heritable property beyond the simple case of land. Perhaps the most important are: (1) things that become legally connected to land are considered heritable property; (2) "rights with a tract of future time", which means rights that a debtor cannot pay off immediately and which provide an annual benefit, such as pensions and annuities, for example; and (3) titles of honour.

Corporeal and incorporeal

1.12 The second distinction that is made when classifying different types of property is that between corporeal and incorporeal property. Corporeal property is the name given to the things that are manifested physically in the world. A bicycle, a field, an apple and a pen are all examples of corporeal property. A piece of incorporeal property is a thing that has no physical manifestation. For example, shares in a company are incorporeal property, as are other personal rights such as the right to be paid a debt.

1.13   A classificatory distinction is drawn between these different types of property, using the concepts of heritable/moveable property and corporeal/incorporeal property, for two reasons. The first reason related to the law of succession and inheritance—broadly, it used to be a male heir who inherited land, though that set of rules is really now only a matter of historical interest. Secondly, and far more importantly, the other reason that property is classified in this way is because in some instances it is appropriate for different rules to apply to different sorts of property. Thus, for example, the rules governing the transfer of land are different from those governing the transfer of a moveable, such as a car, for example. Furthermore, the availability of different types of rights in security, and certain rules in the law of succession, also rely upon the distinction between heritable and moveable property.

CONTEXT

History

Overview
The law of property in Scotland is the product of centuries of evolution. The **1.14** law has been influenced by Roman law, often mediated by canon law or the shared medieval and early modern concept of Roman law known as the *jus commune*. Indeed, the law of property has probably been influenced more by Roman law ideas than any other area of the law in Scotland. The historically strong influence of Roman law on Scottish property law explains much of the structure of the law, as well as the enduring use of a fair number of Latin maxims. While English common law has influenced some areas of Scottish property law, such influence has traditionally been confined in scope and insubstantial. Therefore, although Scots law generally draws upon the dual influences of Roman and English law, it is important to be warier about using English authority, in the context of understanding Scottish property law, than might otherwise be the case in other areas of Scots law.

Heritable property: feudal tenure and registration
There are two leading concepts which have shaped the development of the **1.15** law relating to heritable property in Scotland: (1) the feudal system; and (2) the idea of land registration. These two concepts have had an important influence upon the development of modern land law, and it is to them that we now turn.

Feudal system
Today, the core ideas underlying feudalism are so far away in time that they **1.16** seem utterly alien to our modern views about society, and the law that serves it. The theoretical concept of feudalism, with its idea of feudal lords who had claims and jurisdiction over other men, and the ability to compel those men to do their will, including fight for them and risk injury or death, was as much a political system as it was a legal system. The ideas that informed that political system ceased to command respect in this country many hundreds of years ago. Yet, while the substance of the feudal system as an oppressive and coercive instrument of political governance was discarded long ago, that societal model left its mark upon the form and structure of the law in Scotland for much longer than in many other jurisdictions. That form was characterised overwhelmingly by a hierarchical system of landholding. Over the years legislative reforms heavily amended the position so that the law was almost devoid of the substantive effects of feudalism, but the hierarchical structure remained and still held substantive and symbolic significance. What then was the legal feudal structure?

1.17   The dominant characteristic of the feudal system of holding land was hierarchy: for almost every piece of land there was a hierarchy of different forms of landholding, which were something like multiple ownership interests piled on top of each other. Ownership is seen as an indivisible real right that is held by one person by the current law, but the feudal system did things differently. In the feudal system's hierarchy, there could be many people who held land "of" each other—the idea being that a person could grant a perpetual right to use a piece of land to a person who was in legal form (and normally in class) below them in the hierarchical chain. At the top of the (earthly) food chain stood the sovereign, that is to say the King or Queen. The sovereign was at the apex of the feudal chain, and hence, on one level, the owner of all the land in Scotland. The King could (only) "subinfeudate" land to another person, which meant that the right a person received from the King was a perpetual right to use land that was not technically full ownership. In modern terms, it would look something like a perpetual lease. Part of the bargain was that the person below another in the feudal chain was obliged to render services or to pay to their immediate superior a *reddendo* which was like a form of rent; therefore, a knight who held land "of the" King was obliged to attend him to provide military service, for example. Furthermore, the person to whom the King had granted this feudal title could himself create a similar title, whereby he could grant a right of perpetual use to another person, thereby inserting that person into the feudal chain below them. This can be illustrated pictorially:

Feudal Chain

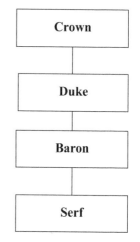

dominium eminems
(Duke's 'superior';
Baron's 'over-superior'; Serf's 'over-over-superior')

dominium directum
('Vassal' of the Crown; Baron's 'superior';
Serf's 'over-superior')

dominium directum
('Vassal' of Duke; Serf's superior)

dominium utile
(Baron's 'vassal'—bottom of the chain)

Chains of interests in land like this one existed under the feudal system when one person subinfeudated the land to another person. Each person had a different level of right within the land, and each person in the chain owed duties to their immediate superior. The Crown is at the top of the chain, and the Duke holds of the Crown. The Crown is known as a "superior" and the person holding of the superior is called a "vassal". Thus, the Duke is the Crown's vassal. But the Duke has subinfeudated the land to Baron, who in turn has subinfeudated the land to Serf. Each time a person in the chain subinfeudated the land, another link was added to the chain.

Abolition of Feudal Tenure etc (Scotland) Act 2000 (AFT(S)A 2000)

It was possible for the holder of a right in the feudal chain to "dispone" the **1.18** property (*a me*) instead of "subinfeudating" property (*de me*). The effect of disponing property was to substitute one person for someone who was already in the feudal chain, rather than the addition of a new link to the chain which occurred when land was subinfeudated. Disponing property was by far the most common means of transfer in practice by the latter part of the twentieth century, and the writing was on the wall for legal feudalism in Scotland with the passing of the Land Tenure Reform (Scotland) Act 1974, which prohibited the creation of new feuduties (the only remaining form of *reddendo*). The end of feudal tenure came on 28 November 2004, when s.1 of AFT(S)A 2000 came into force. At a stroke, the mass of confusing chains of feudal interests came to an end—the person at the bottom of the chain, with the *dominium utile*, became simply an owner of the property with no superiors: all superiorities were abolished. Yet, while the Act necessarily deprives the Crown of its "rights" in most of the land in Scotland it is careful not to touch the Crown's prerogative—in particular, the Crown's rights relating to the *regalia majora* and ownerless property were specifically saved.

The vast majority of the law of landownership was fundamentally **1.19** altered, in terms of form and underlying structure, albeit that not all of the substantive elements of the law were changed, at least by AFT(S)A 2000. Feudalism has, however, left traces of its presence. The *regalia majora* have already been mentioned. Another significant area of law that still bears an organisational scheme borne of feudalism is the law of real burdens. Feudal real burdens were essentially planning devices used by a superior to insert enforceable conditions on the use of land, thereby ensuring some form of continuing control over the land. So, in our example, if Serf decided to subinfeudate the land to another person, but did not want there to be any commercial activity on the land, the Serf would include a condition (a real burden) to that effect in the feudal grant and the Serf's vassal(s) and their successors would be perpetually bound by this. Indeed, the continued existence of the feudal system owed much to the efficacy of real burdens as instruments of planning control. When the feudal system was finally abolished the former superior (whose superiority had ceased to exist anyway) was expressly said to be unable to enforce real burdens created in this way: AFT(S)A 2000 s.17; though some feudal burdens were capable of being converted into various different kinds of burden: AFT(S)A 2000 s.18.

Registration

The concept of registration has been of major historical importance for **1.20** the development of Scottish land law, and remains fundamental to any understanding of the way in which the transfer of land is carried out in

Scotland. As we have seen, the feudal system existed in Scottish law up until November 2004. In order to complete the transfer of land under the feudal system—whether the transfer was effected by substitution using a disposition, or by adding another link in the feudal chain using subinfeudation—it was necessary to take what was known as an instrument of sasine in order to "take infeftment". By becoming infeft the transfer process was completed. Many years ago, the act of taking infeftment by way of an instrument of sasine involved an elaborate ceremony that had to be conducted upon the land which was being transferred. Transferees (vassals) would have a symbolic item delivered to them depending on the nature of the land conveyed: earth and a stone for land; clap and happer for a mill; and a staff or a baton for the transfer of a superiority. When that delivery occurred, a notary had to be present to record the event in an "instrument of sasine" which was a document drawn up by the notary. In the seventeenth century, this document, the "instrument of sasine", had to be recorded in a register by virtue of the Registration Act 1617. The register in which these instruments were to be recorded was, and, indeed still is, known as the General Register of Sasines (GRS). The significance of the ceremony and the fact that it was recorded was the public nature of the process. In the nineteenth century, a series of reforms were enacted which meant that it was no longer necessary to conduct the sasine ceremony. After a series of reforms, it became competent to simply record a deed in the GRS in order to convey an interest in land. That system of registration continued until the late 1970s, when legislation was passed that provided for the (slow) replacement of the GRS with a system of land registration that created a new register known as the Land Register. We will see later how the substance of land registration works. For present purposes, it is sufficient to appreciate the central role that the concept of registration has in Scottish land law.

Reform

1.21 The law of property in Scotland has been the subject of sustained and fundamental reform for over a decade, and the reform process continues. Almost all the reforms have come about as a result of legislation, enacted by the Scottish Parliament, to implement reports of the Scottish Law Commission. In order to understand the process of reform, and the rationale behind it, it is necessary to understand what was being reformed in the first place. In a nutshell, land in Scotland was held upon feudal tenure up until 28 November 2004 when the AFT(S)A 2000 came into force. This Act abolished the feudal system and changed the underlying basis of property law in Scotland. In the wake of the abolition of the feudal system, a number of other statutes were passed to complement this fundamental change in the underlying system of land tenure. Further statutory reforms of property law followed, which were not directly related to the abolition of the feudal system but nevertheless fit within an overarching programme of law reform in connection with land holding in Scotland.

Sources

In common with many other areas of law, Scottish property law is not to be **1.22** found in one place or period. There is no single statute or code that sets out the entirety of Scottish property law. The law is to be found in a number of statutes, cases, institutional writings, and, occasionally, guidance can be found in respected modern monographs. In the last 20 years, there has been significant legislative activity in relation to property law, and a number of important statutes have been enacted, including the following Acts: AFT(S)A 2000; Land Reform (Scotland) Act 2003; Title Conditions (Scotland) Act 2003; Tenements (Scotland) Act 2004; Land Registration etc (Scotland) Act 2012; Land Reform (Scotland) Act 2016, and Private Housing (Tenancies) (Scotland) Act 2016.

Human rights

Property law is increasingly concerned with human rights law. The right to **1.23** own property, and to have that ownership protected, has long been recognised by the common law. More recently the protection of the right to property has been significantly strengthened by Art.1 of the First Protocol (A1P1) to the European Convention on Human Rights (ECHR) to the extent that it permeates domestic law as a result of the "incorporation" of the ECHR into domestic law by the Human Rights Act 1998. Although A1P1 is the most obvious provision of the ECHR with importance for property law, other provisions have been interpreted in ways that have potential implications for domestic property law.

2. OWNERSHIP AND POSSESSION

CONCEPTUAL INTRODUCTION

Ownership is the most comprehensive property right that a person can have **2.01** over a thing. We encountered the real right of ownership earlier in this book when discussing the concept of real rights, and the closed list of real rights known as the *numerus clausus*. Ownership is the primary real right. Unlike many subordinate real rights, ownership is not normally temporary and continues until the owner decides to relinquish ownership, though there are exceptions. Erskine's institutional description, which is succinct and comprehensive, of the content of the right of ownership is: "…the right of using and disposing of a subject as our own, except insofar as we are restrained by law or paction." (Erskine, *Institute*, II.1.1.)

This authoritative sentence captures the key elements of ownership, and **2.02** the powers that an individual has over a thing by virtue of holding the right of ownership. An owner can dispose of, or transfer, the property. Owners are entitled to use or enjoy the property, and to take any benefits that flow from the property. An owner can even opt to destroy the property, if so inclined. These elements of ownership's content are captured in the Latin phrase: *jus utendi, fruendi and abutendi* [the right to use, the right to fruits, and the right to abuse]. Most Latin phrases are ancient and often reflect ideas developed from interpretations of Roman law. This phrase, *jus utendi, fruendi and abutendi,* captures an ancient Roman idea of ownership: an essentially unlimited power for an owner to do whatever they like with a thing.

In modern times, the actual content of the right of ownership is no longer **2.03** as absolute. This was recognised by Erskine when he noted the following condition inherent within his definition of ownership: "except insofar as we are restrained by law or paction." There are a number of such potential restraints upon the rights and powers of an owner, including elements of public law and the law of nuisance, but for present purposes we cannot go into all those limitations. However, an example might help. If Ann owns a 16th century townhouse in Edinburgh that is a listed building she cannot wake up one day and decide to burn it down, or even paint it luminous pink—public and criminal law prevent this. Further limitations upon the powers of an owner come from property law itself in the form of subordinate real rights. Although most subordinate real rights can only be granted by the owner of property, they can remain attached to the thing after it passes to another owner—indeed, that is the essence of a subordinate real right. Therefore, the key concept is that ownership gives a person expansive powers and rights over a thing, but there can be a number of limitations that affect the owner's powers.

PHYSICAL EXTENT OF OWNERSHIP

2.04 What does it mean to say that someone is the owner of a thing in terms of the physical manifestation of that ownership? The answer depends on the type of property. The physical extent of a piece of corporeal moveable property will normally be easily identified, and so, in turn, will the physical extent of its owner's interest. The owner of a corporeal moveable will normally be the owner of the whole thing. Matters are more complex in relation to corporeal heritable property. The physical boundaries marking the extent of one owner's interest are unlikely to be as clearly demarcated as in the case of corporeal moveable property by virtue of the nature of land. The law has developed rules which allow us to identify and demarcate the extent of a piece of corporeal heritable property, and hence the extent of the owner's interest. It is necessary to consider both horizontal and vertical boundaries.

Horizontal boundaries
2.05 The horizontal boundaries of a piece of land depend on the system of land registration used to register that land. If the land is registered in the Land Register the horizontal boundaries of the land are described in the property section of the title sheet relating to that plot of land: Land Registration etc (Scotland) Act 2012 s.6(1)(a)(i). Furthermore, that description must refer to the "cadastral map", which is like a "master-map" of all registered land in Scotland and is based on maps drawn up by the Ordnance Survey: Land Registration etc (Scotland) Act 2012 s.11. In turn, the horizontal boundaries of land registered in the Land Register should be easy to ascertain using this map.
2.06   The determination of the horizontal boundaries of land registered in the General Register of Sasines (GRS) is more challenging because the GRS does not use such a map. Some land registered in the GRS will have been accompanied by a plan of the land, but such inclusion of such plans was not compulsory, and the plans which are registered are not consistently formatted. Land that has been registered without an accompanying plan in the GRS is identified by description. There are two types of description: "bounding descriptions" and "general descriptions". A bounding description is one that incorporates some means of identifying the extent of the land: references to previous deeds, references to local geography, references to other properties etc. General descriptions give very limited information in terms of identification and may simply state the location, address or name of the property. Where the description of a piece of land registered in the GRS is unsatisfactory the law of positive prescription becomes important: if land has been possessed for 10 years in a way that is consistent with the operation of positive prescription—in particular the need for a *habile* title—the law of prescription will delineate the horizontal boundaries of the land in question.

Vertical boundaries

The vertical extent of ownership in a piece of land is said to be *a coelo* **2.07** *usque ad centrum*: "from the heavens to the centre of the earth". (Bell, *Principles*, § 940; Erskine, *Institute*, II. 6. 1.; *Forbes v Livingston* (1827) 6 S. 167 at 179; *Dicksons and Laings v The Burgh of Hawick* (1885) 13 R. 163 at 171, per Lord Young.) What does it mean to describe the vertical extent of ownership in this way? In theory, the ownership of land in Scotland extends all the way up to the end of sovereign airspace to the point at which outer space begins. There is no international agreement about where outer space begins (see F. Lyall and P.B. Larsen, *Space Law* (2009), pp.153 et seq). Despite this uncertainty about exactly where outer space begins, we can be sure that ownership extends up to the lower levels of outer space. What are the repercussions of this upward vertical extent of ownership? In theory, any encroachment or trespass in the airspace above land is actionable at the instance of the landowner.

The possibility of trespassing in airspace occurred in *Brown v Lee* **2.08** *Constructions Ltd*, 1977 S.L.T. (Notes) 61. A contractor was carrying out work on land that was adjacent to the pursuer's land. The base of the crane was not situated on the pursuer's land, but in order to access the worksite the arm of the crane had to swing across the airspace above the pursuer's land. The pursuer sought an interdict to prevent the crane passing through his property. It was argued that the crane was merely passing through the airspace of the pursuer and accordingly the lack of permanent encroachment meant that it was not actionable. The court granted the interdict preventing the crane from operating in the pursuer's airspace. Scottish authorities do not expressly set out any limitations on the upwards extent of ownership (at least before outer space). In England, there is authority limiting the upwards extent of an owner's interest. In *Bernstein v Skyviews and General Ltd* [1978] Q.B. 479 the defendant was a company that had planes fly over houses taking photographs for the purposes of offering the homeowner the opportunity to purchase an aerial photograph of their house. Lord Bernstein brought an action based upon a breach of right to privacy and trespass. The court held that an owner did not have an ownership right which extended upwards without limitation—rather, an owner's rights only extended upwards to the extent required for the "ordinary use and enjoyment" of the property: *Bernstein* at 488A–B per Griffiths J. It is likely that a Scottish court would follow this decision or adopt a similar test if confronted with the issue. Now, by virtue of a statute applicable in Scotland and England, aircraft passing over properties at a reasonable height do not commit an actionable trespass: see Civil Aviation Act 1982 s.76; *Peires v Bickerton's Aerodromes Ltd* [2017] 1 W.L.R. 2865 at [58]–[61] per Sir Terence Etherton MR.

So much for the extent of ownership in an upwards direction, what about **2.09** the downwards direction? Ownership extends all the way down to the centre of the earth (excepting separate tenements which we will deal with in a moment) and there is no suggestion in Scottish or English law that there is any "ordinary use" limitation. In *Star Energy Weald Basin Ltd v Bocardo SA* [2010] UKSC 35 there were two neighbouring plots of land. One of the plots of land was used for oil drilling, and at depths of more than 800ft below the surface the drill pipelines crossed the property boundary between the two pieces of land. The plaintiff raised an action for damages due to trespass by the oil drilling company. The oil drilling company argued that the ordinary use limitation that applied to the upwards limit of ownership (see *Bernstein* above) was equally applicable to the downwards ownership of the land. The Supreme Court accepted that the upwards limit of landownership had been tempered by the "ordinary use" test, but that was not the case in relation to the downwards extent of ownership. Although *Bocardo* is an English decision, it is almost certain that Scottish law would follow this lead, particularly because there is no mention of qualification to the upwards extent of ownership in Scottish authorities.

PERTINENTS

2.10 A pertinent is (normally) a small piece of land that is clearly related to another piece of land; indeed, it is functionally adjusted to be used in a way that fits in with the greater piece of land. The small pieces of land are corporeal pertinents. Another type of pertinent is an incorporeal pertinent. Incorporeal pertinents are, essentially, the benefit of rights enjoyed in association with a piece of land—so the use of a servitude is an example of an incorporeal pertinent.

SEPARATE TENEMENTS

2.11 Having considered the horizontal and vertical extent of landownership it is important to examine an exception to the extent of vertical ownership: the concept of a separate tenement. Separate tenements are parts of land, or rights relating to land, which can be owned as a separate interest from the land itself. It is important to distinguish between the technical legal concept of a separate tenement, and a tenement in the colloquial sense of the word, when it is used to describe a tenement building. Separate tenements are things that can be owned as an independent piece of property. In addition to being capable of being separately owned, indeed, because a separate tenement is a thing that can be owned, it is possible for subordinate real rights to exist over a separate tenement. Separate tenements are classified according to how they are created—therefore, there are "conventional" and "legal" separate tenements.

Conventional separate tenements
2.12 Conventional separate tenements are created by an express reservation by an owner of land when transferring that land. Thus, if Adam transfers land to Bob, and the disposition states that Adam reserves the minerals below the

surface, then the minerals do not pass to Bob; in the absence of that reservation, the minerals would be transferred to Bob with the rest of the land under the *a coelo usque ad centrum* rule. It is not uncommon to see an express reservation of mineral rights (which are not legal separate tenements) when land is transferred from one person to another. Above ground, the most common type of conventional separate tenement are flats within a single building (or tenement building). What is physically a single building on a piece of land is legally divided into a number of different conventional separate tenements. Because the creation of a conventional separate tenement is by reservation there will also be an owner with the residual ownership rights that extend *a coelo usque ad centrum*. Let us take an example: Alf owns a piece of land in the centre of Dundee and decides that he would like to develop the land and build some flats. Alf will instruct a builder to construct a building that will be internally divided into the flats. Once the builder completes the construction of the building Alf will own the entire tenement building, as well as the soil below and sky above it. But Alf will want to sell each individual flat separately, therefore conventional separate tenements will be created for each flat in the building: in effect sections of the sky are divided into separately owned portions where the flats are located. The other conventional separate tenements of importance are of sporting rights relating to the hunting of game and fishing (but not salmon). When the feudal system was abolished it was possible for superiors in the feudal chain to reserve their right to fish or hunt for game on a piece of land if they registered that right before a certain date. The deadline for such reservations has now passed and few were registered.

Legal separate tenements

The other type of separate tenement is a "legal separate tenement". Legal **2.13** separate tenements arose because certain things were considered to be so valuable that whenever the Crown granted land to someone it was assumed by implication that the Crown reserved to itself such valuable rights and minerals—these were part of the *regalia minora* (see "Crown Rights" below). Put another way, the thing was so valuable that the Crown would need to say expressly that it was being granted for it to pass to the transferee of the land. If the Crown did expressly grant one of these valuable types of right or mineral to someone, then that right would constitute a legal separate tenement, capable of ownership, which was owned by the grantee. Such a legal separate tenement is a separate thing, distinct from the land, so different people can own the two things; or the same person might own both. Say Abigail owns land with a river on it *and* a separate legal tenement of salmon fishing. If she transfers the land to Boris, and the river contains salmon, but the transfer does not mention the right to fish for salmon, then Boris would not receive the right to fish for the salmon. That right to fish for salmon constitutes a legal separate tenement, and the silence in the transfer means that separate tenement remains with Abigail. Had Abigail expressly mentioned the right to fish for salmon, then the legal separate tenement would have been transferred to Boris, but as a thing distinct from the land. There are a number of different types of legal separate tenement, such as, the right to fish for salmon; the right to gather mussels and oysters; the right to mine gold and silver: Royal Mines Act 1424; the right to bore for petrol: Petroleum Act 1998 s.2(1). A right which is analogous to a legal separate tenement is the right to mine coal, which is vested in the Coal Authority: Coal Industry Act 1994 s.7(3).

CROWN RIGHTS

2.14 There are a series of rights associated with the Crown known as the regalian rights. The regalian rights are split into two different categories—the *regalia majora* and the *regalia minora*.

Regalia majora
2.15 The *regalia majora* are really rights of sovereignty rather than patrimonial rights. As only the sovereign can exercise rights of sovereignty they are limited to the Crown. Although the Crown might hold such rights in favour of the public, they remain in the ownership of the Crown, and they are not usually capable of being transferred to individuals. Therefore, things that fall within the *regalia majora* are not capable of alienation into private hands; rather, they are rights which are vested in the Crown for the benefit of the public. The most important examples of the *regalia majora* are rights to navigate and fish within the sea and rights related to the foreshore.

Regalia minora
2.16 The *regalia minora* are rights which were originally vested within the Crown, but were considered so valuable that an express grant of these rights was required—they would not be carried by a transfer that was silent about those rights specifically. The crucial difference between the regalia minora and the *regalia majora* is that the *minora* are capable of being held by individuals, unlike the *majora*. Because there has to be an express grant of the *regalia minora*, they can often become effectively separate tenements. Many examples of the *regalia minora* have receded into the mists of time, but surviving examples include: rights to gold and silver mines (though there are statutory specialities); rights of port and harbour; rights to a public ferry; rights to hold fairs and markets; rights to treasure, rights to lost property and wreck; rights to collect oysters and mussels, and the right to fish for salmon. Thus, many modern separate legal tenements originated from the *regalia minora*.

CO-OWNERSHIP

2.17 The idea behind co-ownership is quite straightforward—there can be more than one owner of a single thing. Two people can own a house together, and it is certainly a common occurrence for there to be more than one owner of heritable property. It is also perfectly possible for there to be two or more co-owners of moveable property. Say I decide to buy a valuable portrait, but, sadly, my academic wage will not cover the asking price. I might join economic forces with my friend and we could buy the portrait together, becoming co-owners of the portrait. Furthermore, sometimes there is a presumption that moveable property is co-owned, such as the household goods of a married couple or civil partners: Family Law (Scotland) Act 1985 s. 25(1).

Thus, the idea of co-ownership is that there can be multiple owners of a **2.18** single thing. However, it is important to bear in mind that there are actually two different types or forms of co-ownership. On the one hand, there is what is known as "common ownership", and on the other there is "joint ownership". These terms may have an affinity in language, but in law they denote very different legal forms of co-ownership. The key difference between the two lies in the way in which these respective forms of co-ownership are structured. In the case of "common property" each co-owner has a separate and legally distinct ownership share in the common property, which in turn means that they can sell, bequeath, or otherwise burden that distinct interest. In the case of "joint property", which is the less common form of co-ownership, the position is different. There are two instances of joint property: trust property, and the property of an unincorporated association. Where there is joint property there are no individually identifiable shares of ownership. The co-owners are all said to be simple co-owners of the whole piece of property—there are no separate shares, which in turn means that it is not possible for an individual to sell, or otherwise burden, an individual share or interest in joint property.

Common ownership

Instances of common ownership
Common ownership is the most frequently encountered form of co- **2.19** ownership. Well known situations where the form of co-ownership will be common ownership are: (1) when two people buy heritable property as "joint owners" (the use of the word "joint" is confusing); (2) the household goods presumption relating to married couples or civil partners; (3) where a property development is created there are often certain parts of the development which will be co-owned by owners of individual units that make up such a development. If I build a block of flats, it is likely that I will sell the individual flats to other individuals but stipulate that certain areas are co-owned—such as the common close (stairwell) in a tenement building. This third type of common property is somewhat specialised, as we will see when we consider the law of real burdens and the law of the tenement.

Characteristics of common ownership
With common property each co-owner has what is known as a *pro indiviso* **2.20** share of the property. That means a certain proportion of the property is owned by each of the common owners. Nevertheless, it is important to remember that while there is a separate legal share of the property in question

as a matter of title, the use and management of the property is a common and singular one. With most cases, the certain and identifiable shares will be equally split according to the number of co-owners: if there are two people they will have a 50% or half share in the thing. This is reflected by a legal presumption of equal shares, but it is important to be aware that legal presumptions are not decisive—it is possible to set-up unequal shares, and this happens most frequently when the financial contributions made to acquire the thing are not equal. But what are the consequences of there being more than one owner of a piece of common property? More particularly, how are the normal incidences of ownership affected by the fact that there is more than one owner of a single thing? It is easiest to answer these questions by considering different facets of co-ownership.

Possession

2.21 The right to possession of the property, and hence often the factual element of possession, is shared where there is common property. What does that mean? In the words of Erskine, any co-owner is entitled to make use of "every inch" of the whole of the thing co-owned: Erskine, *Institute*, II, 6, 53 and Bell, *Principles*, § 1072. Let us take an example. Cordelia and Hugo are brother and sister. Their parents buy them a flat, and Cordelia and Hugo are registered as co-owners of the flat with equal shares. Hugo loves tiddlywinks, and Cordelia despises tiddlywinks only slightly less than she despises Hugo. However, in their co-owned flat Hugo is entitled to go anywhere—he can sit in her room and have a tiddlywinks marathon with Crispin. Furthermore, even if Hugo had been given only a 1% share of the property, and Cordelia had a 99% share, he would still be entitled to make use of the whole of the property. There are, however, a number of rules that mitigate this basic position. First, it is possible for Cordelia and Hugo to agree that certain areas of the house will be exclusively for the use of one or the other—but that is a contractual agreement, it is not a part of the law of property. Ownership is unaffected by such a contractual agreement, and so anyone who purchased either share would not be bound by such an agreement. Furthermore, it is a further principle of the shared ownership that only "ordinary" use is permitted. In *Carmichael v Simpson*, 1932 S.L.T. (Sh. Ct) 16 a tenant storing a bath chair in the stairwell was not entitled to use the stairwell for that purpose, because a stairwell is used for access normally, not for storage. Thus, while the right to possession might not be limited per se, the use to which common property might be put is subject to the requirement that the use be ordinary. Furthermore, it is possible that the use to which common property may be put might be the subject of a majority agreement. In addition to this rule, is the related no "excessive benefit at the expense of others" rule. There is some uncertainty about the exact limits of this rule, but a co-owner taking exclusive possession of the entire property is clearly not allowed. A matter that remains uncertain is the extent to which differently weighted shares of property interact with the excessive benefit rule—should someone with a much larger share be given more leeway in relation to that rule?

Repairs or alterations to the property

It is a certain aspect of the law of common property that some repairs or **2.22**
alterations to a piece of common property require the unanimous consent
of all co-proprietors. This proposition was clearly demonstrated in
Rafique v Amin, 1997 S.L.T. 1385, which involved an attempt to make
alterations and repairs to a flat that constituted common property.
However, the requirement that any repairs or alterations require
unanimous consent is subject to two rules. In the first place, there is a *de
minimis* rule, that is to say, if the proposed alteration or repair is of a
minor nature unanimity might not be required. In *Barkley v Scott* (1893)
10 Sh Ct Rep 23, the attachment of a brass name plate to a gate owned in
common was held not to require the unanimous consent of all co-
proprietors. Furthermore, in the case of *necessary repairs* it is possible for
one individual to order the repairs without the consent of the other co-
owners, and that co-owner can recover the costs from the other co-owners
in proportion to their shares of the property: *Deans v Woolfson*, 1922 S.C.
221 and *Rafique*.

Legal acts

As we have seen, the concept of common ownership means that each owner **2.23**
has a separate legal share, and each proprietor is entitled to possession of
the whole property. This has implications for the legal acts that a common
owner may undertake. Essentially, a common owner can carry out any act
which does not impinge upon the ownership right of the other co-owner,
more particularly the right to possession that flows from that right.
Therefore, a common owner can sell their share in the property, they can
bequeath their share to their heir, and they can grant a standard security
over their share. However, a common owner cannot grant a servitude, real
burden or lease because each of these real rights involve an interference
with the possession of the other co-owner, and, accordingly, are not allowed
at the hand of one the owners.

Illegal acts?

At the outset of the chapter, it was said that the classical element of an **2.24**
owner's right which allowed them to "abuse" property was circumscribed
by criminal and public law. Common ownership requires that a co-owner
does not impinge unduly on the rights of other co-owners, which means
that one co-owner cannot destroy the property at their own hand. Similarly,
co-ownership of property will not necessarily be a complete defence to a
criminal charge of vandalism to one's own co-owned property: see
Procurator Fiscal (Peterhead) v Elrick, 2017 S.L.T. (Sh Ct) 67, and
Procurator Fiscal (Peterhead) v Elrick (No 2), 2017 S.L.T. (Sh Ct) 157.

Termination of co-ownership

It will be apparent that the rules of common ownership can present serious **2.25**
challenges to those individual co-owners. It has been judicially observed
that common ownership requires "mutual compatibility, goodwill and

understanding": *Bailey's Exrs v Upper Crathes Fishing Ltd*, 1987 S.L.T. 405 at 406, per Lord Weir. Alas, such noble characteristics are not universal. What then? It might be that one of the co-owners wishes to terminate the entire co-ownership arrangement. If there is a residual element of goodwill then the proprietors might agree to sell the property and apportion any proceeds according to their respective shares in the property. If, however, there is no agreement, the law has an action known as division and sale which any single common owner can insist upon. If an action for division and sale is successful there are a number of remedies that might be granted by the court: (1) physical division: the property is physically divided according to the respective shares, with each part being owned outright after the division; (2) sale of the property on the open market: the common property is sold, and each owner receives proceeds from the sale according to their *pro indiviso* share of the property. The court chooses between the two remedies. In theory, physical division is the preferred remedy, though in practice the sale of the property is the more likely outcome. A third possibility, resting upon some uncertain authority, suggests that one proprietor can seek an order requiring the other proprietor to transfer their share to the other. The status of this third remedy is uncertain.

Joint ownership

2.26 Joint property is the second form of co-ownership in Scots law. There are two main types of joint property: trust property and the property of an unincorporated association (a club). The key difference between joint and common ownership is, as we have seen, that in the case of joint ownership there are no separately identifiable shares of ownership. In the case of a trust, all the trustees are said to be joint owners of the property, but they cannot alienate a specific share of the trust property. In turn, all decisions regarding the trust property are taken by a majority decision of the trustees. There is, therefore, no equivalent action of division and sale for joint property. Furthermore, a trustee is a joint owner of trust property only while a trustee—if he resigns the office of trustee he automatically ceases to be a joint owner. In an unincorporated association, the position is similar. An unincorporated association is another name for a club—if you are a member of a local football club then you are likely to be a joint owner of the club's strips. A person is only a joint owner of the association's property as long as they are a member of that association. Finally, one should note that in the case of a trust there can be joint ownership of both heritable and moveable property. In the case of an unincorporated association there can only be joint ownership of moveable property: any heritable property will be held under a separate trust on behalf of the club, and, while it will be joint property too, it is only the trustees that are joint owners of the heritable property, not every member of the club.

POSSESSION

Concept

The concept of ownership and the concept of possession are distinct from **2.27** each other, but it is easy to get confused by linguistic ambiguity. You may have heard people refer to things that they own as their "possessions" when they mean to highlight their ownership of those things. In fact, possession as a concept is different from ownership. One of the causes of confusion is the fact that often an owner will also have possession of a thing. Ownership is the greatest of the real rights, and it is a legal right. Possession, broadly speaking, is more concerned with a factual state of affairs. Therefore, to be imprecise for a moment, possession is the name given to the way a person holds a thing. It is factual in the sense that a person can be in possession of a thing without having a legal right to be in possession: if Arthur steals a television then he will have possession of it, but he has no right to be in possession of it. More commonly, a person can also be in possession and have a legal right to be in possession. The prime example of a right to possess is that held by the owner of thing, which explains the confusion of the two concepts: they overlap to some extent because one of the most important incidents of the right of ownership is the right to possess the thing. Possession is primarily concerned with the control that is demonstrated by the factual interaction between a person and thing.

Acquiring possession

How, then, do we recognise a situation where someone is in possession of **2.28** a thing? In order for a person to acquire possession of a thing they must demonstrate two things (Stair, II. 1. 18): (1) physical control over the thing (known as the *corpus* element from the Latin word for body), and (2) a mental intention to possess the thing (known as the *animus* element from the Latin word for mind).

Corpus

In order to exercise physical control over a thing there must be an initial **2.29** physical act of possession. This is straightforward for (most) moveable property. In the case of heritable property, the act of physical detention reflects the nature of the thing: one need only take physical steps in relation to a portion of the land: Stair, II. 1. 13. If a farmer wishes to take possession of a field they need not walk over every square foot of the field, it is enough that they take physical steps on a part of the land. The physical control required varies according to the thing possessed: *Lord Advocate v Young* (1887) 14 R. (HL) 53 at 54, per Lord Watson. The need to carry out acts of physical detention render the concept of possession problematic in relation to incorporeal property, the argument being that it is not possible to carry out physical acts in relation to property that has no physical manifestation.

Animus

2.30 In addition to the physical requirements of possession, it is also necessary to consider the mental element of possession, which is sometimes known as the animus requirement. There are two elements to the requisite intention required for possession. First, a person must intend to exercise the necessary physical control over the property; secondly, the intention to possess must be an intention to possess for the benefit of the person exercising physical control. These dual requirements can be difficult to assess in cases involving a container: if there is a thing contained inside another thing. Problems arise if the presence (or existence) of the thing inside the container is not known to the person exercising control over the container—does this lack of knowledge mean that possession of the thing inside the container is not possible? In a leading English decision, a valuable golden bracelet was found in the departure lounge at Heathrow airport, and it was held that if sufficient control of the airport lounge could be demonstrated (which, on the facts of the case, it could not) then that would be sufficient to demonstrate possession of the bracelet: *Parker v British Airways Board* [1982] Q.B. 1004. Although there is an old Scottish case that takes a different approach (*Hogg v Armstrong and Mowat* (1874) 1 Guth Sh Cas 438), it seems that modern Scottish cases take a broadly similar approach to that taken in *Parker*: *Harris v Abbey National* plc, 1997 S.C.L.R. 359. The other element of animus is that one must intend to hold something for one's own benefit: see *JA Pye (Oxford) Ltd v Graham* [2003] 1 A.C. 419 at [71], per Lord Hope. If the holder has no intention to hold for their own benefit, then they have mere custody of a thing. Custody is the name given to the situation where there is physical control but no intention to possess.

Natural and civil possession

2.31 The distinction between "natural possession" and "civil possession" can appear to be an exception to the need to show the dual requirements of physical control and intention. Natural possession is the name given to the state of affairs where a person exercises physical control of the thing herself with the requisite possessory intention. Civil possession is a little different, because a civil possessor exercises no direct physical control over the thing—they have possession through the physical actions of another person. Ian owns a flat that he leases to a student named Helen. When Helen moves into the flat she is the natural possessor of the flat because she has physical control and the requisite intention. Ian also has civil possession of the flat through Helen's acts of physical control. A civil possessor can possess through anyone who is exercising physical control of property, whether they are a full natural possessor or have only custody, so long as the natural possession does not deny the civil possessor's right.

Maintaining possession

2.32 Once a person has possession of a thing they are said to continue in possession of that thing *animo solo*: Stair, II. 1. 19 and Erskine, *Institute*,

II. 1. 21. What that means is that possession is continued by an act of the mind alone. In other words, once someone has taken physical control of a thing with the appropriate intention, it is not necessary to continue with physical acts of control: possession is continued by an act of the mind alone. When Amy goes to work she leaves her house, and consequently she is not exercising physical acts of possession; nevertheless, as long as she maintains her mental intention to possess her home she remains in possession of it (assuming no contrary acts of possession by another have taken place). If she is for some reason unable to resume physical possession, such as she has been held in physical captivity, then it is possible that the possession has come to an end: see generally C Anderson, *Possession of Corporeal Moveables* (2015).

Loss of possession

The continued possession of a thing by intention alone can be ended if **2.33** someone else takes possession of it. The other person who takes possession must satisfy both the *corpus* and *animus* elements of possession. Therefore, if Amy has a cleaner who comes to her house when she is at work, the cleaner does not interfere with Amy's possession. Although the cleaner's actions might be sufficient to satisfy the physical element of possession, the cleaner lacks intention to use the house for her own benefit. Alternatively, if a squatter entered Amy's house when she was at work the squatter would probably gain possession because he would demonstrate physical control and an intention to benefit himself. Amy would lose possession because the squatter gains possession; the squatter does not, however, have a *right* to possess the house.

Right to possess

A right on the part of the possessor to have that possession might augment **2.34** the fact of possession. The holders of a real right will often have a right to possess property. Indeed, the key feature of ownership and leases is normally the right to take possession of the thing in order to use it. Such real right holders have a right to possession that is good against the world: they can recover possession of a thing from a third party, making it a real right. This real right to possession is actually parasitic in the sense that it is ancillary: it requires the existence of another real right to ground the right to recover possession if lost. Others might have a personal right to possession, such as possession under a loan in the case of moveable property. That person is possessing "as of right", but the lack of a real right means that if they are dispossessed by a third party they must rely on the holder of a real right to recover the thing—the possessor's personal right is only good against the lender. Some people possess a thing without any right at all: they might be in bad faith and know that they have no right to possess, or, they might be in good faith due to a mistaken belief that they do have a right to possess. A good faith possessor without any right might be entitled to keep any fruits of the property, and to be reimbursed for any expenditure undertaken in improvements to that property.

Importance of possession

2.35 Many areas of property law use the concept of possession. Possession is important for the law of original acquisition through occupancy: in order to claim ownership of an ownerless thing by occupation it is necessary to take possession of it. Positive prescription also utilises possession by giving an individual who has possessed land for 10 years on some kind of title the ownership of that thing. The system of land registration uses possession in the way it frames some of its rules, and, in order to obtain a real right under some types of lease, the tenant must take possession of the leased premises. Furthermore, certain types of rights of security over moveables require possession before they can be constituted. Indeed, possession plays a particularly important role in relation to moveable property: there is an evidential presumption of ownership for the possessor of corporeal moveable property. Finally, the fact of possession is protected by an action, known as spuilzie, which protects any and all possessors—i.e. whether they possess as of right or not—from being dispossessed by unlawful means.

3. ORIGINAL ACQUISITION

CONCEPTS: ORIGINAL AND DERIVATIVE ACQUISITION

Acquisition is how we describe the investiture of a person with the **3.01** ownership of a thing: to acquire a thing is to become its owner. A distinction is drawn between different types of acquisition that is based on the way in which the acquirer obtains the ownership of a thing. If a person acquires ownership of a thing from another person—in other words a transfer from one person to another—that is an example of derivative acquisition. The acquirer derives their ownership from the transferor. If Alfred buys a car from Betsy we can say that Alfred derives his ownership from Betsy. This form of acquisition is by far the most common form of acquisition. If a person obtains ownership of a thing without the involvement of another person—a transferor—then that is an example of original acquisition. The acquisition is original because it occurs without reference to another person. The law bestows title upon the owner. Because this title is a "fresh" title of ownership the process is called original acquisition. Original acquisition can occur where the thing has no owner, or in situations where the property has an owner but an involuntary legal process extinguishes the ownership of the previous owner. Thus, if the prior owner's title is extinguished, the new owner's title is original—it is not a transfer of ownership, it is a newly created ownership. If Alfred captured a wild animal, as opposed to buying a car, then that would be an example of original acquisition. In this chapter, we are concerned with original acquisition.

OCCUPATION

As we have seen, original acquisition occurs when someone obtains **3.02** ownership of a thing, not from another person, but, instead, when a person obtains their title from the law. There are two types of situation where original acquisition operates. In some situations, a thing has an owner, but, because of the rules of original acquisition, the existing owner loses their title to the thing—the law extinguishes the former owner's title and gives a brand new title to the "original acquirer". The other situation where original acquisition occurs is where a thing has never been owned and a person gains ownership of that thing by virtue of the doctrine of occupation, which takes its name from the Roman law doctrine of *occupatio*.

Things that have no owner are known as *res nullius*. Therefore, if a **3.03** person comes across a *res nullius*, they can obtain ownership of that thing by taking possession of it: *quod nullius est fit occupantis* (ownerless things become property of the taker). Someone becomes owner of a *res nullius* by taking possession of the thing. Possession is a form of taking physical control of a thing and having the appropriate intention to own and possess that thing. In practice, there are few truly ownerless things. A list of examples includes: shells, pearls, gems, stones on the sea shore, and wild animals such as birds, beasts and fish. Items on the sea shore are straightforward, but there are a number of points which one should bear in mind about wild animals. A wild animal is ownerless as long as it is said to be roaming freely. Once a wild animal—it must be a truly wild animal (*Valentine v Kennedy*, 1985 S.C.C.R. 89)—has been captured, ownership of it is taken through occupation, though the animal must continue to be controlled. The definition of control extends to having the animal confined within a certain area—hence deer in a fenced deer park would continue to be owned. If a wild animal escapes from its confinement and returns to the wild, then it becomes ownerless again and is open to occupation from another person, provided the owner is not pursuing the wild animal or has no reasonable prospect of recapturing it. There is a limited exception in relation to animals which go into the wild but subsequently return to a certain location habitually, such as pigeons or bees: such animals that habitually return remain owned until they cease to return.

3.04   Finally, there is a further point that should be borne in mind when considering occupation and wild animals—the concept of poaching. There are statutory rules that allow the owner of a piece of land the rights to game on that land, which essentially means the right to pursue certain types of wild animal. Therefore, it is illegal for another to enter land or trespass in order to hunt those animals; however, the fact that it is illegal to go onto someone's land to poach will not prevent a poacher from gaining ownership of the wild animal, though the court may order restitution of the animal to the landowner. The poaching might constitute a crime, but it does not prevent the law of property operating to give the poacher ownership of the captured animal. Imagine that Abe is a poacher, and that he decides to dust down his camouflage outfit, apply some face paint, and drive up into Angus to shoot some deer at night. If Abe shoots a wild deer on another's land, and then puts it into the back of his van, with the intention of taking it, Abe has committed a crime. Nevertheless, Abe has still taken ownership of the deer. Of course, if Abe is caught he is likely to face a criminal penalty, and the court can (and probably will) order him to return the deer to the land of the landowner.

LOST/ABANDONED PROPERTY

3.05 A feature of taking property by occupation is that once a title has been obtained, except in the case of escaping wild animals, that thing will never be ownerless again. Generally speaking, though there are exceptions, the law does not allow an owner to lose ownership by neglect or absent-mindedness. However, the law does have rules which apply to things which have been lost or have been abandoned. Lost property is not the same as abandoned property. If I leave my umbrella at the theatre, which is a not infrequent occurrence, I have not abandoned it—I have misplaced it. Different rules apply depending on whether the property was lost or abandoned.

Abandoned property

Abandoned property is property that the owner has consciously decided to **3.06** give up—they have made a conscious decision that they no longer want the thing. Lost property is property that the owner has misplaced, and hence the ownership of the thing might not be as clear. If it is clear that property has been abandoned, then the abandoned property falls to the Crown. A good example of this rule can be seen in the case *Mackenzie v Maclean*, 1981 S.L.T. (Sh. Ct) 40, a case which resembles a low-budget version of "Whisky Galore". A hotelier ordered some cans of McEwan's Export and McEwan's Pale Ale which were damaged en route—indeed, when the delivery was inspected upon arrival the place was rather poetically described as "swimming in beer". Unsurprisingly, the hotelier declined to accept delivery of the beer, and the seller agreed to effectively write off the consignment. The hotelier then disposed of the cans of beer in a skip. Thereafter a "crowd then gathered and with the aid of vehicles removed the cans from the skip". During the case, which was actually a criminal prosecution based on the fact that the beer was stolen by removing it from the skip, the sheriff pointed out that when the cans went into the skip they became the property of the Crown as abandoned property. It may now be open to question whether the decision in this case is reliable, in terms of the exact moment at which technical "private law" ownership fell to the Crown, in light of the comments suggesting the Crown must take possession of abandoned moveable property to become its owner in a "private law" sense: *Scottish Environment Protection Agency v Joint Liquidators of the Scottish Coal Co Ltd*, 2014 S.C. 372; 2014 S.L.T. 259 at [108]. It seems that heritable property cannot be unilaterally abandoned by its owner: *Scottish Coal Co Ltd* at [100]–[102]. If, however, the owner ceases to exist (such as when a company is liquidated) then the land might become technically ownerless in a "private law sense", but the Crown's public law rights would give it the power to administer and dispose of the land: *Scottish Coal Co Ltd* at [108]. As noted above, the same approach—that the Crown's initial public law right is akin to a power and not technical private law ownership—applies to moveables, but taking possession of the moveables gives the Crown ownership of them; whereas with land the Crown will rarely register its interest: *Scottish Coal Co Ltd* at [108]. If the Crown waives its rights to such land it will lie dormant in an ownerless state unless acquired by prescription: *Scottish Coal Co Ltd* at [109]; presumably, by analogy, moveable property may be similarly rejected by the Crown.

Lost property

Lost property is property that has been misplaced and it might not be clear **3.07** where ownership lies, and, in some instances, the line between property having been abandoned and merely lost can be unclear. Indeed, property which has been discovered as "lost" property might have been abandoned, but equally it might not have been. If it is clear that a thing is merely lost then the rule seems to be that after 20 years the owner's title to the property is extinguished by negative prescription (Prescription and Limitation (Scotland) Act 1973 s.8), whereupon it falls to the Crown because nothing that has been owned can become ownerless. The decision in *Lord Advocate v University of Aberdeen*, 1963 S.C. 533 demonstrates how the Crown's rights to lost or abandoned property can operate. A large number of ancient artefacts were discovered on St Ninian's Island by an archaeological team from the University of Aberdeen. The Lord Advocate sought to recover the artefacts from the University on the basis that abandoned property is owned by the Crown. The Lord Advocate was successful, with the court observing that whether objects were considered lost or abandoned was not of the first importance as it was clear that they had lain under the ground for some time. Hence, they belonged to the Crown either way.

Civic Government (Scotland) Act 1982

3.08 So far, we have considered the common law relating to the location of ownership of lost or abandoned things. The Civic Government (Scotland) Act 1982 (CG(S)A 1982) regulates the procedures that should be followed in relation to lost/abandoned property that has been discovered. If someone finds property they are required under the CG(S)A 1982 to either deliver the property, or report the fact that they have found that property, to the police. If the true owner is found the police may order the finder to deliver the property to the true owner. Failing that, the finder can keep possession of the property, but crucially they do not obtain ownership under this part of the CG(S)A 1982. The rest of the CG(S)A 1982 has rules dealing with disposal which, broadly speaking, mean that if, after two months, the true owner does not appear the police can: offer the property to the finder, sell the property, or otherwise dispose of the property. If the thing is an animal it becomes the property of the finder. Being offered the property as finder gives the finder a good title in principle, but if the true owner appears within a year they may recover the thing; though if the finder sold the thing to a third-party buyer, who was in good faith, the third party's title is protected.

ACCESSION

3.09 Having considered the law relating to the original acquisition of lost or abandoned property, we now turn to the rules of original acquisition which touch upon owned property that has been neither lost nor abandoned. The first doctrine to consider is that of accession, or as the Romans might say, the law relating to *accessio*. Accession is the rule applied when a piece of property becomes part of another piece of property. That one piece of property becomes part of another is an important point. Accession is what happens when two things are attached to each other: one of those things is subsumed within the other, and, in turn, it becomes a part of the other thing.

At the beginning of the process there are two separate things, whereas at the end there is only a single thing. Of the two things, one survives with the same identity, albeit normally with a greater mass, whereas another thing ceases to exist. The thing that survives and consumes the other thing is called the "principal"; the thing that becomes part of the principal, and hence ceases to exist, is called the "accessory"—hence the name accession.

At this point, we ought to think of an example. The most obvious type **3.10** of accession is that of a building acceding to land. When a building is constructed on a piece of land, that building becomes a part of the land: the land is the principal, and the building is the accessory. In formal terms, that is an example of moveable property becoming attached to heritable property, with the result that the attached moveable property is now considered to be heritable property. The heritable property is always the principal, the moveable property the accessory. Accession of moveable property to heritable property is probably the most common form of accession, but it is also possible for moveable property to attach to moveable property through accession, and for heritable property to become affixed to heritable property by accession.

Three factors
Before considering specific instances of how different types of property **3.11** accede to other types of property, there are three generalised factors applicable to all types of property that are necessary to evaluate when considering whether or not a thing has acceded.

Physical attachment
The first and most important requirement for accession in all cases is that **3.12** the principal and the accessory things have been physically attached to one another. It will depend on the nature of the property involved what the extent of attachment is, but some element of physical attachment is necessary.

Functional subordination
Functional subordination is the idea that the accessory thing must in some **3.13** way contribute to the use or function of the principal thing. This can be difficult to show in some instances, but some cases are straightforward: a doorbell and its accompanying wiring are of little use on their own, but clearly contribute to the overall use of a house. Another example is a central heating system—a radiator is of little stand-alone use without its integration within a central heating system, itself part of a building.

Permanency
In many ways the requirement of permanency is linked to the requirement **3.14** of physical attachment. A thing that is affixed without permanency, or at least some form of quasi-permanency, suggests a lack of physical attachment; likewise, a greater degree of physical attachment will in turn suggest a greater degree of permanency. Indeed, it is an aspect of accession

that although these three requirements are requisite, they are also relative. It is not necessary that each of the three requirements need be present to the strongest or absolute degree—the presence of two factors clearly satisfied might mean that the third requirement need not be as strongly evidenced.

Consequences of accession

"Mechanical" process

3.15 It is important to appreciate that accession is what is known as a "mechanical" process: the intentions of the parties involved are irrelevant. The operation of accession is solely governed by the application of the three factors set out above. What does that mean? I cannot stick a post-it note to a wall and say that it is attached permanently because I intend it to be so— it is the factual question of whether the note is actually sufficiently attached with permanence and functional subordination that matters. Furthermore, the mechanical nature of accession also has significance for the owners of the things involved. If an accessory thing is attached to a principal and accession occurs, then that is the end of the story—the accessory becomes part of the principal. It does not matter if different people own the two things, nor does it matter if the person who attached the two things is in good faith or not. Indeed, it does not even matter if one of the things is stolen. In the past, the law seemed to suggest that the identity of the parties could have an effect on the operation of accession—so, for example, the property of a tenant would not accede to rented property. Clearly such an approach was not a mechanical approach. However, that non-mechanistic approach was rejected by the House of Lords in the late nineteenth century: *Brand's Trs v Brand's Trs* (1876) 3 R. (HL) 16. Therefore, the identity of the parties, particularly in a case where the principal and accessory are separately owned, is not relevant to the question of whether accession has occurred or not.

Accessory becomes part of the principal

3.16 The principal thing subsumes the accessory thing. The significance of the accessory becoming part of the principal is that any rights over the principal affect the accessory automatically. If Angelo installs a marble fireplace in his house, then the fireplace will accede to the house. The house has acceded to the land, so the fireplace has actually acceded to the land. Therefore, the owner of the land now owns the fireplace. Likewise, any right in security taken over the land will apply to the fireplace, as it is also now a part of the land. The owner of the principal thing becomes owner of the accessory thing because the accessory becomes a part of the principal. Obtaining ownership by accession is an example of original acquisition because the accessory becomes part of the principal by operation of law; the owner of the accessory thing did not transfer it to the owner of the principal thing.

Conversion

Another notable consequence of accession is the change in the nature of the **3.17** accessory thing. If a piece of moveable property accedes to a piece of heritable property, then the moveable property (the accessory) becomes heritable property. Because the accessory has been subsumed within the heritable principal property it is now heritable property. Hence, the fireplace in the example above is a corporeal moveable before installation, after installation it is heritable property because it is a part of the house, and hence part of the land.

Owner of accessory loses title

Perhaps the hardest aspect of accession is that the owner of the accessory **3.18** thing loses title to it. That is so for the simple reason that there is no longer a separate thing to own once accession has occurred. Had the fireplace in the example above been stolen, but nevertheless installed in the house, the true owner would have lost his ownership of the fireplace when it was installed. Furthermore, any subordinate real rights that existed within the accessory are also extinguished.

Severance

If the accessory is subsequently severed from the principal then some of the **3.19** effects of accession are reversed. If an accessory thing is detached from the principal then it is no longer a part of the principal: once again there are two distinct things. Furthermore, if moveable property is detached or separated from heritable property, then it ceases to be heritable property. To continue our example of the fireplace, if it was removed from the house then it becomes a separate piece of moveable property again. But one crucial consequence of accession is not reversed: the change of ownership, which occurred as a result of accession. The owner of the principal retains ownership of the accessory even after severance. Thus, if the stolen fireplace from our example was to be detached from the house (and hence the land) the original owner does not regain title—ownership of the fireplace remains with the owner of the land.

Compensation

If the owner of the principal thing, who will have gained ownership of the **3.20** accessory thing by virtue of accession, brought about the accession, then the former owner of the accessory has a personal right to compensation if there was no agreement to join the two things. The right to compensation is only a personal right based on unjustified enrichment, and, in turn, it will be of little use if the owner of the principal thing is bankrupt.

Types of accession

Moveable property to heritable property

Having considered the three requirements for the operation of accession **3.21** generally, we should consider the how those rules operate in individual instances. First, we consider the most common form of accession—that of moveable property acceding to heritable property. Items of moveable property that have acceded to heritable property are known as "fixtures" (not to be confused with "fittings" which are merely things in a house that have not acceded). Bearing in mind the three elements that dictate whether accession operates, the case of moveable property acceding to heritable property is the clearest instance of accession. A building is clearly physically attached to land; furthermore, the extent of that physical attachment is often so strong that the other two elements of accession need only be met in a very weak sense (*Christie v Smith's Excr*, 1949 S.C. 572 at 578–579, per the Lord Justice-Clerk (Thomson)). Sometimes a thing's functional subordination will be obvious: the heating system, the doorbell, the plumbing etc. Where, however, an item is purely decorative it may not have the requisite functional subordination to accede—hence a painting or tapestry is a thing which has value as a thing in its own right (*Cochrane v Stevenson* (1891) 18 R. 1208). Permanence might be problematic since the concept of time is inevitably a somewhat fluidic one, but it is settled that certain factors can be used to assist in considering the permanence of an attachment: the degree of attachment, the mutual adaptation of accessory and principal to fit one another, and any relevant customs about whether a thing would normally be detached or removed in the circumstances.

Moveable property to moveable property

3.22 It is also possible for a piece of moveable property to accede to another piece of moveable property. The same three principles are applied as in the context of land, but they can be more difficult to demonstrate. So, for example, an elbow patch sewn onto an academic's tweed jacket will accede to the jacket, as would the gold leaf applied to a picture frame. But the nature of moveable property can make it more difficult to apply the three requirements for accession due to the fact that moveables will often be a similar size. This poses a problem in relation to the distinction between the accessory piece of property and the principal—how does one identify the principal thing? The institutional writer Bell gives some factors to take into account here: Bell, *Principles*, § 1298. If one of the two things ceases to exist separately then it is the accessory: an example would be the paint applied to a car. If a thing is a mere adornment or completion then it is the accessory: an example would be the insertion of a small diamond into a large crown. Finally, if the ceasing to exist or adornment tests are inconclusive then it might be that the bulkiest thing is the principal.

Heritable property to heritable property

3.23 Where a piece of land is adjacent to a body of water, the extent of the water can ebb and flow. If water recedes, and thereby reveals more land, the revealed land accedes to the land which is adjacent to it. This is known as alluvion, and the process has two requirements. First, the change in the extent of the water should be permanent and not simply a seasonal fluctuation; second, it must be a gradual or incremental change. Sudden changes are known as avulsion and do not change ownership.

Fruits

The final form of accession is known as accession by fruits, and it is **3.24**
concerned with natural processes whereby a thing of nature grows and
accedes to that from whence it came. There are three main examples of
accession by fruits.

Crops, trees and plants

Crops, trees and plants generally accede to the soil from which they grow **3.25**
when they take root and draw nourishment. There is an exception in relation
to "industrial growing crops", which remain separate items of moveable
property. Industrial growing crops are those that require annual seed and
labour: e.g. wheat, barley etc remain the property of whoever sows and
harvests them. The exception can be seen in *Boskabelle Ltd v Laird Ltd*,
2006 S.L.T. 1079. A company that had purchased land sought to recover
wheat and barley that had been growing on the land on the basis that crops
had acceded to the land, and hence its purchase of the land entitled it to
claim the crops. This was rejected, and the court observed that there was
long line of authority that industrial growing crops remained the (moveable)
property of the person who sowed them.

Young animals

Young animals which are still *in utero*, which means in the womb, are a **3.26**
part of and accede to the mother. Upon birth the animal is severed from the
mother and becomes a separate thing, but remains owned by the owner of
the mother.

Natural products

The natural products of things from the animal and plant kingdoms accede **3.27**
to the thing from which they grow. So, for example, the milk from a cow
or the apples on a tree, are a part of the thing that they grow from. Again,
like the case with young animals, when they fall or are harvested they
become a separate thing, but they are owned by the owner of the thing from
which they have grown.

SPECIFICATION

Concept

The doctrine of specification is the process whereby a new thing is created **3.28**
using existing things owned by more than one person. It is crucial that a
new thing is created, and it is this creation of a new thing that distinguishes
specification from accession. With accession one thing becomes a part of
another thing; with specification existing things are used to make a new
thing. There are many examples: melting a square of wax and adding
perfume to make a scented candle, mixing flour and eggs to make a cake,
or combining planks of wood to construct a boat etc. The law relating to
specification in Scotland is derived from the Roman law of *specification*,

which was itself extremely unsettled. The question of who owns the newly created thing has long been problematic. While it is possible for the parties to agree who will become owner, see *Wylie and Lochhead v Mitchell* (1870) 8 M. 552, matters are far less clear if ownership of the thing has not been agreed upon in advance. In Scots law, it is the approach set out by Bell that has been adopted and followed in case law. According to Bell there are three requirements for specification.

Requirements for specification

3.29 The first requirement for specification is that a new item has been created through workmanship. In other words, there must be a new thing that is more than simply the sum of its parts. Secondly, the process must be irreversible: this reflects the debates of Roman law about who should own the newly created thing. If it is possible to reverse the process, so that the constituent things might be returned as they were before they were made into the new thing, then ownership remains with the previous owners of the respective constituent things. If, however, the process cannot be reversed, then the ownership of the newly created thing is vested in its maker. The final question to be determined is whether the maker of the new thing was in good faith—if the materials belonged to other people, did the maker know that? In Scots law, there is authority that only a maker in good faith will acquire ownership by specification. In *McDonald v Provan (of Scotland Street) Ltd*, 1960 S.L.T. 231 a car had been made using the parts of two cars, one of which was stolen. The court held that there could be no specification at all because the process was reversible; however, the court observed that even if the process had been irreversible there could have been no ownership in the maker, because the new thing was made in bad faith.

Compensation

3.30 If a maker has created a new thing it might be possible for the owner of the materials used to make it to claim compensation for the value of the materials used to make the new thing. The basis of this claim for compensation appears to be unjustified enrichment. In *International Banking Corporation v Ferguson Shaw and Sons*, 1910 S.C. 182 a quantity of margarine was made using vegetable oil owned by another person. The maker of the margarine was in good faith but was still ordered to pay the value of the oil used to the former owner.

CONFUSION AND COMMIXTION

3.31 The final forms of original acquisition in moveable property are the doctrines of confusion and commixtion. These doctrines apply where things are mixed together without becoming physically attached enough to trigger accession, and where no new thing is created by specification. The different terms refer to different types of mixture: confusion is concerned with mixtures of liquids, whereas commixtion is concerned with mixtures of solid things. The rules are designed for a situation where it is impossible to separate individual items from the mixture. If Adrian has 10 tonnes of wheat, and Barbara has 10 tonnes of wheat, and all that wheat is mixed together in a (large) cement mixer it will be impossible to distinguish which specific grains belong to which owner. Likewise, if Alfonso and Beth both pour a bottle of their finest malt whisky into the same decanter it will be impossible to separate the mixed (perhaps blended) whisky. Specification cannot easily be relied upon as it is difficult to say that a new thing has been created (with the possible exception of the whisky in the unlikely event that a drinkable blend was created). If mixing the component parts together has created a new thing, then the rules of specification apply. If separation is possible, then there is no confusion or commixtion: each owner retains ownership of his or her part of the mixture as constituted before the mixing. If separation is impossible then the mixture is said to be co-owned: the mixture is common property. If there is no agreement relating to the proportional shares of the common property, then the mixture is divided according to proportional contribution if the components were of equal value. If the components were not of equal value then the ownership is divided according to value. So, in the example of the grain above, both Adrian and Barbara have a 50% share in the mixed grain. If Adrian had contributed 75 tonnes of grain and Barbara 25 tonnes of grain, then they would have a 75% and 25% share respectively. If, however, Arnold has a bottle of wine worth £99 and Bob has a bottle of wine worth £1, and the two are mixed together, then it would appear that Arnold would have a 99% share in the resulting mixture.

4. DERIVATIVE ACQUISITION

CONCEPTS AND PRINCIPLES

Transfers generally

If a person acquires ownership of a thing from another person—a **4.01**
transfer from one person to another—that is an example of derivative
acquisition. The acquirer derives their ownership from the other person.
In such a transfer, there are two key persons: the person who owns the
thing and is transferring it (the transferor) and the person who will
receive ownership once the transfer has been completed (the transferee).
When ownership has been derived from another person the acquirer's
title is limited by any factors that might have affected the transferor's
title, or by the process by which that title was transferred. There are a
number of different factors that might have such an effect. A valid
transfer requires consent on the part of both the transferor (*animus
transferendi dominii*) and the transferee (*animus transferendi dominii*):
a person cannot (normally) be forced to take, or part with, the ownership
of a thing. In order to give legally effective consent, a person must have
sufficient legal capacity to do so. Furthermore, in order to make an
effective transfer, it is necessary to focus this consent by identifying a
specific thing. If a purported transfer does not identify a thing with
sufficient accuracy, then consent cannot be applied to that particular
thing to authorise its transfer; though a personal right might arise on the
basis that the words used refer to things of that general nature. If Andrew
says "I will sell you *this* red ball" (and he is holding a red ball) then that
particular red ball is identified and can be transferred (assuming all other
requirements are met) because his consent is focused on that specific red
ball (as is the consent to receive on the part of the transferee). On the
other hand, if Andrew says "I will sell you *a* red ball" (and he is not
holding a red ball) then a thing has not been sufficiently identified to
which his consent to transfer (or the transferee's consent to acquire) can
attach. The effect is that personal (contractual) rights to obtain (the right
of the transferee), and to receive payment for (the right of the transferor),
an as yet unidentified red ball might be formed—but no transfer of
ownership can occur. Consent is required in order to carry out a transfer,
and that consent must be focused upon a particular thing. This need for
focus is part of an important exercise in differentiation: it is important to
distinguish between dispositive intention and contractual intention. The
parties' contractual intentions are what constitute the consent needed to
form a contract. Dispositive intentions are those that form the consent
that is focused on a particular thing in order to transfer it. In order to
make sense of this distinction it is necessary to distinguish between a
contract and a conveyance.

Contract and conveyance

4.02 The distinction between real and personal rights has been considered above. We have also just alluded to a situation whereby non-specific things might be the subject of a contract, but not of a transfer. What does that mean? In order to understand this concept, it is important to be familiar with a fundamental distinction in property law: the distinction between contract and conveyance (conveyance is just another name for transfer). Take the following example: Ariella sells a farm to Boris. Two separate legal actions occur. First, a contract of sale between Ariella and Boris is formed. As with all contracts, this creates mutual rights and duties between Ariella and Boris. The main obligations and rights are that Ariella will transfer the farm to Boris, and, on the other hand, Boris will pay Ariella money. These mutual *obligations* under the contract do not transfer the property to Boris. The transfer is brought about by a second legal action known as the conveyance or transfer. Boris registering a deed transferring the farm, which was granted by Ariella, achieves the transfer. The contract is only the prelude to the transfer and is, therefore, sometimes known as the "cause" because it is what sets in motion the separate act of transfer. In most cases there will be a cause that sets in motion a transfer; the transfer itself is achieved by some kind of public act.

Public acts and the "publicity principle"

4.03 What is meant by a public act? A requisite of any transfer is the presence of consent, but it is not enough in itself to complete the transfer: a further "public act" is required be undertaken. That a public act is required comes back to the fundamental idea of real and personal rights. A real right is a right in a thing that can be enforced against the world, and, thus, it is important that the world should be able to see if someone has such a right. This is the "publicity principle". The type of publicity required depends on the type of property involved. Constituting real rights over land normally requires some form of registration, while constituting rights over corporeal moveables traditionally required delivery of the moveable thing. The public act for the transfer of incorporeal property is "intimation" (see below). Public acts are also necessary to constitute any real rights, and so includes subordinate real rights. Normally, the moment the public act is carried out is the moment the real right is created. Ownership of a thing is in the transferor until the moment of the public act, whereupon ownership moves instantaneously to the transferee.

Void, voidable and absolutely good

4.04 In addition to the process of transfer it is important to examine what is being transferred. In order to consider what is being transferred it is important to understand what different qualities of title a person may have. Someone can have an "absolutely good title", which is a title that is valid and is not amenable to any challenge. Alternatively, someone may have a less straightforward and weaker title. A voidable title is a title that is valid for the time being, but, for some reason, which is also vulnerable to challenge. A voidable title is a valid title, but it is vulnerable. If a voidable title is successfully challenged it comes to an end. This can be contrasted with a void title, which is not really a title at all. Invalid from the outset, a void title is a title which has never been valid. Someone may think that they have a good title, but it might in fact be void or voidable. How do void and voidable titles arise? Whether a title is good, void, or voidable depends on a number of factors. The title of the person from whom the current holder received the property can be relevant, as might the circumstances surrounding the way a person came to have the property.

Void title

A void title occurs if the transferor had a void title. If Alf had a void title **4.05** (that is no title) to a pen and purported to transfer ownership of the pen to Bill, then what Bill receives is a void title (which is no title). Alf had nothing and so gave nothing. Other situations where a void title can arise are those where the transfer was made with an absence of consent. Therefore, if a purported transfer was made, but, in fact, the transferor lacked capacity or was labouring under force and fear, then only a void title can be obtained by the transferee.

Voidable title

A voidable title is subtly different from a void title. A voidable title is a **4.06** valid but vulnerable title. Voidable titles arise if the transfer of a thing has been validly concluded, but some aspect of the transfer process meant that another person's rights have been violated. Fraud is the classic means by which such voidable titles are created. Frank transfers a valuable painting to Lucifer after being fraudulently induced to do so. Frank has actually consented to the transfer, albeit that the consent was imperfectly obtained, and so the law states that a valid transfer has occurred. However, the title that Lucifer receives is said to be voidable because Frank can subsequently challenge the transfer, but Lucifer's title is valid until successfully challenged. Frank can seek a "reduction" of the transfer, which is the name given to the process used to challenge and extinguish a voidable title. If the transfer is reduced, the ownership of the painting returns to Frank. Voidable titles can also arise if property is improperly transferred by a person subject to insolvency proceedings in order to defeat his creditors. A transfer made in contravention of an existing contractual obligation (the "offside goals" rule) also gives rise to a voidable title. It is important to appreciate that the concept of a voidable title is distinct from a voidable contract. As we saw earlier, there is a difference between the contract relating to a transfer and the conveyance itself. The fact that a contract is voidable does not mean that the transfer, and hence title, will necessarily be voidable. Likewise, it is possible that the transfer is voidable but not the contract. It is possible that both might be voidable, but they are intellectually distinct and should be considered separately.

Implications of quality of title: the importance of the transferor's title

4.07 What is the broader relevance of all this discussion about the different types of title that a person might have? Why does it matter what sort of title someone has? The broader importance of the quality of someone's title is the effect that this will have on any future transfer of the property. In other words, how does the title of the transferor affect the title of the transferee? If the transferor of property has an absolutely good title then the transferee, their singular successor, will also have an absolutely good and valid title. However, even though the title itself is fine, there might still be problems associated with the process by which the transfer was made. A voidable title is one that is vulnerable to challenge, but until it is challenged it is a perfectly valid title. The fact that the title is valid, albeit precariously so, can have a number of effects on the transferee. The effects on the transferee depend on the knowledge of the transferee on the one hand, and also the nature of the transaction. If the transferee knows that the transferor's title is voidable, then the transferee's title is voidable too. Abraham is fraudulently induced to sell a tomato to Buchanan, and then Buchanan sells the same tomato to Carter. If Carter knew about the fraud, then Carter's title is voidable. If, however, Carter did not know about the fraud then he buys in good faith, and because he is in good faith he receives an absolutely good title (the rule is given statutory form for sales of corporeal moveables by the Sale of Goods Act 1979 s.23, but the principle is a general one). The state of knowledge on the part of the transferee is crucial. However, if the transfer is made as a gift—i.e. the transferor is getting no material benefit in return for making the transfer—then it does not matter whether the transferee is in good faith or not: his title will be voidable. If Buchanan had transferred the tomato to Carter as a gift it would have made no difference whether Carter was in good faith or not—Carter's title to the tomato is voidable. Thus, the title that a grantee will get from a granter with a voidable title will depend upon circumstances. Bear in mind the nature of a voidable title as a vulnerable one—a voidable title is only valid until challenged, and the moment that it is successfully challenged it becomes a void title. This has an obvious importance with regard to timing—if a voidable title has been reduced (and made void) the question of knowledge does not arise because the transferor has nothing to give to the transferee. If the fraudulent sale of the tomato had been challenged and reduced then Buchanan would have had a void title, and, in turn, all he could give to Carter was a void title. If the transferor's title is void then the transferee's title is also void. This is expressed in the latin maxim *nemo plus juris ad alium transferre potest quam ipse haberet*: no-one can transfer what he does not himself have. That idea is perhaps the golden rule of property law. This ties in with the fact that a void title is not really a title at all: when we accept that a void title is, in effect, nothing, the result of the *nemo plus* rule is that a transferor with nothing can grant nothing. There are, however, exceptions to the *nemo plus* rule. Furthermore, it is important to be aware of timing, especially when answering a question about this subject. The question of timing is important in a situation where a granter purports to make more than one transfer: Adam agrees to sell his house to Bert, and delivers a disposition (the conveyance) to Bert on Monday. On Tuesday, Adam agrees to sell the same house to Craig, and delivers a disposition to Craig. On Wednesday Craig registers his disposition. Remember that a public act is required to complete a transfer. When Craig registered his disposition on Wednesday he carried out a public act that completed the transfer. Bert did not register his disposition, and, even though he contracted with Adam before Craig, the fact that Craig completed the entire process first means that he is now the owner of the thing. If Bert tried to register his disposition he would not gain a good title to the house. Why? Craig became the owner when he registered his disposition, and so, in turn, from that moment Adam was no longer the owner: he had a void title. In turn, because Bert's disposition relies upon Adams's title, any attempt to register it could only give Bert a void title because of the *nemo plus* rule. The *nemo plus* rule applies to the creation of all real rights, and so only an owner of property can grant a subordinate real right. If Anthony granted Brian a lease over Holyrood Palace that grant would be void. Anthony is not the owner of Holyrood Palace and so his title is void, and, because of the *nemo plus* rule, Brian's lease is also void.

Prior tempore est potior jure

If there are two competing attempts to create a real right the first duly **4.08** constituted real right takes precedence over the other. This is sometimes explained in the maxim *prior tempore est potior jure*: first in time, stronger by right. This means that the first person to secure a public act to complete a transfer is stronger in right and will defeat another party who is still to secure the public act to complete the transfer. The significance of the completion of the public act is that it is the point at which a contractual right to a conveyance is augmented by the occurrence of the conveyance— it is when the real right moves from the granter to the grantee. In many respects, the prior tempore rule is the other side of the *nemo plus* rule coin. In the case of Adam, Bert, and Craig, above, we saw that Craig's registration meant that Adam no longer had ownership, and, in turn, Bert could not derive a valid title from him. The *prior tempore* rule merely states that because Craig registered before Bert he is stronger in right than Bert; but the reason that he is stronger is because the *nemo plus* rule means that Adam no longer had a good title to transfer. The *prior tempore* rule applies to a competition between the holders of any type of real right, but the result of the competition might be different. That is because certain types of real right are incompatible with others. In the case of the transfer of ownership of a thing, if there are two competing dispositions the winner takes all. That is not the case in other circumstances. Anna owns a farm and has granted a standard security to Bank of Bonds and another to Bank of Crowns. Bank of Crowns registers its standard security on 1 January, and Bank of Bonds registers its standard security on 3 January. In this situation Bank of Crowns and Bank of Bonds will both get a real right. That is because a standard security is a subordinate real right, and so, even though Bank of Crowns has registered its standard security, Anna is still the owner of the farm and so she has title to give Bank of Bonds its standard security. However, Bank of Crowns takes "priority" in the "ranking" between Bank of Bonds and Bank of Crowns' securities. If Anna were to become insolvent and the farm had to be sold, then Bank of Crowns will be paid first—Bank of Bonds must wait to see if there are any proceeds of sale leftover following the payment of Bank of Crown's debt. Thus, it is important to carry out a public act to complete a real right as quickly as you can: if you're not fast, you're last.

Offside goals

4.09 One of the significant features of a real right being a right in the thing is that when a thing is transferred to a successor the real right survives the transfer. That is because the right is in the thing, and not against the holder of the thing (which would normally be a personal right). A personal right can only be enforced against the person who owes the concomitant duty associated with it, and so it cannot be enforced against singular successors. There is, however, an exception to this general rule that a personal right cannot be enforced against a singular successor: the exception is known as the "offside goals rule" (the name of the rule comes from a metaphor used in one of the leading cases: *Rodger (Builders) Ltd v Fawdry*, 1950 S.C. 483 at 501, per the Lord Justice-Clerk Wheatley). The content of the rule is that if a person obtains a real right, in the knowledge that someone else has a contractual right to obtain a real right, then their title is voidable. The person with the pre-existing contractual right can challenge the transferee's voidable title and have it reduced. If that title is reduced then a personal right, that is the pre-existing contractual right, is essentially prevailing over a real right. Annabel decides to sell her house. On Monday, she agrees a contract to sell the house to Bob for £1 million. Bob tells his friend Hamish that he is getting a great deal on the house. Hamish turns out to be no friend. On Tuesday, Hamish contacts Annabel and offers to buy the house for £1.1 million. Annabel is greedy and agrees to Hamish's offer and grants him a disposition which he then registers. Hamish has become the owner of the house—he has registered a disposition making him owner. However, Hamish knew about the pre-existing contract between Bob and Annabel: he has scored an offside goal. Hamish's title is voidable, and so Bob can challenge and reduce it. To show that there has been an offside goal it is necessary to show that there was either (a) knowledge of the prior personal right, or (b) that the transfer in breach of the pre-existing personal right was a gratuitous transfer. The rule applies to double sales, but it is also possible to have other grants of real rights reduced as voidable if there was a prior personal right. When the owner of a house concluded missives with A, but, before A could register, the owner granted another standard security to bank C which registered its security, it was held that the standard security was voidable as it was granted in contravention of the pre-existing personal right: *Trade Development Bank v Critall Windows Ltd*, 1983 S.L.T. 510.

Accretion

The final concepts of this examination of the general elements of transfer **4.10** are both related to the *nemo plus* rule. The doctrine of accretion is concerned with situations involving a chain of void transfers. When someone who does not own something purports to transfer it, such a transfer is void; meaning the transferee also has a void title. However, if the transferor subsequently becomes the owner of the thing that they previously purported to transfer, then that purported transfer is automatically validated retrospectively. This an exception to *nemo plus* rule insofar as a transfer made by a non-owner gives a valid title to the transferee (eventually). However, the fact that the non-owning granter must still gain title, albeit later, makes it an exception in a temporal sense only. The most important application of the doctrine is in relation to heritable property, though it appears there is some scope for the doctrine in relation to incorporeal moveable property, and perhaps, though less so, in relation to corporeal moveable property. Angelo grants Brenda a disposition of Princes Street Gardens in Edinburgh, which Brenda registers. Angelo does not own Princes Street Gardens, and the transfer is void. If, however, 10 years later the owner of the Gardens transferred ownership of them to Angelo, then Brenda would automatically get a good title to the Gardens. There is no need for another disposition or registration—the transfer is automatic. It is a legal fiction. Furthermore, the transfer is considered to be retrospective; so, even though Angelo only received title 10 years after the void transfer, the law holds that the transfer occurred on the day of that original (void) transfer. This can be important if there have been multiple transfers by the owner. The final doctrine is also related to the *nemo plus* rule and constitutes another form of exception. The doctrine is concerned with heritable property and relates to the position of an unregistered holder of heritable property. An unregistered holder of heritable property is not the owner of the property: to own property one must be registered. On the other hand, an unregistered holder is someone who has a delivered disposition (the deed which conveys land, see below) and only needs to register it in order to complete their title—the ability to become owner is entirely in their own hands. A person in this position is accorded certain privileges by the law. The most important of these is the power of an unregistered holder to grant a disposition to another person, which, if registered, will give the transferee a good title of ownership. The chain of dispositions forming the underlying title—known as "midcouples" or "links in title"— is no longer examined by The Keeper of the Registers of Scotland upon registration, but the ultimate transferee's solicitor will check the links in title upon applying for registration: see K.G.C. Reid and G.L. Gretton, *Land Registration* (2017) at [8.11], [8.16]. This is a clear exception to the *nemo plus* rule, hence the need to demonstrate these "midcouples". If Alf has delivered a disposition transferring land to Bert it is perfectly acceptable for Bert not to register it (and hence not complete the transfer), and instead grant a disposition of the land in question to Charles. If Charles registers the disposition from Bert, then Charles will become the owner.

MOVEABLE PROPERTY

Corporeal moveables

4.11 The transfer of a moveable from one person to another varies according to the type of property involved. Certain rules govern the transfer of corporeal moveable property, and others govern transfer of incorporeal moveable property. Bear in mind throughout this analysis that we are looking at derivative acquisition—a transfer from one person to another—and that involves one person being divested of ownership while another is simultaneously invested with ownership. A corporeal moveable is a thing that is not land, and which has a physical manifestation. The transfer of the ownership of a corporeal moveable can occur in different ways depending on the underlying "cause" of the transfer. The three most common causes of a transfer are gift, exchange and sale.

Exchange and gifts: delivery

4.12 In each case the common law requirements reflect the general position we considered earlier: there must be mutual consent to the transfer and a public act of perfection to complete the transfer. Historically, the public act required in the case of moveable property was an act of delivery. Delivery is still required to perfect the transfer of ownership in all cases except sales. Arnold buys a law book so that he can give it to his daughter Babs for her studies. Arnold tells her that he has bought her a book on the phone. At this point, there has been no transfer of the book from Arnold to Babs. Babs must wait until Arnold delivers the book to her before she will become its owner. "Delivery" can have a specialised meaning that goes beyond physically handing over a thing. Physically handing over a thing is known as "actual delivery". Constructive delivery is where "delivery" of a thing is made without the need for a physical transfer of possession. The transferor can inform a third party, who is holding goods on behalf of the transferor, that he now holds on behalf of the transferee: that is called a constructive delivery. If Arnold had bought the book in a bookshop, he could tell the manager to hold it on behalf of Babs, which would represent a constructive delivery, and hence give Babs ownership. It is essential that the third party is informed because this constitutes a public act: merely telling Babs on the phone, or giving her the receipt alone, is not enough: *Inglis v Robertson and Baxter* (1898) 25 R. (HL) 70. An alternative form of delivery is known as symbolic delivery. In practice, the most commonly encountered instance of symbolic delivery is concerned with a document of title called a "bill of lading". A bill of lading details corporeal moveables on a ship somewhere, and, for the purposes of the law, it symbolises the goods themselves. Handing over the bill of lading is to symbolically hand over the goods, and in turn constitutes delivery: *Hayman and Son v McLintock*, 1907 S.C. 936. Therefore, if there is a mutual intention to transfer a piece of corporeal moveable property, as a gift or as part of an exchange, it is necessary for the corporeal moveable property to be delivered by one of these methods.

Sale

4.13 It was formerly the case that to complete a sale of corporeal moveables it was necessary to deliver them. However, that requirement for delivery in the case of sales was abolished and replaced by the rules contained in the Sale of Goods Act 1979 (SOGA 1979). According to the SOGA 1979, the transfer of the ownership of a corporeal moveable in a sale takes place at the moment intended by the parties: SOGA 1979 s.17(1). Therefore, the main rule is that ownership passes when the parties choose—there is no need for delivery. Of course, because it is open to the parties to choose the moment of transfer they may opt for delivery as the moment of transfer; but to do so would be their choice—it is not a requirement. Sometimes the parties will not expressly state when they intend ownership to transfer, and so various default rules provide further guidance. There are five "rules" which apply to assist with determining when ownership will pass: SOGA 1979 s.18. The most important rule is that when there is an unconditional contract for specific goods (goods = corporeal moveables), ownership passes upon completion of the contract: SOGA 1979 s.18, r.1. The remaining rules deal with conditions relating to the goods that must be satisfied; once the conditions are satisfied ownership passes: SOGA 1979 s.18, rr.2–5. Special mention should be made of the fifth rule, which applies to a contract for the sale of goods that have not been specifically identified or do not yet exist: SOGA 1979 s.18, r.5. Until these goods are specifically identified, or come into existence, it is impossible to apply the necessary consent to transfer to them, in accordance with the specificity principle identified above. A special rule applies to goods in an "identified bulk". If the bulk itself is identified, and the buyer (transferee) has paid for the goods, then the buyer is a co-owner of that entire identified bulk: SOGA 1979 s.20A(2)(b). The undivided share assigned to the buyer as a co-owner is allocated in proportion to the share of the bulk that they have paid for: SOGA 1979 s.20A(3). Astrid is a grain merchant with 100 tonnes of wheat in a warehouse. Bea and Carlos are grain buyers for two bakeries. Astrid agrees to sell 50 tonnes of the grain to Bea, and the remaining 50 tonnes to Carlos. Bea pays for the grain, but Carlos agrees that he will only pay upon delivery. The grain is still in the warehouse. In this situation Beth is a co-owner of this identified bulk, and her assigned share is 50%. Carlos has no co-ownership interest because he has not paid.

Exceptions to the *nemo plus* rule

4.14 The *nemo plus* rule states that nobody can transfer title to a thing when they themselves do not have title. The rule also applies to sales of corporeal moveables (for sales see SOGA 1979 s.21(1)), though there are statutory exceptions to the rule as it applies to corporeal moveables. Remember that ownership passes when the parties intend, and so the parties can stipulate that ownership of the goods does not depend on possession. Goods can be possessed by the seller even though ownership has passed to the buyer; alternatively, the goods can be possessed by the buyer even though ownership has not been transferred. In these situations, the person with possession is not the owner, but, nevertheless, they may appear to third parties as the owner. In publicity terms, the possession of a corporeal moveable suggests ownership. Indeed, there is a presumption that the possessor of corporeal moveable property is the owner of that property (Bell, *Principles*, § 1313, *Chief Constable of Strathclyde v Sharp*, 2002 S.L.T. (Sh. Ct) 95; *Prangnell-O'Neill v Skiffington*, 1984 S.L.T. 282). Therefore, there are exceptions to the *nemo plus* rule for certain situations involving the sale of goods where possession and ownership have been detached. The first exception is where the seller is left in possession of the goods after ownership has passed to the buyer: SOGA 1979 s.24. If the "seller in possession" transfers those goods to a third party, who is in good faith, the essential effect (the wording is convoluted) of s.24 is to give that third party ownership of the goods. Allowing the seller to give the third party title is an exception to the *nemo plus* rule because the seller had no title (a void title) to give. Similarly, the second exception is where the buyer has obtained possession of the goods but is not yet the owner: SOGA 1979 s.25. If the "buyer in possession" transfers the goods to a third party, who is in good faith, then, again, the essential effect (the wording is even worse than s.24, and contains fiddly exceptions to the exception) of s.25 is to give that third party ownership of the goods: *Archivent Sales and Development Ltd v Strathclyde Regional Council*, 1985 S.L.T. 154. This represents an exception to the *nemo plus* rule because the buyer is not the owner, but their actions have given someone a good title. The rationales for both exceptions come from the publicity element of possession: the world is entitled, in some circumstances, to assume that the possessor is the owner of the goods, and so the world ought to be able to rely upon that perception. Possession of the goods must be taken in the capacity of seller or buyer in order to rely on the sections: *Fadallah v Pollak* [2013] EWHC 3159 (QBD). References to ss.24 and 25 of the SOGA 1979 are often accompanied by references to ss.8 and 9 of the Factors Act 1889 respectively. These provisions of the Factors Act 1889 are substantially the same as the *nemo plus* exceptions found in the SOGA 1979, and, to some extent at least, are interchangeable. Section 2 of the Factors Act 1889 creates a distinct exception to the *nemo plus* rule: if possession of goods has been given to "a mercantile agent" (as opposed to a buyer or seller of goods under a contract of sale), they can give good title to a third party in good faith.

Incorporeal moveables

Concept

4.15 Incorporeal property is the name that we give to property that has no physical manifestation, and the most common example of that sort of property is a personal right. The most commonly transferred incorporeal moveable is a right to be paid money by someone else: a debt. If Abner owes Brett £20 we say that Brett has a personal right to be paid £20 by Abner. Brett might want to get the money early or avoid the hassle of enforcing the debt, so he might want to transfer his right (the claim to £20 from Abner) to Chic in exchange for money. Brett can transfer his right to receive £20 from Abner to Chic. A creditor can transfer a personal right without seeking consent from the debtor; the idea is that the debtor is not really bothered about who he will ultimately pay. The transfer is called an "assignation" in Scotland, though the terms assignment and cessio are sometimes used.

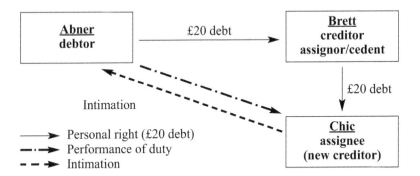

Transferability
The first question that has to be addressed is whether the incorporeal **4.16** moveable can be the subject of a transfer at all. Most personal rights can be transferred by assignation, but not all can. Certain rights cannot be transferred by statute: for example, any purported assignation of universal credit, a jobseeker's allowance, or child credit is void (Social Security Administration Act 1992 s.187(1)(za),(aa) and (c). Likewise, the original contract that gives rise to the right being assigned may prohibit assignation of that right. If the contract between Abner and Brett expressly prohibited the assignation of Brett's rights under the contract, that would be effective. In common with most elements of contract law, the prohibition against assignation can also be implied. Related to the question of transferability is a question about what sort of person can assign a right. The most important rule here is that while a creditor can assign a right without requiring the debtor's consent, a debtor cannot unilaterally assign a duty or obligation. The reason for this can be illustrated using our example: Abner cannot transfer his obligation to pay £20 to another person because he might transfer the obligation to someone without good credit. When Abner and Brett entered their contract, Brett expected Abner to perform the contract and calculated his risk and the terms of the loan accordingly. If Abner could unilaterally transfer his obligation to Dodgy Dave, a bankrupt, it is unlikely that Brett would be paid the money he is owed. However, while a debtor cannot unilaterally transfer an obligation to a third party, it is possible to make such a transfer if the debtor, creditor and third party all agree. Such a transfer of an obligation is not an assignation, it is known as "delegation".

Transfer process: three steps

1. Contract

4.17 If it has been established that the personal right is transferable then the assignation process can take place. The process follows the general rules of property law: there is (1) a contract, and (2) a distinct conveyance that is perfected by (3) a public act. The first step is that a contractual agreement has been reached (there is no need for writing, but often it will be in writing) with respect to the assignation. Normally this will be a sale, whereby the assignee (the transferee) agrees to pay the assignor or cedent (both mean the transferor) to transfer the right.

2. Assignation (conveyance)

4.18 Somewhat confusingly the term "assignation" is the name given to the entire process of transferring an incorporeal moveable, as well as the name given to the conveyance element of the overall process. It is not necessary for the conveyance of an incorporeal moveable to be in writing, but in practice almost all conveyances of incorporeal property are done in writing by granting a deed of assignation. That deed of assignation is often in the style suggested by the venerable Transmission of Moveable Property (Scotland) Act 1862, though other styles are valid if worded correctly. Such a deed of assignation will normally be delivered to the assignee, but, crucially, the ownership of the personal right has not yet been transferred by delivery the deed of assignation.

3. Intimation (public act)

4.19 As with all types of property, the final requirement for the transfer of incorporeal moveable property is a public act that perfects and completes the transfer. The public act that completes the process of assignation is intimation to the debtor of the assignation. In other words, the debtor must be informed of the transfer. Intimation constitutes a public act because it involves a third party, and it is important because the debtor needs to know the identity of the person to whom he should make payment or render performance of the obligation. In our example, for Brett to transfer the £20 claim to Chic there must be intimation of the transfer to Abner. In practice, the assignee will be the person who gives intimation to the debtor—because it is in his interest to do so—though it is perfectly valid for the cedent/assignor to give the intimation. Two statutory options exist for the form in which the intimation may be given: (1) notarial delivery of a copy of the assignation; and (2) the postal delivery of a copy of the assignation to the debtor: Transmission of Moveable Property (Scotland) Act 1862 s.2. In both cases the intimation is only complete, and hence so is the whole transfer, when the debtor receives a copy of the assignation. The statutory forms of intimation are most commonly used, but they are not exhaustive. While it is possible to give intimation in different ways, the law insists on some degree of formality, and a debtor finding out about the assignation through private knowledge does not constitute intimation in Scottish law. The most important alternatives are performance by debtor to assignee or an action brought by the assignee against the debtor.

Effect of the assignation

At one level the effect of a valid transfer is an obvious one—the right is **4.20** transferred. However, the content and characteristics of the right that has been transferred are more complex. The most important concept is the idea that the assignee gets no better right than the assignor had: *assignatus utitur jure auctoris*. The effect of the rule is that the right that the assignee receives is exactly the same as the right that the assignor had. If the right transferred is a contractual right, then any defences available to the debtor to a claim by the original creditor are also available against the assignee: *Scottish Widows Fund v Buist* (1876) 3 R. 1078. In the Scottish Widows case a Mr Moir took out a policy of life insurance, a condition of which was (as now) full disclosure of medical health. Mr Moir lied and said that he was in good health and of sober living; in fact, he had syphilis and was an alcoholic. The effect of that lie was to invalidate the life insurance. However, Mr Moir assigned his rights under the insurance document to Mrs Buist, who was in good faith—she knew nothing of the lie, or of the invalidity of the insurance. Mrs Buist tried to claim when Mr Moir died, but her claim was denied on the basis of the *assignatus utitur jure auctoris* principle. Mr Moir could not have claimed on the basis of his rights under the policy, and transfer of the right to Mrs Buist did not cure the defect: she had no better right than Mr Moir, even though she was an innocent third party giving value. There is an exception to this rule in the case of latent trust rights: the debtor cannot set up a defence based on a latent trust if the assignee was in good faith and takes for value: *Redfearn v Somervail* (1813) 1 Dow 50. The material time for fixing the content of the right assigned for the purposes of the *assignatus* rule is the state of the right at the moment of intimation. When a person sells something they normally give what is known as "warrandice". This is the name given to a personal undertaking on the part of seller that operates as a warrant or guarantee that some state of affairs exists. In the case of assignation there is an implied warrandice that the debt that the assignor is transferring exists and is due to the assignor. The warrandice does not extend to undertaking that the debtor will actually pay, only that he is legally obliged to pay. If Herman purports to assign a right to Igor and it turns out that the debt does not exist, then Herman is personally liable for breaching his undertaking to Igor that the debt existed.

HERITABLE PROPERTY

The transfer of heritable property follows the general principles of transfers: **4.21** a distinction is drawn between contract and conveyance, and a public act is needed to perfect the transfer. In the case of heritable property, the public act is the act of registration. The rules governing the process of registration are governed by statute, and so it will be considered in some detail when the topic of registration is addressed below.

Three stages of transfer

1. Missives (contract)

4.22 Most transfers of land are sales, so the first stage in the transfer of land is conclusion of the contract, which is the cause of the transfer. The contract underlying the transfer of land is often referred to as the "missives". Concluding missives is the first stage in the transfer process. The terms of the missives themselves tend to follow fairly standard terms for the type of heritable property to which they relate. The Law Society of Scotland's website hosts a number of model or standard missives which solicitors can choose to use for residential transactions, including the *Scottish Standard Clauses*, 2nd edn (2016), which are designed for use across Scotland, and to replace the selection of regional standard missives (currently there are regional missives for Aberdeen, Ayr, Borders, Dumfries and Galloway, Edinburgh and Glasgow, Tayside, Highland, Inverclyde, Moray, and Paisley): see *https://www.lawscot.org.uk/members/rules-and-guidance/ rules-and-guidance/*. The core terms are that the transferor will transfer the property to the transferee, and that, in turn, the transferee will pay the price to the transferor. The key concept is that the missives are a contract for sale, therefore they contain important terms and information, but they are not a conveyance of the property.

2. Disposition (conveyance)

4.23 After missives have been concluded the transfer process moves to the second stage. Once missives have been concluded the parties will move towards "settlement" which is the time (and often place) that the conveyance will take place. Before settlement the buyer's solicitor will (or should) have been busy checking the register to check the quality of the title that has been marketed, and also arranging the details of the mortgage etc (see A. Stewart and E. Sinclair, *Conveyancing Practice in Scotland*, 7th edn (2016) Chs 7, 8). When the date of settlement arrives two things will happen: (1) the buyer (transferee) will hand over the money to seller; and (2) the seller (transferor) will hand over a "disposition", which is the conveyance of the land in question, to the buyer. Often these two events are considered to be interconnected and contemporaneous under the contract, but that will not always be the case: *AMA (New Town) Ltd v Law*, 2013 S.C. 608. The disposition itself is a unilateral deed: one person grants a right in favour of another person: the buyer simply accepts the disposition, they are not involved in executing it. Once the buyer has the disposition they are still not the owner of the land, but they are very close to becoming the owner. Sometimes a buyer with the disposition is referred to as an "uninfeft proprietor", but this term should not be taken to mean that they are the owner—they are not. There are number of things that a buyer in this position can do which are like the powers that can be exercised by an owner, but delivery of the disposition alone does not transfer ownership.

3. Registration (public act)

Once the buyer has possession of the disposition they must register the **4.24** disposition in order to complete the transfer process: the registration is the requisite public act that perfects a transfer of land. The idea of registration is fairly straightforward—the deed is taken to the appropriate register and is duly registered—but it is important to examine the basic features of the register and the registration process in order to understand the effects of registration fully.

Registration of land

In order to transfer ownership of land the transfer must be registered. **4.25** Beyond saying that registration is necessary it is important to understand how the registration process works, and what happens at the moment of registration. Some understanding of the historical development of the system of registration is necessary to understand the current law.

Introduction of registration of title

The system of "registration" in the Land Register was created by the Land **4.26** Registration (Scotland) Act 1979 (LR(S)A 1979) to replace the "recording" of deeds in the General Register of Sasines (GRS). The system of registration in the Land Register is known as "registration of title". The registration system was significantly reformed by the Land Registration etc (Scotland) Act 2012 (LRe(S)A 2012); however, as significant as these reforms were, the LRe(S)A 2012 builds upon the scheme of the LR(S)A 1979 and retains many of its objectives and features. The Scottish Law Commission, which was responsible for developing the LRe(S)A 2012, stated: "Our recommendations are evolutionary: the great achievements of the 1979 Act should be consolidated and developed." Scottish Law Commission, *Report on Land Registration* (SLC No 222 (2010)) at xxxiii.

General Register of Sasines: recording of deeds

The old system of recording deeds involved the transferee going to the **4.27** Keeper of the Register and handing over the deed transferring the property. The Keeper (or their staff) would then take the deed, make a copy of it, and stamp it with the date they received it. The date stamped on the deed was the date the transferee became the owner of the land following a valid transfer. The Keeper would keep a copy of the deed, and return the original to the transferee. However, simply recording a deed in the General Register of Sasines did not guarantee that the transferee would become the owner of the land. It was necessary for a transferee to record their deed in order to gain ownership, but it was not necessarily sufficient. That is because the GRS is merely a register of deeds: it is an enormous analogue evidential data-set. All the copies of deeds that are recorded in the register are merely evidence of whether the transferor, or their predecessors in title, had a deed made out to them in the past. There is no guarantee that any of the deeds are correct: the GRS gives no explicit guarantee that anyone is the owner of land. What is the point of it then? Because it is a big pile of evidence it was up to the transferee to carry out a search of previous deeds relating to the land they were seeking to purchase. In practice, a transferee would hire a solicitor or other search professional to search the register—which is open to the public—and the solicitor would check whether the transferor had herself been the transferee in a deed, and, if so, the solicitor would then check who was the transferor in that prior deed, and then check if there was a deed made out to them, and so on. Ideally, there would be an unbroken chain of deeds that could be followed that would strongly suggest that ownership had passed down the chain accordingly, but even then, there was no guarantee that it had. All the GRS offered was evidence of what different people were purporting or trying to do—it did not guarantee that they had necessary good titles in order to be successful in those attempts. Positive prescription was important for the functioning of the GRS, even if the various deeds in the register were only evidence, because if a person or their successors in title had possessed land for 10 years, then he definitely would have become the owner, and hence any dispositions made by them would have been perfectly valid. This had a dual effect—it made searching much easier, as solicitors only had to look back 10 years to check if there was possession by someone recorded in the GRS as owner, which made the likelihood of receiving a good title very high. Nevertheless, having to hire a solicitor to carry out a long and complicated search through old deeds, that contained rather unreliable or ambiguous descriptions of land, and which might be inaccurate in terms of actual ownership, was a suboptimal system.

Land Registration (Scotland) Act 1979: the introduction of registration of title

4.28 The recording of deeds in the GRS was replaced with a system of registration of title in the Land Register. The main feature of the registration of title model was to give transferees greater confidence that they would receive a valid title. This was achieved by the effect of the registration (LR(S)A 1979 s.3(1)(a)), which was that anyone registered as the owner became the owner, regardless of the surrounding circumstances and title of the transferor. In other words, if you could reach the register you were the owner. Once a person was on the register it could be rectified, but, in most cases, if the register was rectified so that ownership was lost, the person losing out (i.e. the transferee who had become owner) was indemnified in respect of the rectification: LR(S)A 1979 s.12(1). Similarly, if rectification was barred (if the person registered as the owner was in possession of the property, the Keeper was not normally allowed to rectify the register) or refused by the Keeper, then a person who lost out on that basis was also indemnified against that loss. So, if someone managed to get onto the register, even though the transferor had no title, then if the register could not be rectified the "true" owner who had lost ownership was indemnified. The registration of title system operates as it is named—the Keeper registers ownership of the land itself, rather than recording a deed that purports to give ownership. Although it is included here within the discussion of derivative acquisition, the effect of registration under s.3 of the LR(S)A 1979 was to create a new ownership title for the person registered. The effect of registration was akin to original acquisition, because title was derived from the effect of the law, not the transferor's title (or lack thereof). In turn, there were really two transfer systems operating: (1) the "normal" law which followed the general principles of transfer, such as the *nemo plus* rule; and (2) the effect of registration under the LR(S)A 1979, which made someone an owner by the sole fact of registration alone. This bijuralism caused instability within the law. A welcome element of the registration of title system was increased accuracy in the identification of the registered land. Under the recording system in the GRS the registered deeds might include a plan of the property, or it might only describe the extent of the property without an attached plan. This led to some inaccuracy and uncertainty. The LR(S)A 1979 system of registration of title identified the land by reference to an Ordnance Survey Map. Therefore, the introduction of registration of title by the LR(S)A 1979 represented a fundamental change to the system of registration. The most important change related to the guarantee of title upon registration, which, when taken alongside the rules on indemnification, operated to provide a state guarantee of title.

Land Registration etc (Scotland) Act 2012: refining registration of title
The introduction of registration of title by the LRe(S)A 1979 brought about **4.29** a fundamental change in the essence of the law relating to the registration of land. The LRe(S)A 2012 does not fundamentally alter the law relating to the registration of land; however, it does introduce significant alterations. The intention behind the LRe(S)A 2012 was to consolidate and develop the registration of title system, while retaining many of its policy objectives. The significant reforms introduced by the LRe(S)A 2012 include: increasing the use and coverage of the Land Register; reforming the way that the register is rectified if there is an inaccuracy (in particular bringing an end to bijuralism); improving and regulating the Keeper's duties and practice; improving the quality of the information held by the registration authorities in terms of mapping and supporting documentation; facilitating electronic registration, and, attempting to provide a solution to the "gap problem". Furthermore, although the LRe(S)A 2012 repeals the LR(S)A 1979, much of the substance of the LR(S)A 1979 is re-enacted by the LRe(S)A 2012.

Getting registered
Registration of the disposition remains a necessary element of a transfer **4.30** ownership of land: LRe(S)A 2012 s.50(3). Crucially, it must be a *valid* disposition which is registered in order to transfer ownership to the transferee: LRe(S)A 2012 s.50(2). Indeed, the creation of almost all real rights over land requires registration: the formula used by the LRe(S)A 2012 is that rights which are constituted by a "registrable deed" may be registered: see LRe(S)A 2012 ss.21(1) and 49. All such registrations will be

in the Land Register. Under the LR(S)A 1979 the manner in which some rights were created over land meant that they were to be registered in the Land Register; but, in other situations, registration might still take the form of recording in the GRS. This state of affairs, which evolved from the gradual introduction of registration in the Land Register, was criticised because the transfer of land into the Land Register from the GRS was taking a long time. The LRe(S)A 2012 changes the rules about what may be registered so that in time any registration of a disposition, or, indeed, any other real right, will have to be made in the Land Register, thereby phasing out recording in the GRS entirely: LRe(S)A 2012 s.48. This approach is to meet the policy objective of bringing all land onto the Land Register: see K.G.C. Reid and G.L. Gretton, *Land Registration* (2017) Ch 7.

4.31 It is useful to say something about the mechanics of achieving the registration necessary to transfer ownership. A person (the transferee) who would like to register their disposition must make an application to register to the Keeper of the Register: LRe(S)A 2012 s.21(1). The Keeper, in turn, must accept the disposition if the application meets the conditions of registration: LRe(S)A 2012 s.21(2); likewise, if the application does not meet the conditions of registration, the Keeper must reject the application: LRe(S)A 2012 s.21(3). It falls to the applicant to convince the Keeper that the application does meet the conditions: LRe(S)A 2012 s.21(2). What are the conditions for registration? There are general conditions that apply to all applications for registration, including: that the application is sufficiently detailed to allow the Keeper to meet their obligations to note certain information about the registration (LRe(S)A 2012 s.22(1)(a)); the deed is probative in accordance with s.6 of the Requirements of Writing (Scotland) Act 1995 (LRe(S)A 2012 s.22(1)(c)); the registration is made in accordance with the land register rules (LRe(S)A 2012 ss.22(1)(d) and 115) and, that the registration fee has been settled (LRe(S)A 2012 s.22(1)(e)). In addition to these general conditions, the application for registration must satisfy requirements for registration that depend on the nature of the deed being registered. Thus, applications for the registration of a disposition of, or a notice of title to, unregistered land (LRe(S)A 2012 ss.21(2)(a) and 23), applications for the registration of (qualifying) leases and standard securities in relation to unregistered land (LRe(S)A 2012 ss.21(2)(b), 24 and 25), and applications in any other case (LRe(S)A 2012 ss.21(2)(c) and 26) are treated separately. The last category, applications "in any other case", is the most important and will be the most frequently used as more and more land is registered in the Land Register. Furthermore, these conditions will be applied to dispositions transferring property as well as to deeds creating subordinate real rights. Therefore, the more specific conditions are that the deed is valid (LRe(S)A 2012 ss.26(1)(a) and 113(2)), the deed relates to a registered plot of land (LRe(S)A 2012 s.26(1)(b)), and that the deed refers to the title number of the title sheet of the land which the application relates to (LRe(S)A 2012 s.26(1)(c)). If these conditions are met then the Keeper must accept the registration.

Effect of application for registration
The register and its administration
The Land Register itself is made up of four components or sections: (1) the **4.32**
title sheet record; (2) the cadastral map; (3) the archive record, and (4) the
application record: LRe(S)A 2012 s.2(a)–(d). Each section fulfils an
important role in the land registration process and helps ensure accuracy,
detail and integrity permeate the contents of the register. The cadastral map
is, essentially, a map of the whole of Scotland which is divided into units; the
units being things that sustain a distinctive title of ownership: LRe(S)A 2012
ss.11–13. In turn, the map is based on the Ordnance Survey map and is
supposed to illustrate the detailed boundaries of landownership in Scotland.
The archive record's function is almost adjectival in the sense that it augments
and supports information in the register by providing for the creation and
retention of copies of all documents submitted by or associated with any
registration: LRe(S)A 2012 s.14. So, for example, if a disposition is submitted
for registration, it will be copied and the copy retained. A copy of a document
like this might be important for, say, any application to rectify the register.
The application record fulfils a similar administrative purpose by ensuring
that a record of all pending applications and advance notices (see below) is
maintained: LRe(S)A 2012 s.15(a)–(b). The title sheet record is perhaps the
most important because it is the section of the register that shows the legal
position with respect to each unit on the register. There is a "title sheet" for
every plot of land that is registered in the Land Register: LRe(S)A 2012
s.3(1). A title sheet is essentially a summary of the ownership of, and
registered subordinate real rights relating to, a registered plot of land. A title
sheet is split into four sections: (1) the property section; (2) the proprietorship
section; (3) the securities section; and (4) the burdens section: LRe(S)A 2012
s.5(1)(a)–(d). The property section describes the plot of land, by reference to
the cadastral map, as well as the nature of the proprietor's right in the plot of
land: LRe(S)A 2012 s.6(1)(a)(i)–(ii). Furthermore, if the registered plot of
land is a separate tenement, then the nature of the tenement must be
described: LRe(S)A 2012 s.6(1)(a)(iii). The property section of the title sheet
is concerned with the definition and identification of both the ownership
interest and the thing over which it is being registered. The proprietorship
section of the title sheet identifies the person who holds the ownership interest
over the plot of land identified in the property section: LRe(S)A 2012
s.7(1)(a). If the land is co-owned the distinct *pro indiviso* shares of the co-
owners will be listed: LRe(S)A 2012 s.7(1)(b). Similarly, a person's
"designation" will be noted—this means that if, say, the owner is a company
then the company number will be noted; in other cases, a designation might
be made that is based on holding an office, such as a trustee: see LRe(S)A
2012 ss.7(1)(a) and 113(1). The securities section is where standard securities
are noted: LRe(S)A 2012 s.8(1); whereas, the burdens section is where other
registered real rights, such as real burdens, servitudes, and registrable leases
are noted: LRe(S)A 2012 s.9. Taken together, the different sections of the
title sheet provide an overview of the legal interests associated with a piece
of registered land, and, in turn, feed into the publicity associated with

registration. The title sheets section of the Land Register is the totality of all the individual title sheets associated with registered properties: LRe(S)A 2012 s.3(3). Therefore, when unregistered land is registered in the Land Register for the first time, a consequence of that registration is that the Keeper must create a title sheet: LRe(S)A 2012 ss.3(1) and 30(2)(a). Once the land has been registered the title sheet, title number and entry on the cadastral map will make information easily accessible; the characteristics of the title sheet also explain the framing of the conditions for registration of registered land under s.26 of the LRe(S)A 2012.

Legal effects of an application for registration
Timing

4.33 When an application for registration has been made there are a number of legal consequences, and the timing of those consequences is crucial. When an application for registration is made to the Keeper it will take some time to process the application. If the application is accepted the registration takes effect from the date of the application, not the date on which the Keeper decided to accept the application: LRe(S)A 2012 s.37(1). Graham grants a disposition to Adam on 14 May 2018. If Adam submits an application to register a disposition on 1 June 2018, and the Keeper does not decide to accept the application until 1 December 2018, the date of registration is 1 June 2018. In other words, Adam becomes the owner on 1 June 2018. However, there is a potential problem—what about the period between 1 June to 1 December 2018? Anyone looking at the register on 1 July 2018 would see Graham registered as owner (which he was) and might rely upon that information. The LRe(S)A 2012 deals with this potential difficulty by requiring the Keeper to maintain the application record, which, by detailing any pending applications and advance notices, means that people consulting the register would be able to see not only that an application had been made but also the date that it was made, and hence would become effective if accepted by the Keeper. Similarly, the date of application governs the "ranking" of applications. The fact that the Keeper must deal with applications in order of receipt (LRe(S)A 2012 s.39(1)) means, when taken together with the rule that the date of application is the date of registration, that the first person to apply for registration will (assuming acceptance) become owner first. Gareth grants a disposition to Harry on 1 February 2018, and he then grants another disposition to Ivan on 17 February 2018. Ivan applies for registration on 20 February 2018, and Harry applies for registration on 22 February 2018. Ivan's application must be considered first; if it is accepted, then Ivan becomes owner by registration effective from 20 February. Furthermore, because Ivan was the owner as of 20 February, that means that Harry's deed cannot take effect from 22 February (the date of his application) because it would be invalid under the *nemo plus* rule—Gareth was no longer the owner on 22 February, and, therefore Harry's disposition is invalid. In turn, the Keeper would refuse to register Harry's disposition as the Keeper's decision must be based on the position as "at the date of application": LRe(S)A 2012 s.21(2).

Mind the gap

Because the transfer of ownership of heritable property involves three stages—   **4.34**
the missives, disposition and registration—there are opportunities for delays
to occur between these events. A particularly problematic "gap" in the past
was that which occurred between the delivery of the disposition and
registration. Once a disposition is delivered the transferor has little or nothing
left to do—it is up to the putative transferee to register the disposition.
However, during the period between delivery of the disposition and
registration the transferor remains the owner: only registration has the effect
of transferring ownership by simultaneously divesting the transferor and
investing the transferee. The period between delivery of the disposition and
registration represented a dangerous gap: the transferor might grant a
disposition to someone else (*Ceres School Board v Macfarlane* (1895) 23 R.
279); or, they might become insolvent, with the result that the land would be
attached by their creditors and the buyer would lose out: compare *Sharp v
Thomson*, 1997 S.C. (HL) 66 (receivership did not affect the buyer) with
Burnett's Tr v Grainger, 2004 S.C. (HL) 19 (sequestration did affect the
buyer). Furthermore, the problems associated with the gap were compounded
by the fact that payment by the buyer was normally made at the same time as
delivery of the disposition: therefore, the transferor had the price as well as the
ownership of the property during the gap. If the transferor became insolvent
their creditors would have both the price and the land to satisfy their claims,
and the transferee would rank as a simple ordinary creditor with a personal
right. The gap was a major feature of litigation in property law and caused
considerable unease. Before the LRe(S)A 2012 a system of "letters of
obligation" was used whereby the solicitors acting in a transaction, bolstered
by their professional insurance policy, undertook to bear the costs of dealing
with any nasty surprises which occurred during the period of "the gap"; but
the system was less than ideal. The LRe(S)A 2012 introduced a new device
to deal with the problem of the gap: the "advance notice". A person planning
to grant a disposition of land can apply for an advance notice in relation to that
disposition: LRe(S)A 2012 s.57(1)–(2). If the Keeper accepts the application
they must enter the advance notice in the application record section of the
register: LRe(S)A 2012 s.57(4). Once accepted, the advance notice creates a
"protected period" (LRe(S)A 2012 s.58(3)) which lasts for 35 days beginning
with the day after the notice was entered in the application record: LRe(S)A
2012 s.58(1). So, in other words, a transferor seeks an advance notice before
a disposition has been granted in order to provide a protected temporal space
in which that disposition can be used by the transferee to obtain ownership.
Protection is provided by the operation of the protected period. If someone
applies to register a deed other than the protected disposition two outcomes
may occur: (1) the non-protected deed might have been registered (remember
each application is considered according to the date of application), however,
in that situation the Keeper must consider the application to register the
protected deed as if the non-protected deed had not been registered: LRe(S)A
2012 s.59(2). If the Keeper then decides to accept the application relating to
the protected deed then *the effect of the non-protected deed's registration on*

the protected deed is to be as if the non-protected deed was not registered: LRe(S)A 2012 s.59(3)(a). In other words, even though the non-protected deed has been registered it is subordinated to the protected deed, and so the protected deed can still be given effect to, and the register must be altered so that any effect that the non-protected deed has is postponed to the protected deed: LRe(S)A 2012 s.59(3)(b). If both deeds are protected deeds then the deed with the earlier protected period prevails: LRe(S)A 2012 s.59(1)(b)(ii). Therefore, the protected period creates a relative advantage between the two deeds in favour of the protected deed—it does not deprive the non-protected deed of all effect, it merely postpones it to the protected deed. In order for the protected deed to take precedence over other deeds in this way an application for registration of the protected deed must be made during the protected period: LRe(S)A 2012 s.59(1)(a)(ii). In other words, if the protected deed is registered on the 36th day after the advance notice was registered then it falls outwith the protected period, and, in turn, it will not take priority over that other deed—the situation will be regulated in the same way as it would have been if there was no advance notice.

4.35 Let us return to the example given earlier when Gareth granted a disposition to Harry on 1 February 2018, and then granted another disposition to Ivan on 17 February 2018. Ivan applies for registration on 20 February 2018, and Harry applies for registration on 22 February 2018. Ordinarily, Ivan's application is considered first, and, if it is accepted, Ivan becomes owner by registration effective from 20 February. The effect would be that Ivan was owner as of 20 February, and so Harry's application of 22 February would be invalid and fail due to the *nemo plus* rule. What if Gareth had applied for an advance notice with respect to the deed granted in favour of Harry on 1 February, and that advance notice was entered in the application record on 31 January? That would make Harry's deed a protected deed, and the protected period would be 35 days beginning on 1 February. Ivan's application to register (a non-protected deed) on 20 February would fall within the protected period, as would Harry's later application to register (a protected deed) on February 22. Even if the Keeper accepted Ivan's application, and registered him as the owner of the property, the Keeper must make a decision on Harry's application as if Ivan's deed had not been registered—therefore, the *nemo plus* rule, which rendered Harry's deed invalid under normal circumstances, is suspended for this limited purpose. If the Keeper decides to accept Harry's application then Harry's deed is registered as if Ivan's was not registered, and it is given effect as if it was registered before Ivan's. Thus, Harry becomes the owner and Ivan's deed is invalid because treating it as being registered after Ivan's makes it invalid: the effect of the advance notice means that Ivan's deed falls foul of the *nemo plus* rule. On the other hand, if these facts were tweaked so that Harry applied for registration on 1 April, he would not be able to take advantage of this rule, because his application falls outwith the protected period, with the result that the "normal" rules apply and Ivan becomes the owner in the way outlined in the original variant of the example.

Inaccuracy and rectification

Inaccuracy

It will be recalled that registration is necessary to complete the transfer of **4.36**
land: LRe(S)A 2012 s.50(3). However, the mere fact that someone has been
registered as the owner does not necessarily mean that they are in fact the
owner. It is true, as noted above, that if a valid disposition is registered then
ownership is transferred to the transferee (LRe(S)A 2012 s.50(2)); but the
key element of that statement is that registration of a *valid* disposition will
transfer ownership. By requiring a valid disposition the law requires the
transfer to accord with the general principles of transfer set out above.
Similarly, other rights are not constituted by registration in the land register
alone: the effect of registration is to allow the general law of transfer, or
other common law rules and statutory provisions, to take effect: LRe(S)A
2012 s.49(2). If Albert draws up a disposition that purports to transfer land
that he does not own to Bob, that disposition is invalid: the *nemo plus* rule
applies. Even if Bob registers the disposition, and he makes it onto the
register, he is not the owner: an invalid deed is only valid to the extent that
a statute provides (LRe(S)A 2012 s.49(4)). These effects of registration
represent a significant change from the position under the LR(S)A 1979,
which provided that if a transferee registered their disposition then they
became the owner by virtue of registration alone: LR(S)A 1979 s.3(1)(a). In
turn, that system gave rise to the bijuralism mentioned earlier: the "curative"
effect of registration meant that the register said one thing, and the general
law of transfer said another thing. The system under the LRe(S)A 2012
avoids this bijuralism by returning to the general principles of transfer.
LRe(S)A 2012 means that it makes more sense to talk about the
"inaccuracy" of the register: if a person is registered as the owner, but the
general law of transfer means that the purported transfer was ineffective,
the register is inaccurate because it misstates the position in fact or law:
LRe(S)A 2012 s.65(1)(a). Returning to the example of Albert and Bob, the
position in law was that Albert's status as a non-owner meant that the
transfer was void under the *nemo plus* rule; however, the register states that
Bob is the owner, and is therefore inaccurate. In addition to such legal
inaccuracy, the register can be factually inaccurate by reason of mistakes in
the demarcation of boundaries or the cadastral map. The test for inaccuracy
is that the register misstates the position in fact or law (LRe(S)A 2012
s.65(1)(a)). But there may be mistakes on the register, which are sufficiently
minor so as not to constitute inaccuracies in the technical sense of
"misstating the position". Such minor mistakes are deemed "typographical
errors" on the register and *may* be corrected by the Keeper: Land Register
Rules etc. (Scotland) Regulations 2014 (SSI 2014/150) reg 17.

Rectification

When a "manifest inaccuracy" occurs on the register the Keeper must take **4.37**
some form of action: LRe(S)A 2012 s.80(1). If the manifest inaccuracy can
be easily rectified, because the means of achieving rectification is also
"manifest", then the Keeper must rectify the register in that way: LRe(S)A

2012 s.80(2). So, for example, if the register shows an incorrect name the way that rectification could remove the inaccuracy is manifest, and so the Keeper must rectify by replacing the incorrect name with the correct one. If there is an inaccuracy on the register that cannot be so easily rectified—the means of rectification are not "manifest"—then the Keeper must simply note the inaccuracy on the title sheet: LRe(S)A 2012 s.80(3). Thus, where an inaccuracy is detected the Keeper must take some kind of action.

Protections and remedies
Keeper's warranty

4.38 When the Keeper accepts an application for registration the Keeper warrants to the applicant that the title sheet to which the application relates is accurate: LRe(S)A 2012 s.73(1). In other words, the Keeper gives a financial undertaking to the applicant (e.g. a transferee holding a disposition) that the information in the register is correct and can be relied upon. The reliability of the register is important to the applicant for all sorts of reasons: for example, the ability of the transferee to obtain a valid title from the transferor depends on the transferor having a good title, and so the transferee would like to be able to rely on what the register says in that regard. If it becomes clear that the register is inaccurate then the Keeper's warranty is breached, and they must compensate the claimant for any loss sustained as a result of that breach: LRe(S)A 2012 s.77(1). The Keeper's liability to compensate such loss only arises when the inaccuracy on the register has been rectified: LRe(S)A 2012 s.77(2). Alan grants a disposition to Bernard, and Bernard successfully applies to register the disposition. The register showed Alan as the owner, and so when Bernard's application was accepted the Keeper warranted that the register accurately stated Alan was the owner of the land. In fact, the true owner of the land is, and always has been, Carla. Alan's presence on the register was an inaccuracy; removing Bernard's name, and entering Carla's in its place as the owner, will rectify the register making it accurate. Bernard can claim against the Keeper for compensation for breach of warranty: the Keeper warranted that the register was accurate in stating that Alan was the owner, but the register was inaccurate and has been rectified. Note, however, that the Keeper's warranty relates to the accuracy of the register only—just because the Keeper warranted that the title sheet stating Alan was the owner was accurate that did not mean that Alan (or Bernard) was actually the owner. In this example, the title was void: Carla was the true owner, and hence Alan's title was void even though he appeared on the register. If the facts were exactly the same except that Alan had a voidable title, instead of a void title, the result would be different. Alan would appear on the register and *would in fact have been* the owner, and so Bernard would have become the owner when the Keeper accepted his application for registration. Thus, by granting a warranty, the Keeper is providing some protection to an applicant who relies on the register. In this way, the policy of providing a form of state administered protection for titles is achieved.

Transferors in possession and good faith transferees

When the transferor is not the owner, but appears on the register as the **4.39** owner, the situation is normally regulated by the Keeper's warranty. The register will be rectified with the result that the true owner will keep their property, and the transferee who missed out will be compensated according to the terms of the Keeper's warranty. Thus, in the example above, when the register was rectified to recognise Carla's ownership she retained her land, and Bernard obtained compensation. However, if the transferor was not only registered as the owner (when he was not in fact), but was also in possession of the land itself, then the transferee might receive ownership of the land upon registration of the *a non domino* disposition: LRe(S)A 2012 s.86(2). In order for the transferee to receive ownership, the land in question must have been possessed by the transferor (or a combination of the transferor and transferee) for a continuous period of one year: LRe(S)A 2012 s.86(3)(a). Furthermore, the transferee must be in good faith—i.e. they must not know about the transferor's lack of title—and the Keeper has warranted title: LRe(S)A 2012 s.86(3)(f). Finally, the disposition itself would have conferred ownership on the transferee if the transferor had in fact been the owner: LRe(S)A 2012 s.86(3)(d). In other words, the rule will only operate if the only problem with the disposition is that it is *a non domino*: the rule will not operate if the deed is invalid for another reason, such as not complying with the appropriate formalities or it is a forgery. The rule is an exception to the *nemo plus* rule: a transferee derives a valid title from someone with a void title. However, the true owner is entitled to compensation for the loss of their land: LRe(S)A 2012 s.94(1). In addition to the rule relating to *a non domino* transfers of ownership, there are similar rules dealing with some subordinate real rights: LRe(S)A 2012 ss.88 et seq. Thus, in some situations the law adopts a policy decision to allow a true owner to keep their property and limit the transferee to compensation; in other situations, such as when the transferor is in possession, the law adopts a policy decision to allow the purported transferee to obtain ownership and limits the true owner to compensation for the loss of their property. Of course, in the middle of all this is the non-owning transferor. If the transferor can be found the Keeper will seek to recover the compensation they have paid to either the true owner or the transferee because of their attempted transfer. Unfortunately, the transferor is often, though not always, a fraudster and will have disappeared.

Prescriptive claimants

The doctrine of positive prescription is where ownership of a piece of **4.40** property is obtained by possessing the property for a certain period of time. It is not clear if Scots law recognises positive prescription of moveables, but it is clear that positive prescription is possible in relation to land. If a person possesses land for 10 years, and does so on the basis of a void or voidable title registered in the land register, then they become the owner of the land possessed: Prescription and Limitation (Scotland) Act 1973 s.1. Therefore, a person who is registered as the owner of land will receive ownership of it after 10 years possession even if they were not in fact the true owner during those 10 years. Therefore, prescription provides protection for individuals registered by creating or fortifying titles after 10 years of possession.

Reduction and rectification of deeds

4.41 It was noted above that voidable titles are valid until they are challenged. Therefore, if someone has been registered as the owner of land on the basis of a voidable deed, then they are the owner of the land (for the time being). Challenging a voidable deed in court might result in that voidable deed being judicially reduced by a decree of reduction. However, even if a voidable deed is reduced, the ownership of the land remains with the person who was registered if they had a voidable title—the decree of reduction must be registered in the Land Register in order to alter the ownership of the land: Conveyancing (Scotland) Act 1924 s.46A(1)(b). Similarly, where a deed has been the subject of judicial rectification—that is to say a problem with a deed has been rectified by a court so that the problem has been removed—it must be registered in order to have effect: Law Reform (Miscellaneous Provisions) (Scotland) Act 1985 s.8A.

5. REAL BURDENS

INTRODUCTION AND CONCEPTS

Statutory developments

The rules governing real burdens have been codified in statutes, though **5.01** many of the rules are restatements of the common law rules regarding real burdens. Rationalisation of the law of real burdens was necessary because many real burdens were feudal burdens—that is to say they were related to the feudal system, and so when the feudal system was abolished it was necessary to rationalise the law of real burdens. The vast majority of the rules governing real burdens can be found in the Title Conditions (Scotland) Act 2003 (TC(S)A 2003) and the Abolition of Feudal Tenure etc. (Scotland) Act 2000 (AFT(S)A 2000).

What is a real burden?

"A real burden is an encumbrance on land constituted in favour of the **5.02** owner of other land in that person's capacity as owner of that other land": TC(S)A 2003 s.1(1). A real burden is an obligation upon the owner of a piece of land that requires them (the owner) to do or refrain from doing something. This is an important definition as it provides the basis for distinguishing real burdens from servitudes. Generally speaking, a servitude gives someone the right to access or use land owned by someone else; whereas a real burden places an obligation on an owner of land to do something or not to do something in relation to that land. Another crucial element of a real burden is that it is said to "run with the land", in that its terms are binding upon the singular successors of the owner of the piece of land that the real burden affects. If there is a real burden that prevents the owner of 25 Hyacinth Drive from conducting commercial activities it applies to whoever is the owner of 25 Hyacinth Drive at the time. Special names are given to the two properties that are linked by a real burden. The property that is the subject of the real burden that imposes an obligation upon its current owner is known as the "burdened property", the property that benefits from the real burden is known as the "benefited property". There are many examples of real burdens. A real burden might require the benefited property to be kept in good condition, or in tenements there can be real burdens that impose obligations upon the owners of flats to contribute to the costs of maintaining communal areas. Real burdens can impose an obligation to build something on the burdened property, or they might prohibit the owner of the burdened property from using it in a certain way. A common real burden is a prohibition against using the burdened property for commercial purposes or for keeping livestock.

Types of real burden

Feudal and non-feudal real burdens

5.03 The feudal system has been abolished, and with it went "feudal burdens". A feudal burden was a real burden constituted in favour of a superior that they could enforce against the *dominium utile* of their vassal. The *dominium directum* was the benefitted property, while the *dominium utile* was the burdened property. In this way, the superior was able to continue to exercise control over the use of a piece of land. Furthermore, if the vassal transferred the *dominium utile* to a singular successor the superior could enforce the real burden against the singular successor. Although feudal burdens have been abolished, provision was made so that some existing feudal burdens were converted into non-feudal burdens when the feudal system was abolished. If the superior owned land that was adjacent to the land that was burdened by the feudal burden, and there was a building used as a place of habitation within 100m of the burdened property, the superior could register a notice preserving the substance of the feudal burden by converting it into a non-feudal burden: AFT(S)A 2000 s.18. Likewise, the substance of a number of other feudal burdens were preserved by being converted into "personal burdens" (AFT(S)A 2000 ss.18A–C).

Affirmative or negative real burdens

5.04 Some types of real burden are named so as to reflect the content of the real burden itself. If a real burden imposes an obligation upon an owner of property to do something then that is known as an affirmative burden: TC(S)A 2003 s.2(1)(a) and (2)(a). So, for example, a real burden that states that the owner of a burdened property must build and maintain a wall on the burdened property is an affirmative real burden. A negative real burden is simply the opposite of an affirmative real burden. A negative real burden imposes an obligation on the owner of a burdened property to refrain from doing something on the burdened property: TC(S)A 2003 s.2(1)(b) and (2)(b). So, for example, a negative real burden might prevent the owner of the burdened property from building a wall that was over a certain height, or from using of the land for a commercial purpose.

Ancillary real burdens

5.05 Affirmative and negative real burdens impose an obligation upon the owner of a burdened property to do, or refrain from doing, something on the burdened property. However, these burdens do not impose an obligation on the owner of a burdened property to allow another person to use the burdened property—that is the normally the role of a servitude. There is, however, a small exception to this rule which relates to a type of real burden known as an "ancillary real burden". An ancillary real burden is one that allows access to, or the use of, the burdened property in connection with another primary real burden: TC(S)A 2003 s.2(3)–(4). If there is an affirmative real burden that requires Amy to build and maintain drains on her land, there might be an ancillary real burden that allows someone to access Amy's land in order to verify compliance with the primary real burden by checking that the drains are being maintained. Similarly, ancillary burdens can extend to providing for the management or administration of the burdened property in connection with a primary real burden.

Praedial or personal burdens

Another important distinction to draw between different types of real **5.06** burden is the distinction between praedial and personal real burdens. A praedial real burden is the most commonly encountered type of real burden. A praedial real burden links a benefited property with a burdened property: both properties must be present. A real burden that imposes an obligation on the owner of a burdened property in favour of the owner of a benefited property is a praedial burden. A personal burden is quite different. Where there is a personal burden there is only a burdened property—there is no benefited property. Only certain designated persons can enforce the obligation imposed by a personal real burden, who those designated persons are will depend on the type of personal burden involved. There are a number of different types and form of personal burden: TC(S)A 2003 s.1(3). The key thing to remember is that there is only a burdened property where there is a personal burden: enforcement rights are given to designated people, not to the owner of a benefited property.

Community burdens

A community burden is another type of real burden that should be borne in **5.07** mind. When examining the nature of a community burden it is easiest to begin by considering the manner in which it is created. In a simple case the creation of a real burden normally involves the division of a piece of land whereby a single real burden is imposed on the newly separated land. If Archibald owns two acres of land and sells one of those acres to Barbara, he might insert a real burden prohibiting the commercial use of that land into the disposition transferring the newly separated acre of land. Archibald would have created a simple negative burden. The creation of community burdens follows a different process. The typical situation when a community burden will be created is where a builder or property developer has built multiple properties and would like those properties to be the subject of the same real burdens. A community burden is created if real burdens are imposed under a "common scheme" on two or more units of land, and some of those real burdens are mutually enforceable: TC(S)A 2003 s.25. Therefore, in order to create a community burden the burden must have been imposed as part of a "common scheme": what does that mean? Let us take an example. Albert is a property developer who owns 100 acres of land, and he has split the 100 acres into 100 individual plots of one acre each. Before selling the plots, Albert imposes a number of real burdens relating to maintenance, which each plot owner will be able to enforce against each other—thus making all 100 units both benefited and burdened properties in relation to those burdens. That is an example of a common scheme of real burdens being imposed to give mutually enforceable burdens, and therefore those burdens are known as community burdens. The significance of community burdens becomes clearer when we consider benefited properties and discharge of burdens.

Facility and service burdens

5.08 A facility burden is a burden which regulates the "maintenance, management and use of a facility": TC(S)A 2003 ss.56(1)(a) and 122(1). Facility burdens tend to be feudal burdens that have been converted into "non-feudal" burdens. The superior would have held the benefited property that enforced these maintenance and management burdens on behalf of a number of properties. For example, real burdens might have imposed liability for the maintenance of the common stair upon all the flats in a tenement building, thereby making them all burdened properties while the superior held the benefited property. When the feudal system was to be abolished it became clear that in order to prevent the loss of these useful burdens they would need to be converted into non-feudal burdens. Hence the creation of facility burdens where the facility itself, and the properties that it benefits, are all benefited and burdened properties with respect to the facility. Service burdens are similar: a burden that required the provision of services to other properties might have been enforceable only by a superior. Therefore, burdens providing that properties were to receive a service were converted into service burdens, the benefited properties being those entitled to receive the service: TC(S)A 2003 ss.56(1)(b) and 122(1).

CREATION OF REAL BURDENS

5.09 In order to create a real burden a number of requirements must be satisfied. These requirements can be broken down into two distinct conceptual requirements: (1) the content of the real burden that is being created must be permissible; and (2) the formalities required in order to create a real burden.

Permissible content

5.10 It is a requirement when creating a real burden that the content of the real burden is allowed by the law. The requirement that the content of the burden should be one allowed by the law should not be confused with the "fixed list" requirement that exists in relation to the creation of servitudes: there is no "fixed list" of real burdens like that which exists for non-expressly created servitudes. Nevertheless, it is important that real burdens conform to a number of rules and requirements.

Praediality

5.11 It is important that real burdens are sufficiently "praedial": *Tailors of Aberdeen v Coutts* (1840) 1 Rob App 296. Praediality is the concept that two pieces of land—a benefited and a burdened property—are linked by a real burden. Normally a real burden must be sufficiently praedial: the content of the burden must be directed at the burdened property in some way, and not just at the owner: TC(S)A 2003 s.3(1)–(2); see S*tewart v Duke of Montrose* (1860) 22 D. 755 at 803–804, per Lord Deas. There must be some physical proximity, though not necessarily contiguity, between the benefitted and burdened properties: *Hill of Rubislaw (Q Seven) Ltd v Rubislaw Quarry Aberdeen Ltd*, 2015 S.C. 339 at [13] per Lord Drummond Young. Therefore, a real burden cannot impose an obligation on the owner of the burdened property to smoke a pipe or read a particular newspaper: obligations of this nature are in no way related to the burdened property. Likewise, a further aspect of the praedial test comes from the perspective of the benefited property. The content of the real burden must also benefit the benefited property, not just the caprice of the benefited property's owner: TCSA 2003 s.3(3). That praedial benefit is defined in monetary terms in modern law: "a real burden must benefit the owner, tenant or occupier of property in such a way that the value of the property itself is enhanced or at least protected." (*Hill of Rubislaw (Q Seven) Ltd v Rubislaw Quarry Aberdeen Ltd*, 2015 S.C. 339 at [14] per Lord Drummond Young.) While the owner of a benefited property might like the idea of requiring their neighbour to perform interpretative dance every morning at 7am that does not benefit the benefited property. Sometimes it will be difficult to determine if a burden complies with the praedial rule if that burden confers an obvious personal benefit on a person. A provision restricting the extent to which a piece of property could be used as office space was considered to be praedial, despite the fact it could be argued that it provided a personal benefit to the owners of the property by protecting their commercial interests, because there was a demonstrable benefit to the benefited properties themselves: see *Hill of Rubislaw (Q Seven Ltd) v Rubislaw Quarry Aberdeen Ltd* [2013] CSOH 131; 2013 G.W.D. 27-545 at [16]–[22], per Lord Malcolm; as approved by the Inner House in *Hill of Rubislaw (Q Seven Ltd) v Rubislaw Quarry Aberdeen Ltd*, 2015 S.C. 339 at [17], [24] per Lord Drummond Young.

Public policy

The content of a real burden cannot be contrary to public policy: TC(S)A **5.12** 2003 s.3(6). Generally speaking, the limits of "public policy" can be difficult to identify and this is so with respect to real burdens in particular. Although the TC(S)A 2003 provides some assistance by identifying a particular example of public policy—unreasonable restraints upon trade—the potential scope of public policy remains broad. On the particular point concerning restraint of trade, guidance can be sought from factual examples from a number of decisions. An owner of two grocery shops sold one of them and attempted to impose a real burden prohibiting the use of the shop as a butcher or a grocer, but the burden was held to be unenforceable as an unreasonable restraint upon trade: *Philips v Lavery*, 1962 S.L.T. (Sh Ct) 57; see also *Giblin v Murdoch*, 1979 S.L.T. (Sh Ct) 5 (similar situation involving hairdressers); *Aberdeen Varieties Ltd v James F Donald (Aberdeen Cinemas) Ltd*, 1939 S.C. 788; 1940 S.C. (HL) 52 (owner of two theatres). A different conclusion was reached in relation to a restriction on the sale of alcohol by a supermarket in a shopping precinct on the basis that the burden contributed to the viability of the precinct as a whole: *Co-operative Wholesale Society* *v Ushers Brewery*, 1975 S.L.T. (Lands Tr) 9. Most recently, the courts have stated any such restraint on trade must be "reasonable as between the parties" and "consistent with the interests of the public": *Hill of Rubislaw (Q Seven Ltd) v Rubislaw Quarry Aberdeen Ltd* [2014] CSIH 105; 2015 S.C. 339 at [20]–[22] per Lord Drummond Young. It seems that the burden of justifying the restraint in these terms will lie with the party relying upon the restraint: *Hill of Rubislaw* at [21] per Lord Drummond Young. The court's assessment of the reasonableness of the restraint and parties' interests will take account of the commercial context, and, in particular, it will "consider the particular trade or profession or business that is affected by the restriction, and also the overall economic context in which it operates." (*Hill of Rubislaw* at [22] per Lord Drummond Young).

Illegality and repugnancy with ownership

5.13 Similarly, it is well established that the content of a real burden cannot be illegal: TCSA 2003 s.3(6). So, for example, a real burden would be unenforceable if it stipulated that a property should only be used for the manufacture of "crystal meth". Likewise, real burdens that prohibit the use of property by persons of a certain race or gender might well be illegal by virtue of legislation such as the Equality Act 2010. Finally, the content of a real burden cannot be such that it is "repugnant to ownership": TC(S)A 2003 s.3(6). In other words, the real burden's content cannot be so arduous or expansive that it effectively removes the rights of the owner of the burdened property. The courts have been lukewarm about the applicability of the concept: *Sheltered Housing Management Ltd v Bon Accord Bonding Co Ltd*, 2010 S.C. 516 at [35]. Nevertheless, the principle seems to strike at burdens that limit the ability of an owner to carry out common juristic acts—so, for example, a real burden that purports to prevent the sale or leasing of the property is clearly not allowed: *Grant v Heriot Trust* (1906) 8 F. 647 (prohibiting a common owner from exercising the remedy of division and sale was repugnant with ownership). Whereas restrictions relating to certain types of trade or use, especially in residential properties, are unlikely to be repugnant to ownership: *Earl of Zetland v Hislop* (1882) 9 R. (HL) 40 (prohibition upon the sale of alcohol was not repugnant with ownership). The matter is really one of fact and degree. A burden that states you may not keep chickens is probably not repugnant to ownership; a burden that states that all you can do on your land is keep chickens is repugnant to ownership.

Formalities required to create a real burden

Dual registered deed

5.14 In order to create a valid real burden it must be created by a deed granted by the owner of the property that is to be the burdened property: TC(S)A 2003 s.4(1) and (2)(b). Thus, the creation of a real burden requires a written instrument creating the burden to be registered. The deed must be sufficiently descriptive to identify both the benefited and burdened properties (TC(S)A 2003 s.4(2)(c)(i)–(ii)), and to provide details of the terms of the burden: TC(S)A 2003 s.4(2)(a). Crucially, that deed must be registered against both properties: TC(S)A 2003 s.4(5). The need for dual registration was introduced by the TC(S)A 2003 and it is a major improvement on the old law which only required registration against the burdened property. The old rule caused a great deal of difficulty when it came to enforcing real burdens, because it was not always clear what property was the benefited property. If the burden is a personal real burden then the deed must identify the person in whose favour it is constituted: TC(S)A 2003 s.4(2)(c)(iii), and it need only be registered against the burdened property (because there is no benefited property): TC(S)A 2003 s.4(5).

"Real burden"
In addition to the formalities mentioned above it is vital that the deed **5.15** creating the real burden uses the actual words "real burden": TC(S)A 2003 s.4(2)(a). These magic words must be used in addition to describing the substance of the burden itself. If the real burden is a nominate or nameable real burden then it is permissible to use the nominate term for the burden instead of the phrase "real burden": TC(S)A 2003 s.4(2)(a) and (3). Thus, for example, if the deed purports to create a "community burden" (TC(S)A 2003 s.25(1)) or a "rural housing burden" (TC(S)A 2003 s.43(1)) then using those nominate terms, instead of "real burden", is acceptable; nevertheless, that means that magic words are still required—they are just different magic words. The requirement for a deed to use specific terminology is aimed at preventing ambiguity concerning what terms are intended to be real burdens. The express creation of a servitude does not require the use of the term servitude, though it would be wise to do so in order to avoid ambiguity.

"Four corners of the deed"
It was a rule of the common law (which has been continued: TC(S)A 2003 **5.16** s.4(2)(a)) that the terms and extent of any real burden should be written in the deed creating the burden; furthermore, it could not refer to any extraneous document to fill in any gaps. Thus, the terms of the burden were limited to what was contained within the "four corners of the deed". The idea behind the rule is that, because a real burden can affect singular successors, the public should be able to see what the terms of the burden are without having to go away and carry out a detailed search and investigation of various documents. A burden that referred to an Act of Parliament that was used to regulate performances in theatres violated the rule (*Aberdeen Varieties Ltd v James F Donald (Aberdeen Cinemas) Ltd*, 1939 S.C. 788), as did a burden that referred to the terms of other real burdens constituted over other properties: *Botanic Gardens Picture House v Adamson*, 1924 S.C. 549. The rule has been relaxed by s.5 of the TC(S)A 2003 with respect to burdens that refer to public documents in connection with the calculation of liability for costs only.

ENFORCEMENT OF REAL BURDENS

Title and interest

5.17 The enforcement of real burdens is a rather tricky area of law, even though it has been simplified by the TC(S)A 2003. A significant factor behind the complexity of the law in this area are the effects of the old rule that burdens only needed to be registered against the burdened property. Because it was not always easy to identify which properties were benefited by the burden, a number of rules have been developed which allow us to identify benefited properties in order to allow enforcement of those burdens. However, before we consider those rules, we need to consider how real burdens are enforced. In order to enforce a real burden a person must demonstrate that they have *both* "title" and "interest" to enforce the burden in question: TC(S)A 2003 s.8(1).

Title

5.18 A person will have title to enforce if that person has a relevant relationship with the benefited property. The owner of the benefited property has title: TC(S)A 2003 s.8(2). In addition to the owner of the benefited property, a number of other persons have title. A tenant or liferenter with a real right in the benefited property has title (TC(S)A 2003 s.8(2)(a)), as do non-entitled spouses or partners with statutory occupancy rights (TC(S)A 2003 s.8(2)(b)). However, if the burden provides for a right of pre-emption, redemption, reversion, or any other option to acquire the burdened property, then only the owner of the benefited property has title: TC(S)A 2003 s.8(4). Thus, in order to have title to enforce the burden a person must stand in one of these designated legal relationships to the benefited property. That is why it is crucial to identify the benefited property as part of the enforcement process: it must be possible to identify the benefited property before a person can demonstrate that they stand in a relevant relationship to it.

Interest

5.19 In order to enforce a real burden a person must have title, but title on its own is insufficient—the person must be able to show that they have interest to enforce as well. A person has interest to enforce a real burden if they can show that a breach of the burden in question would, in the circumstances of the case, result in a material detriment to the value or enjoyment of their right in the benefited property: TC(S)A 2003 s.8(3)(a). What is meant by material detriment? It is generally thought that the proximity of the benefited and burdened properties is relevant to determining the materiality of a breach (see e.g. *Ferguson v Gunby* 2015 S.L.T. (Lands Tr) 200 at [14]), as indeed is the extent of the breach. The fact that the test stipulates that the determination must take account of the circumstances of the case makes it a fairly subjective and fact specific determination. A number of decided cases have added some flesh to the meaning of material detriment. When a bed and breakfast was opened in breach of a burden prohibiting commercial activity it was held that there was no interest to enforce the burden because the breach was not sufficiently material: *Barker v Lewis*, 2008 S.L.T. (Sh Ct) 17; see also *Clark v Grantham*, 2009 G.W.D. 38-645. In *Barker* the Sheriff Principal noted that the word materiality could not sensibly be interpreted out of its factual context, and suggested that it was an "adjective of degree": *Barker* at [21] and [27]. More recent authority has suggested that to suggest materiality is a matter of degree might be misleading, and that material detriment means detriment that is something more than fanciful or insignificant: *Franklin v Lawson*, 2013 S.L.T. (Lands Tr) 81 at 83–84. When a charity sought to use a residential property to house vulnerable or disabled adults, in breach of a burden requiring the property to be used only as a residence for a single family, it was held that the likely effects on parking outside and the value of the benefited properties would be materially detrimental to the enjoyment and value of the properties respectively: *Kettlewell v Turning Point Scotland*, 2011 S.L.T. (Sh Ct) 143 at 154–157, per Sheriff Sinclair.

Identification of the benefited property
In order to enforce a real burden there must be both title and interest on the 5.20 part of the person seeking to enforce the burden. However, real burdens will not always be registered against the benefited property, which can make finding them difficult; but the benefited property must be identified in order to demonstrate title to enforce. The TC(S)A 2003 contains rules which identify implied rights of enforcement in certain situations—in other words, if there is no express identification of the benefited property in the constitutive deed the law has rules to identify benefited properties in order to imply enforcement rights.

Burdens created after 28 November 2004
If a burden was created after 28 November 2004—the date that the relevant 5.21 provisions of the TC(S)A 2003 came into force—matters are simple. Since that date all real burdens have had to be registered against both the benefited and burdened properties. Thus, the benefited property will be identified in the deed that created the burden, hence there is no need for implied rights of enforcement.

Burdens created before 28 November 2004
Matters are more complex with respect to burdens created before 5.22 28 November 2004 because there was no need for dual registration. Seven different rules are used to identify whether there is a benefited property, and which property it is that is benefited.

1. Express identification
Although dual registration was not a requirement before 28 November 5.23 2004, some pre-2004 burdens do identify the benefited property expressly in the constitutive deed: if that is the case, then that is normally the end of the matter.

2. Related property in a common scheme

5.24 If a number of real burdens have been imposed upon multiple properties as part of a common scheme they are mutually enforceable: TC(S)A 2003 s.53(1). In other words, any property that is the subject of one of these identical burdens is both a benefited and burdened proprietor in relation to all the other properties that are subject to such burdens. Remember, it is possible to see which properties are subject to the burden—i.e. burdened properties—because the burden would have had to have been registered against them. Thus, in order for s.53 of the TC(S)A 2003 to apply, there must be a common scheme making the burdens "community burdens", and the properties must also be "related properties". Whether properties are related is to be inferred from all the circumstances (TC(S)A 2003 s.53(2)), which has been interpreted to mean that the court has discretion to determine whether the properties are related: *Russel Properties (Europe) Ltd v Dundas Heritable Ltd* [2012] CSOH 175 at [22], per Lord Woolman; see also *Thomson's Excr*, 2016 G.W.D 27-494 (Lands Tribunal). When exercising discretion in order to draw such an inference the following circumstances are expressly suggested by the legislation to be of potential relevance: (1) the properties share facilities or features that suggest common management of them would be convenient (TC(S)A 2003 s.53(2)(a)(i)–(ii)); (2) there is shared ownership of common property (TC(S)A 2003 s.53(2)(b)); (3) the properties are part of the common scheme by virtue of the same deed of conditions (TC(S)A 2003 s.53(2)(c), see also *Franklin v Lawson*, 2013 S.L.T. (Lands Tr) 81 at [7]–[9]); and (4) the properties are flats in the same tenement building (TC(S)A 2003 s.53(2)(d)).

5.25 **Example:** In 1990 a builder constructed 100 houses in a housing scheme, and he built a play park in the middle of the housing scheme. He wanted to ensure that the housing scheme remained solely residential, so he inserted an identical real burden upon all 100 properties stating that the properties are not to be used for commercial purposes. He also provided that all 100 properties will own the play-park in common. These are valid community burdens, but he did not identify any benefited properties. By virtue of s.53 of the TC(S)A 2003, all 100 properties are part of a common scheme, and they are related properties because of their co-ownership of the play-park. Thus, all the properties are benefited and burdened properties—they have mutual enforcement rights. If the owner of plot 67 tries to turn their house into a dental practice, then the owners of the other 99 properties can seek to enforce the burden as the owners of a benefited property. The word "seek" to enforce is used advisedly here: all 99 have title to enforce the burden, but they will need to show that they have interest to enforce in order to be successful.

3. Unrelated properties in a common scheme

5.26 If there is a common scheme but the properties are not "related", in the technical sense discussed above, then different rules apply (on the difference between ss. 52 and 53, see *Thomson's Excr*, 2016 G.W.D 27-

494 (Lands Tribunal)). Where there is such a common scheme without related properties, it is necessary for the title of a piece of property to refer to the common scheme expressly if it is to be identified as a benefited property: TC(S)A 2003 s.52(1). There are two ways in which this can happen. First, if the real burden originally applied to a single plot of land that covered a large area, and then subsequently that single plot was subdivided, the newly divided properties are part of a common scheme and have mutual enforcement rights. However, if there was a prohibition against subdivision, then no mutual rights of enforcement will be implied: *Girls School Co Ltd v Buchanan*, 1958 S.L.T. (Notes) 2. Secondly, if an individual deed imposing burdens on the burdened property makes reference to some kind of common scheme—such as undertaking to impose the same burdens on other properties—then it might be a benefited property with implied mutual enforcement rights against any other property that meets the criteria in the common scheme. In order for an unrelated property in a common scheme to be identified as a benefited property there must be nothing in the deeds imposing the burdens to suggest that such mutual enforcement rights were not intended to be created: TC(S)A 2003 s.52(2).

Subdivision example: In 1980 Bob the farmer owned 10 acres of land. He **5.27** planned to sell the land to a property developer called Hamish. Before selling the land to Hamish, Bob imposed a real burden on the 10 acres that prohibited the commercial use of buildings. Hamish bought the land and built 10 houses before splitting the land into 10 separate plots and selling each plot. Each of the 10 plots of land is subject to the same burden, and, because the original deed referred to the broader area, the owners of all 10 plots have mutual enforcement rights.

Single deed referring to common scheme example: In 1970 Anna was a **5.28** property developer. She owned 50 acres of land and had built 25 houses; she planned to build another 25 houses, but first she had to sell the first 25 plots to raise funds. She inserted the same real burden into the deeds disposing of the first 25 plots of land, each burden prohibited use of the plots for commercial purposes and stated that "these burdens are imposed on all built properties, and will be imposed on those subsequently built". In 1980, she built the remaining 25 houses and inserted the same burden into the dispositions that disposed of each of the remaining 25 plots. In this situation, all 50 plots of land have mutual enforcement rights.

4. Facility burdens
Separate rules apply to the implication of enforcement rights in relation to **5.29** facility burdens. Facility burdens regulate the maintenance, management, reinstatement or use of heritable property which constitutes, and is intended to constitute, a facility of benefit to other land: TC(S)A 2003 s.122(1), see *Greenbelt Property Ltd v Riggens*, 2010 G.W.D. 28-586. Furthermore, the TC(S)A 2003 gives further information about what constitutes a facility by providing an indicative list of examples which includes: common parts of a

tenement (TC(S)A 2003 s.122(3)(a)), common recreation areas (TC(S)A 2003 s.122(3)(b)), private roads (TC(S)A 2003 s.122(3)(c)), private sewerage systems (TC(S)A 2003 s.122(3)(d)), and boundary walls (TC(S)A 2003 s.122(3)(e)). In this situation, the benefited properties are the heritable property that constitutes the facility itself and any properties to which the facility is (and was intended to be) of benefit: TC(S)A 2003 s.56(1). Thus, if there is a real burden regulating the use of a private road that is owned in common, then any property that receives, and was intended to receive, a benefit from that road will be a benefited property, as is the road itself. Thus, the owner of the facility itself (the road in the example) can enforce the burden as well as the owners of the properties that benefit from the facility.

5. Service burdens

5.30 A real burden that requires a service to be provided to land other than the burdened property is a "service burden": TC(S)A 2003 s.122(1). If there is a service burden and the benefited properties are not expressly identified then the rule is that any land which receives that service is a benefited property: TC(S)A 2003 s.56(1)(b).

6. Converted feudal burdens

5.31 If a feudal burden has been converted into a non-feudal burden it would have been necessary to have registered a notice in order to do this: AFT(S)A 2000 s.18(1) and Sch.5. The terms of the necessary notice must include a description of both properties which will constitute the burdened and benefited property of the newly converted burden: AFT(S)A 2000 s.18(2)(b). Therefore, identifying the benefited property should be straightforward.

7. Non-feudal burdens not part of a common scheme

5.32 The final rule applied to real burdens that were created by dispositions: i.e. not in a feudal deed. The factual situation where such a real burden would be imposed was where a piece of land was "broken off" another piece of land by a disposition which contained the real burden, but that real burden did not mention the benefited property. This is another example of subdivision, except in this case the land is being split into two properties only (if the subdivision is into more than two plots this rule does not apply as it would be a common scheme: TC(S)A 2003 s.50(6)). In such a situation, the benefited property was the nearby property retained by the owner of the original whole when they divided the land by granting the disposition containing the real burden and dividing the land: TC(S)A 2003 ss.49(2) and 50. The rule previously existed at common law: *J.A. Mactaggart and Co v Harrower* (1906) 8 F. 1101. The rule was a transitional one and ceased to operate on 28 November 2014. Any implied rights under this rule that were not preserved in accordance with the requisite formalities (which entailed registration of the burden against both the benefited and burdened properties) before 28 November 2014 were extinguished on that date: TC(S)A 2003 ss.49 and 50.

Example: In 1990 Anna owned a two-acre property and decided to split it **5.33**
into two plots so that she could sell one of them. Anna inserted a real burden
into the disposition she granted to transfer the land to Bob, but the terms of
the disposition do not identify the benefited property. The acre that Anna
retained is the benefited property with regard to the real burden that burdens
the land broken off and sold to Bob.

EXTINCTION OF REAL BURDENS

Express discharge

A real burden can be extinguished, and so cease to exist, if it is expressly **5.34**
discharged by the person who is entitled to benefit from it. In the case of a
praedial burden it will be the owner of the benefited property who can
discharge the burden (TC(S)A 2003 s.15(1)); whereas, if the burden is a
personal real burden the discharge is granted by the holder of the burden:
TC(S)A 2003 s.48(1). In both cases the express discharge is carried out by
granting a deed of discharge (sometimes called a minute of waiver). The
grant can be gratuitous, but it can also be granted pursuant to a payment to
encourage the discharge. Once a deed of discharge has been granted it must
be registered against the burdened property in order to take effect: TC(S)A
2003 ss.15(1) and 48(1). The use of the word "discharge" is specialised in
this context in that it encompasses a variation of the burden (so as to make
it less arduous), as well as its complete discharge: TC(S)A 2003 ss.15(2)
and 48(2). Thus, if a real burden stated that no more than three cars could
be parked on the burdened property, a deed of discharge could be granted
which removed the restriction on parking entirely, or it could be varied so
that no more 10 cars could be parked. However, the owner of the benefited
property could not vary the burden so that no more than two cars could
park on the burdened property—to do so would be to make the burden more
arduous.

Community burdens

The express discharge rule presents a potential problem in relation to **5.35**
community burdens—where there are multiple benefited properties, must
the owners of all those properties sign a deed of discharge? The answer is
no. If all the owners of the community do in fact grant the discharge then
that will be valid, but it is impractical, especially in large communities.
Therefore, there are two possible ways of discharging (or varying) a
community burden without requiring all the benefited proprietors to sign
the deed. First, if a simple majority of the owners of the benefited properties
that constitute the community (including the property seeking the
discharge: TC(S)A 2003 s.33(3)) sign the deed of discharge or waiver then
that is sufficient: TC(S)A 2003 s.33(2)(a). The deed granted by the majority
must be registered against each of the burdened properties: TC(S)A 2003
s.33(1). If a deed is so granted by a majority, the owners who did not sign
the deed must be given notice of it: TC(S)A 2003 s.34(1)–(2) and Sch.4. An

owner who did not sign the deed can challenge it by applying, within eight weeks of receiving notice of the deed, to the Lands Tribunal to preserve the burden unaltered: TC(S)A 2003 s.34(3), see *Fleeman v Lyon*, 2009 G.W.D. 32-539. Another method by which a community burden may be expressly discharged is if *all* of the owners of the benefited properties that are *adjacent to* the burdened property grant the deed of discharge: TC(S)A 2003 s.35(1). A benefited property is "adjacent" to the burdened property if part of it is within 4 m of the burdened property (excluding public roads less than 20 m wide and pertinents of either property): TC(S)A 2003 ss.32 and 125(a)–(b). If a deed is granted by all adjacent owners, then notice of that fact must be given, but, unlike s.23, there are two routes to giving notice: (1) intimate a copy of the deed and a statutory form to all the other owners in the community (TC(S)A 2003 s.36(1)); or (2) affix certain types of notice to nearby lampposts: TC(S)A 2003 s.36(1)–(2). Once again, a non-adjacent owner can challenge the deed by applying to the Lands Tribunal for preservation of the burden: TC(S)A 2003 s.37(1). Where a deed has been granted using either the majority or adjacent proprietor rule it must be accompanied by an endorsement from the Lands Tribunal, stating that there is no live challenge to the discharge, before it can be registered: TC(S)A 2003 ss.34(4)–(6) and 37(2). The owner of the burdened property must also swear an oath before a notary public that the intimation requirements have been complied with: TC(S)A 2003 ss.34(4) and 37(4). Complying with the adjacent proprietors rule will often be the easiest approach: it involves procuring less signatures, and, if the "notice by lampost" approach is followed, it sidesteps having to use the potentially complicated rules to identify implied enforcement rights (because it does not require identification of *all* the benefited properties in the community).

Sunset

5.36 Some old real burdens can be brought to an end by using a specific process that is formally known as "termination", though the subject matter means that the process is sometimes described as the "sunset rule": TC(S)A 2003 s.20. A real burden can be terminated using a process initiated by the owner of the burdened property if at least 100 years have elapsed since the deed creating the burden was registered: TC(S)A 2003 s.20(1). The burdened proprietor (known as "the terminator" in this context) may register a notice of termination (TC(S)A 2003 s.20(1)), which identifies the terms of the burden and the burdened property (TC(S)A 2003 s.20(4)(a)–(c)), and which will have the effect of extinguishing or varying the burden: TC(S)A 2003 s.24(1). However, before the notice of termination can be registered the terminator must comply with a number of requirements. The terminator must intimate their intention to register a notice of termination to the owner of each benefited property if the burden is praedial (TC(S)A 2003 s.21(1)(a)), or to the holder of a personal burden (TC(S)A 2003 s.21(1)(b)). Intimation of the intention to register a notice of termination can be given by: (1) sending a copy of the proposed notice of termination (TC(S)A 2003 s.21(2)(a)); (2) affixing a statutory notice to lampposts (TC(S)A 2003 s.21(2)(b)); or, (3) advertising in a local newspaper, but only if the lamppost method is impossible or the burdened property is a separate tenement of minerals or salmon fishing (TC(S)A 2003 s.21(3)(c)). The terminator must also swear an oath that the intimation requirements have been met: TC(S)A 2003 s.22(1). After receiving intimation of the intention to register a notice of termination a benefited proprietor can apply to the Lands Tribunal to have the burden in question renewed: TC(S)A 2003 s.90(1)(b)(i), see *Cook v Cadman*, 2014 G.W.D. 3-66 and *Macneil v Bradonwood Ltd*, 2013 S.L.T. (Lands Tr) 41. In order to be registrable, a notice of termination must be endorsed by the Lands Tribunal to the effect that no such application is live: TC(S)A 2003 s.23(1). If all these requirements have been complied with the burden will be extinguished when the notice of termination is registered: TC(S)A 2003 s.24. The purpose of the sunset rule is to allow real burdens that are anachronistic or ill-suited to their modern context to be dispensed with.

Negative prescription and acquiescence
A real burden can be extinguished by negative prescription if the burden is **5.37** breached for a period of five years, and the extent to which the burden is extinguished correlates to the extent of the breach: TC(S)A 2003 s.18(1). The owner of a benefited property who is aware of a breach of a burden, but does nothing to challenge that breach, might be taken to have acquiesced in that breach: TC(S)A 2003 s.16. In order to demonstrate acquiescence three requirements must be met: (1) the breach involved material expenditure (TC(S)A 2003 s.16(1)(a)); (2) any benefit derived from that expenditure would be substantially lost if the burden were to be enforced (TC(S)A 2003 s.16(1)(b)), and (3) either the owner consented to the breach, or *every* person with an interest to enforce the burden (see above) consented to or was aware (or ought to have been aware) of the breach and did not object to it (TC(S)A 2003 s.16(1)(c)(i)). Objections must be made within a reasonable period of time after the breach commenced, and in any event not later than 12 weeks after the date the breach commenced: TC(S)A 2003 s.16(1)(c)(i). Furthermore, once 12 weeks have elapsed after the commencement of the breach a presumption arises that there were no objections and so acquiescence has occurred: TC(S)A 2003 s.16(2). The presumption is an evidential device which means that an objector will have to prove that they did object which might be difficult. If acquiescence has occurred the burden is extinguished to the extent of the breach: TC(S)A 2003 s.16(1).

6. SERVITUDES

CONCEPTS

Introduction

Servitudes are real rights that give someone a right to use or do something **6.01** on another person's land. Servitudes can arise in a number of different ways: a servitude can be created expressly or by implication (unlike a real burden, which can only be created expressly). Although some elements of the law relating to servitudes are statutory, many of the rules are common law rules. Like real burdens, servitudes are concerned with the relationship between two different properties. Furthermore, again in common with (most) real burdens, there must be a benefited and burdened property. The benefited property is the property that benefits from the servitude; the burdened property is the property that is subject to the servitude. The two properties are normally corporeal heritable property, but it is possible to have a servitude where the benefited property is a legal separate tenement. If there is a separate tenement of salmon fishings, for example, there might be a servitude allowing access to the separate tenement.

Confusion

It was once thought necessary for there to be two separately owned pieces **6.02** of land in order to create a servitude. The argument was that if the land was in single ownership the servitude would be extinguished by a doctrine known as confusion (*confusio*): ownership would simply subsume the subordinate real right. It is now possible to register a servitude over a piece of land that is owned by a single person that will take effect when ownership of the land is divided: Title Conditions (Scotland) Act 2003 (TC(S)A 2003) s.75(2). A typical example would be a builder who is developing land and wishes to create an express servitude with a view to the future division and transfer of the land.

Positive and negative

In the past there were what were known as "negative servitudes" as well as **6.03** "positive servitudes". Positive servitudes allow someone to enter another person's land and use that burdened property in some way. Positive servitudes continue to exist today. Before 28 November 2004 there was a type of servitude known as a "negative servitude". A negative servitude essentially prevented the use of the burdened property in some way or for some purpose. As a category, negative servitudes were somewhat redundant, because their purpose could be achieved by using a real burden. Hence, on 28 November 2004 it was made incompetent to create any new negative servitudes (TC(S)A 2003 s.79) and all negative servitudes which existed at the time were converted into real burdens by force of law: TC(S)A 2003 s.80(1). Any such "converted servitude" which was not registered (servitudes can be created without registration in some circumstances) before 28 November 2014 was extinguished: TC(S)A 2003 s.80(2)–(3).

Essentials elements of a servitude

Praediality

6.04 As with most real burdens, the content of a servitude must be sufficiently praedial. The servitude must provide a benefit to the benefited property itself, rather than a benefit that relates to the personal whims of the owner of the benefited property. If a servitude is insufficiently praedial the most it can amount to is a personal contract of some sort, which will not bind singular successors: see *Patrick v Napier* (1867) 5 M. 683 at 710, per Lord Ardmillan.

Repugnancy with ownership

6.05 Once again like real burdens, the content of a servitude must not be repugnant with ownership: it must not confer so expansive or detailed a right on the benefited property that it becomes unduly invasive of the owner of the burdened property's right of ownership. The rule exists at common law, and is applied by statute to any servitude that is created by virtue of the statutory provisions that permit the creation of servitudes that are not on the fixed list (see below): TC(S)A 2003 s.76(2). The most recent examples of arguments based upon repugnancy with ownership have arisen in relation to cases considering the existence and scope of a servitude of parking: see *Holms v Ashford Estates Ltd*, 2009 S.L.T. 389; *Johnson, Thomas and Thomas (A Firm) v Smith*, 2016 G.W.D. 25-456 at [38]–[45].

Known to the law (sometimes)

6.06 Traditionally, in order for a servitude to be created it had to be of a type that was known to the law (cf *Johnson, Thomas and Thomas (A Firm) v Smith*, 2016 G.W.D. 25-456 at [19] et seq). This requirement meant that only certain types of servitude could be created, and in turn it was said that there was something akin to a "fixed list" of servitudes. The reason that servitudes were limited to known types was because servitudes could, and indeed still can, be created by implication rather than expressly. A servitude that was not expressly created would not appear on the register; in turn, servitudes had to be of a recognised kind so that anyone purchasing the property would not be subjected to an unwelcome surprise in the form of an unusual servitude that did not appear on the register. The fixed list meant that only servitudes of a certain type could lurk unseen by a prospective transferee, and hence this would minimise the impact on the transferee if there were in fact unregistered servitudes. However, the position has been liberalised for servitudes which are expressly created by a deed registered against both the burdened and benefited property: TC(S)A 2003 s.76(1). A servitude created in this way need not be known to the law because its content will be apparent to any transferee due to its presence on the register. Nevertheless, the fixed list remains important because a servitude created by means other than registration must still adhere to the requirement that it be of a type known to the fixed list. Furthermore, although the list is theoretically not closed—i.e. new servitudes might be added to it—it is added to extremely infrequently and it is arguable that it is functionally closed. A number of recent attempts to extend the list have failed: *Mendelssohn v The Wee Pub Co Ltd*, 1991 G.W.D. 26-1518 (no servitude right of signage recognised), *Neill v Scobbie*, 1993 G.W.D. 13-887 (no servitude to run overhead power cables), *Romano v Standard Commercial Property Securities Ltd*, 2008 S.L.T. 859 (no servitude of signage reiterated). However, the tone of a recent shrieval decision was amenable to the recognition of new servitudes: *Johnson, Thomas and Thomas*. Having established the importance of the fixed list, it is useful to set out those servitudes that have been recognised by Scots law, which follows the Roman law quite closely. The servitude of access, which allows someone to access the burdened property, can be subdivided according to the nature of its exercise, such as by people or vehicles. A servitude allowing the benefited property to use a neighbouring burdened property for support is recognised, as is a servitude allowing the benefited property to run water or drainage onto the burdened property. Staying with the water theme, servitudes allowing the owner of the benefited property to draw or lead water from the burdened property are recognised. Furthermore, servitudes that allow a benefited proprietor to graze animals or wash/dry clothing on, or to extract materials such as peat or minerals from, the burdened property are recognised. Recent additions to the list include a servitude of parking (see *Moncrieff v Jamieson*, 2008 S.C. (HL) 1; *Johnson, Thomas and Thomas*, and a statutory servitude that provides a right to lead pipes, cables or wires over or under land: TC(S)A 2003 s.77(1). It is arguable whether the servitude of "overhang" is a new addition to the list or not: *Compugraphics International Ltd v Nikolic*, 2011 S.C. 744.

CREATION OF SERVITUDES

Express creation

Express grant
The first way that a servitude can be created expressly is if there is an express **6.07** grant of the servitude. In this situation, the grant of the servitude is made by the owner of the burdened property in favour of the benefited property. The owner of a piece of land is granting a servitude that can be exercised over their land. This accords with the *nemo plus* rule. Astrid cannot grant a servitude that allows someone to use Bill's land—only the owner of a piece of property can create subordinate real rights that burden it. A number of technicalities must be observed to create a servitude by express grant. The deed creating the servitude must adequately describe both the benefited and the burdened properties. If the deed fails to describe each property adequately the court is likely to consider the right granted a simple personal right that is incapable of transmitting against singular successors: *Howie v Kirkcudbright County Council*, 1963 S.L.T. (Sh Ct) 60. The servitude, as a real right in land, must also be created in writing: Requirements of Writing (Scotland) Act 1995

s.1(2)(b); but there is no formal requirement to use the word "servitude" akin to the rule for real burdens. Crucially, in order to create a valid servitude by express grant it is now necessary for the deed to be registered against both the benefited and the burdened properties: TC(S)A 2003 s.75(1). An express grant can be made using one of two types of deed: a conveyance (disposition) or a deed of servitude. A disposition is the deed that transfers the ownership of land—remember the three-step process of missives, disposition, and registration when transferring land (see above). The person who is selling a piece of land will become the burdened proprietor, and the person buying the land is going to become the benefited proprietor. Alan owns two acres of land and decides to sell one of those acres to Bob. In order to make the acre marketable it might be necessary to create a servitude of access over the acre to be retained in favour of the acre to be sold. Alan will insert the servitude into the disposition that transfers the land from Alan to Bob. The servitude is created when the disposition is registered. The acre retained by Alan (the seller) is the burdened property, the acre purchased by Bob (the buyer) is the benefited property. Using a deed of servitude is more straightforward. A deed of servitude is a one-off grant that stands alone and has no purpose beyond creating a servitude. Once again, it must be the owner of the property that is to become burdened that grants the deed of servitude. If Farmer John wants to graze his cattle on Farmer Giles's land, he might ask Farmer Giles if he can have a servitude of pasturage in order to facilitate this. Farmer Giles might agree to do this by granting a deed of servitude in favour of Farmer John (probably in return for something), but Farmer John cannot grant himself the servitude by a deed of servitude because he is not the owner.

Express reservation

6.08 In addition to the express grant of a right of servitude, a servitude right can be expressly reserved. A person transferring land may wish to create a servitude that will benefit their own property (the property they are going to retain). As with an express grant of a servitude, the express reservation of a servitude must be in writing (Requirements of Writing (Scotland) Act 1995 s.1(2)(b)), and the deed must be registered against both the burdened and benefited properties: TC(S)A 2003 s.75(1). An express reservation can only be achieved by a disposition: a deed of servitude cannot be used, because the transfer of the property means that there is no way to reserve a right because the transferor is no longer the owner. If a servitude is created by express reservation the land being transferred by the disposition becomes the burdened property. Adrian owns two acres of land and decides to sell one of those acres to Brenda. Unlike the example above Adrian wants to ensure that he can access the acre of land that he is retaining, and to do that he would like to ensure that he has a servitude of access over Brenda's land (the acre to be sold). A deed of servitude is no use because Adrian cannot grant himself a right in the land of another because of the *nemo plus* rule; instead, Adrian must expressly reserve the servitude right when he transfers the land to Brenda.

Creation by implication

It is also possible for servitudes to be created by implication (unlike real **6.09** burdens). When the creation of a servitude is implied, the law considers that the creation of a servitude was the presumed intention of the parties as objectively assessed: *ASA International Ltd v Kashmiri Properties (Ireland) Ltd*, 2017 S.C. 107 at [15]. That is rather different from the creation of a servitude by prescription, for example, where there is no agreement between the parties, express or implied. Demonstrating the creation of a servitude by implication is not easy. As with express creation, it is possible for servitudes to be created by both implied grant and reservation.

Implied grant

For there to have been an implied grant of a servitude the first thing that is **6.10** required is that there must have been a conveyance of land to a new owner. The question is whether the transfer of a piece of land to a new owner impliedly granted a servitude in favour of the transferred land? Thus, like an express grant, an implied grant creates a servitude that burdens the property retained by the transferor, and, in turn, benefits the property transferred. In what circumstances will a grant of a servitude be implied? The answer is: few. The servitude that is said to have been impliedly granted has to be "necessary for the reasonable enjoyment of the property". The test of necessity for the reasonable enjoyment of the property comes from the leading case: *Cochrane v Ewart* (1861) 4 Macq 117. In *Cochrane*, it was explained that "necessary" meant necessary for the convenient and comfortable enjoyment of the land in the same way as it had been enjoyed before the transfer. Thus, in order to successfully argue that there has been an implied grant of a servitude it might be necessary to show that activities akin to those claimed as the subject of the claimed servitude were already going on. In the *Cochrane* case the land that was transferred (the benefited property) had previously drained into a cesspool on the land that was retained (the burdened property) when the same person owned both properties. The test is somewhat open textured and has proven difficult to satisfy: *Fraser v Cox*, 1938 S.C. 506; *Moncrieff v Jamieson*, 2008 S.C. (HL) 1; *Harton Homes Ltd v Durk* 2012 S.C.L.R. 554. Recent Inner House authority provides helpful guidance by explaining that the law's suspicion of such implied grants rests upon a number of policy reasons: when dividing property the parties could have created the servitude expressly, but they did not; the implied rights claimed are necessarily less certain than express servitudes, and could even be "dubious or extravagant"; servitudes are real rights of potentially indeterminate duration, so uncertainty is especially undesirable in this context; finally, and most importantly, as real rights bind the world at large they must be particularly clearly established when they are created by means other than registration (as an implied grant is): *ASA International Ltd v Kashmiri Properties (Ireland) Ltd*, 2017 SC 107 at [17]–[18]. In *ASA International Ltd* a servitude right of access was denied because the existence of alternative routes meant that an implied grant was not reasonably necessary for the convenient and comfortable enjoyment of the putative benefited property.

Implied reservation

6.11 The other way in which a servitude can be created by implication is where the servitude is reserved by implication. Once again there must be a transfer of land, and, like with an express reservation, the property transferred forms the burdened property and the property retained is the benefited property. The question is of presumed intention: did the parties to the transfer impliedly reserve a servitude in favour of the retained property? Demonstrating an implied reservation in Scotland appears to involve satisfying an even stricter test than that which applies to an implied grant. The transferor must demonstrate that the reservation of the servitude is a necessity: *Fergusson v Campbell*, 1913 1 S.L.T. 241 (water for a mill an utter necessity); *Murray v Medley*, 1973 S.L.T. (Sh. Ct) 75 (water for people not an utter necessity). The rationale for the stricter test is that a transferor should not be able to turn around after the transfer, and say that she actually meant to retain various rights in favour of herself: a transferor should not "derogate from the grant". A transferor is not to be allowed to water down the content of a transfer after the fact.

Prescription

6.12 The final way in which a servitude can be created is by positive prescription: if someone exercises a servitude right for a sufficient amount of time, while also satisfying a number of other conditions, they will acquire the servitude right. In order to create a servitude by prescription there must be possession of the servitude for a period of 20 years: Prescription and Limitation (Scotland) Act 1973 s.3(1)(a). It is not necessary for there to be a foundation deed like in the case of positive prescription of ownership because servitudes can be created in ways other than express grant. The possession must be "adverse", which means the possession must be as of right. If the possession is merely tolerated then that is not sufficient for the purposes of possession required to constitute a servitude by possession. One of the ways in which a servitude can be said to have arisen by virtue of adverse possession is if the "user", that is to say the amount of use, suggests that a right is being asserted: *Aberdeen City Council v Wanchoo*, 2008 S.L.T. 106; *Greig v Middleton*, 2009 G.W.D. 22-365; *Jones v Gray*, 2012 G.W.D. 2-18; *Baron of Bachuil v Paine*, 2012 G.W.D. 35-707 at [27]. If a person nips across their neighbour's land once every six months when it is raining to shorten their walk then that is probably not sufficient possession; however, if they cross their neighbour's land every day, morning and night on the way to and from work, then that would suggest that a right to a servitude of access could be claimed.

EXERCISE OF SERVITUDES

6.13 The rules governing the exercise of servitudes seek to balance the interests of the benefited and burdened proprietors by imposing rights and obligations on the owners of each: see *Rattray v Tayport Patent Slip Co* (1868) 5 S.L.R. 219 at 220, per Lord Ardmillan, and *Bain v Morrison* (1871) 8 S.L.R. 539 at 540, per the Lord President (Inglis). If a servitude is created expressly, rather than by implication or prescription, determination of the content and extent of the servitude right will rely upon the appropriate interpretation of terms of the deed: *Dunlea v Cashwell*, 2017 S.C.L.R. 675 at [15] et seq.

Benefited property

Rights

The owner of the benefited property (i.e. the person who can exercise the **6.14** servitude) has a number of rights that protect their ability to exercise their servitude effectively. The owner of the benefited property may carry out physical acts on the burdened property in order to exercise their right fully. Obviously, the benefited proprietor can go onto the burdened property and use the servitude in accordance with its normal content, but they can also undertake related ancillary activities. Where a servitude provided a right to draw and pipe water from the burdened property it was accepted that building a dam and plumbing tanks were necessary ancillary works that could be undertaken: *Chalmers Property Investment Co Ltd v Robson*, 2008 S.L.T. 1069 (the case is actually from 1967). Similarly, the benefited proprietor has a right to enter onto the burdened property in order to carry out operations to protect the exercise of the servitude. The most common example of this is the ability to enter the land of another to carry out repairs: *Central RC v Ferns*, 1979 S.C. 136. Finally, the burdened proprietor has a right to enforce remedies against anyone who interferes with their servitude—whether that is the burdened proprietor or others.

Duties

The owner of the benefited property is also subjected to duties that are **6.15** implied by the law. The servitude can only be used for the benefit of the benefited property and it cannot be used to benefit other properties for sheer convenience: *Alvis v Harrison*, 1991 S.L.T. 64 at 67, per Lord Jauncey; *Irvine Knitters Ltd v North Ayrshire Co-operative Society Ltd*, 1978 S.C. 109. In a related rule, the benefited proprietor must exercise their servitude civiliter: it must be exercised so as to impose the least possible burden on the burdened property: *Hill v McLaren* (1879) 6 R. 1363 at 1366. Where a servitude of access has been exercised on an established route, it is not open to the benefited property to unilaterally alter the route: *Pollock v Drogo*, 2017 G.W.D. 14-221 at [23]-[25] per Lady Wise. Finally, the exercise of the servitude must not cause an unacceptable increase in the burden of the servitude: *Alvis v Harrison*, 1991 S.L.T. 64; *SP Distribution Ltd v Rafique*, 2010 S.L.T. (Sh Ct) 8; *Garson v McLeish*, 2010 S.L.T. (Sh Ct) 131.

Burdened property

Rights

6.16 Just because there is a servitude burdening a property does not mean that
the burdened proprietor is limited in the manner in which they may exercise
their normal rights of ownership: "[t]he proprietor may make every use of
the ground he pleases, if such use is not inconsistent with the servitude":
Rattray v Tayport Patent Slip Co (1868) 5 S.L.R. 219 at 219, per Lord Deas.
The burdened proprietor also has the right to enforce the duties that are
imposed upon the benefited proprietor, i.e. to use the servitude only for the
benefit of the benefited property, to exercise the servitude *civiliter*, and to
exercise the servitude in a manner that does not unreasonably increase the
burden and extent of the servitude right.

Duties

6.17 The owner of the burdened property is not allowed to interfere with the
exercise of the servitude right: to do so is to derogate from the grant by
undermining the servitude. When a burdened proprietor placed an obstacle
on the burdened property that prevented a servitude holder from watering
their cattle this was an unacceptable interference: *Beveridge v Marshall*,
Nov. 18 1808 F.C. The standard used to determine what amounts to
interference will be calculated according to what would affect an objective
benefited proprietor: *Drury v McGarvie*, 1993 S.C. 95.

EXTINCTION OF SERVITUDES

6.18 A servitude can come to an end in a number of different ways. A servitude
can be expressly discharged by the benefited proprietor, perhaps in
exchange for a payment. An express discharge must be done in writing
(Requirements of Writing (Scotland) Act 1995 s.1(2)(a)(i) and (2)(b)), and
the deed executing the discharge must be registered against the burdened
property: TC(S)A 2003 s.78. A servitude can also be extinguished by
negative prescription after 20 years: Prescription and Limitation (Scotland)
Act 1973 s.8. If the benefited and burdened properties are united in
ownership—i.e. they become owned by the same person—then the
servitude will be extinguished by confusion. Acquiescence can also operate
in relation to a servitude if the benefited proprietor does not object to an
interference with the exercise of the servitude. The acquiescence rules are
similar to those applicable to real burdens, though they are not statutory. It
is also possible for the burdened proprietor to apply to the Lands Tribunal
for the discharge or variation of a servitude: TC(S)A 2003 s.90(1)(a)(i),
sometimes with the agreement of the benefited proprietor: see e.g. *Young
v Markey*, 2014 S.L.T. (Lands Tr) 61. The Tribunal must have regard to a
range of factors when determining whether to make an order for discharge,
variation, etc, under s.90 of the TC(S)A 2003: TC(S)A 2003 ss.98, 100.
Though decisions are necessarily fact-specific, there is a growing body of

helpfully indicative authority: see *United Investment Co Ltd v Charlie Reid Travel Ltd*, 2016 G.W.D. 1-13; *Yule v Tobert*, 2015 G.W.D. 39-620; *Cope v X*, 2013 S.L.T. (Lands Tr) 20; *Mackay v Bain*, 2013 S.L.T. (Lands Tr) 37. The Tribunal operates in an accessible manner and can adopt an approach encouraging agreement between the parties: see e.g. *Pollachi v Campbell*, 2014 S.L.T. (Lands Tr) 55. Where the Tribunal makes an order varying or discharging a servitude (or any other relevant title condition) it can also order the payment of compensation to the benefited proprietor whose servitude right has been distinguished or diminished: TC(S)A 2003 s.90(6)–(7); see *Young*. If the burdened property ceases to exist or is acquired by compulsory purchase then any servitudes are extinguished. Compulsory purchase essentially creates a new ownership title which destroys the existing ownership title, and in turn all the subordinate real rights associated with the existing title are extinguished. Likewise, destruction of a thing (normally) causes the destruction of the ownership interest and subordinate real rights associated with it.

7. LEASES

CONCEPT

A lease is the means by which the owner of a piece of land can grant to **7.01** another person the right to possess that piece of land for a period of time, in exchange for a payment known as rent. This is an area of property law that is commonly encountered: many people across Scotland reside in flats or houses under a residential tenancy, and many retailers possess premises on commercial leases. The widespread use of leases is reflected by the age of the concept of a lease—leases have been around for many years, and one of the oldest statutes still in force in Scotland relates to leases: Leases Act 1449. The law regulating leases in Scotland is a mixture of statutory and common law, and there is no single statutory consolidation. Part of the reason for the mixture of source material relates to the fact that there are a number of different types of lease. In addition to residential leases there are commercial and agricultural leases, and although these different types of lease have shared features, their different subject matters make them necessarily different in terms of design and scope. A lease is another potential example of a real right, though it is important to appreciate that not all leases are real rights. It is only in certain circumstances that the tenant under a lease will have a real right in the subject matter. What is the significance of the tenant having a real right in the subject matter? The significance of any real right is that it can affect singular successors. If the owner of land subject to a lease that is a real right sells it to another person, the tenant under the lease is entitled to continue in possession for the duration of their lease, even though the ownership of the land has changed. It is in this way that a lease is a real right and is therefore of significance in property law. Leases can, however, be purely contractual, and so would not give the tenant a real right. If the land is sold the new owner can evict the tenant, and the tenant must raise their action against the former owner as a matter of contract law—their right is not real, and therefore they cannot insist that the new owner allow them to remain in possession for the duration of the lease. All leases are contracts, but not all of them create real rights. For the moment, we shall concentrate on the creation of a lease of land as a matter of contract law. Demonstrating that a lease of land exists as a matter of contract law is important because it is only then that a subsequent question arises: does that lease bestow a real right upon the tenant?

CREATION OF A LEASE

7.02 Since it is necessary to demonstrate that there is a contractual lease, we must first consider what is required to create a contractual lease. Four elements are required in order to constitute a valid contract of lease. Before examining these four elements, some matters of formalities must be noted: most leases with a duration of more than one year must be in writing if they are to have real effect according to the Requirements of Writing (Scotland) Act 1995 s.1(2)(b) and (7). However, a verbal lease in excess of one year might be given effect to as a matter of contract: *Gray v Macneil's Excr*, 2017 S.L.T. (Sh Ct) 83 at [21]. A "private residential tenancy" created in the terms of the Private Housing (Tenancies) (Scotland) Act 2016 (PH(T)(S)A 2016) need not be created in writing (PH(T)(S)A 2016 s.3), but in such a case the landlord is obliged to provide written terms of the tenancy if they have not already been put into writing: PH(T)(S)A 2016 s.10. The four elements necessary to constitute a valid lease are sometimes described in case law and textbooks as the "cardinal elements" of a lease. The four elements are: (1) that the subject of the lease is heritable property; (2) that consensus has been reached on the terms of the lease; (3) an agreement has been reached as to the duration of the lease; and (4) the rent payable under the lease has been determined.

1. Heritable property

7.03 In order to execute a valid lease the subject matter of the lease must be an identified piece of land. This may see obvious, but there are some nuances here. The requirement is that the subject matter of the lease is heritable property, and, therefore, this includes incorporeal heritable property. It is possible to grant a lease of a separate tenement, and various other incorporeal heritable rights, for the purposes of creating a *contractual* lease. For example, the owner of the separate tenement of the right to fish for salmon can grant a lease over that incorporeal heritable right in the same way that farmer can grant a lease over a field. The subject matter of the lease must be clearly identified as well as being heritable property: *Andert Ltd v J and J Johnston*, 1987 S.L.T. 268.

2. Consensus

7.04 As with any contract there must be a sufficient level of contractual agreement to constitute a lease. In turn, the requisite consensus should be determined in accordance with the normal rules of contract law. One facet of contract law is that in order to have a meaningful consensus it is necessary to have two separate persons (legal or natural) who can come together to form a consensus. In order to have a lease it is necessary to have two separate persons as parties to the lease: one party as the landlord and the other party as the tenant: *Kildrummy (Jersey) Ltd v Commissioners of Inland Revenue*, 1991 S.C. 1. As Lord Hope of Craighead noted, in *Clydesdale Bank plc v Davidson*, 1998 S.C. (HL) 51 at 56: "For one individual to grant a lease in favour of himself over his own property is therefore a legal impossibility."

3. Duration

A lease must specify the duration of the tenant's right to use the heritable **7.05** property. In other words, there must be a set period in which the tenant is to have possession of the property. At this stage, we must divide certain types of leases because there are restrictions relating to the permissible duration of a lease that depend on the nature of the property involved. At common law, there were no restrictions on the duration of a lease: it was possible to create a lease for a thousand years, or even a perpetual lease. Nevertheless, it was still necessary for some kind of period of time to be identified for the lease to be valid. Today, there are more arduous restrictions on the duration of a lease. A starting point is that a lease of residential property cannot normally have a duration in excess of 20 years: Land Tenure Reform (Scotland) Act 1974 s.8(1), though residential leases created before 1974 can have a duration in excess of 20 years. What will become a more significant exception to the 20 year limitation is the substantial change relating to residential tenancies which was made by the (PH(T)(S)A 2016. A tenancy defined under s.1 of the PH(T)(S)A 2016 as a "private residential tenancy" can have a duration in excess of 20 years: Land Tenure Reform (Scotland) Act 1974 s.8(3ZA). Such private residential tenancies have only been possible to create since 1 December 2017. All residential tenancies (bar the exception mentioned in the next sentence) created after 1974, but before 1 December 2017, are subject to the 20 year limitation. There is a further exception to the 20 year rule for residential leases where the lessee (tenant) is a social landlord or related body: Land Tenure Reform (Scotland) Act 1974 s.8(3A). No lease created after the year 2000 can have a duration of more than 175 years: Abolition of Feudal Tenure (Scotland) Act 2000 s.67(1). This is particularly relevant to commercial leases, and those residential leases to which s.8(1) of the Land Tenure Reform (Scotland) Act 1974 does not apply. Following the abolition of feudal tenure, legislation was enacted to ensure certain registered leases of private dwelling houses, with a duration in excess of 175 years, and which had more than 100 years left to run, were converted from leases into ownership for the tenants on 28 November 2015: Long Leases (Scotland) Act 2012 ss.1, 4 and 70.

Taking these restrictions into account it is important not to lose sight of **7.06** a key point: a lease must normally specify some type of period or duration. This is sometimes described as the need for an "ish", which is the term used for an end date for the lease. If, however, there is no identification of a period of the lease, but the other three "cardinal elements" required to constitute a valid lease have been fulfilled—i.e. the subjects are heritable, there is adequate consensus, and an agreed rent—then the court will imply a duration for the lease. If the tenant has taken possession of the property the implied duration will be a period of one year. In *Gray v University of Edinburgh*, 1962 S.C. 157 a lease was being negotiated but there was no agreement as to the duration or rent. The potential tenant refused to continue, and the owner of the piece of property argued that a valid lease had been created. The court held that there was no lease because there was no agreement as to rent or duration; however, the court observed that if the rent had been agreed, and the tenant had taken possession, then the court would have been prepared to imply a duration of one year. Private residential tenancies have their own statutory version of the rule stating that an agreement which would be a tenancy but for the absence of a specified ish is to be regarded as giving rise to a tenancy: PH(T)(S)A 2016 s.4(a).

4. Rent

7.07   The fourth and final cardinal element that is necessary to constitute a valid contract of a lease is the need for an agreed rent. There must be an agreement about what payment will be made in exchange for the right to possess the land in question. It is not necessary that the rent is necessarily monetary, though in practice it almost always is. The agreed payments must be payable in a way that is somehow periodic—a lump sum at the outset is not a rent: *Mann v Houston*, 1957 S.L.T. 89. Houston had paid £200 up front to rent a garage for 10 years from Renstrom. Renstrom sold the garage to Mann, who in turn wanted to remove Houston from possession of the garage. Mann was successful on the basis that the Houston's single payment was not rent, and therefore there was no lease. Thus, in the absence of a rental payment there will be no lease in most cases. As with the duration of the lease, if the other three cardinal elements have been satisfied then the court might fix a market rate rent: *Shetland Islands Council v BP Petroleum Development Ltd*, 1990 S.L.T. 82. It seems the general rule and approach to the requirement for rent will apply to a private residential tenancy, at least at the outset, though the legislation specifies that if the requirement to pay rent is *subsequently* removed, or ceases to have effect, then the agreement is to continue to be regarded as a tenancy: PH(T)(S)A 2016 s.4(b).

A LEASE AS A REAL RIGHT

7.08   Having considered the cardinal elements required to constitute a valid contractual lease, it now falls to consider what makes a contractual lease a real right. Most leases with a duration of more than one year must be in writing if they are to have real effect: Requirements of Writing (Scotland) Act 1995 s.1(2)(b) and (7). An exception can occur if a putative tenant has occupied a home pursuant to an unwritten private residential tenancy: PH(T)(S)A 2016 s.3(1)(a). The fact that leases can be made real at all is a result of statute: at common law leases were simply personal contracts, and in turn they gave the tenant no right against a singular successor if the land was sold before the end of the lease. Statutory interventions have changed matters, and there are three main statutes that can give a lease real effect— the Leases Act 1449 (the 1449 Act), the Registration of Leases (Scotland) Act 1857 (ROL(S)A 1857), and the PH(T)(S)A 2016. The statutes apply to different types of leases depending on the type and duration of the leases: if a lease is for a duration in excess of 20 years it is known as a "long lease" and it can only be made real using ROL(S)A 1857, or under PH(T)(S)A

2016 if it is a "private residential tenancy". If a lease is for a duration of 20 years or less it is known as a short lease, and it can be made real under the 1449 Act, or, again, under PH(T)(S)A 2016 if it is a "private residential tenancy".

Leases Act 1449: short leases

The 1449 Act is extremely old and if you look at it in a statute book you will **7.09** see that it is written in old Scots. Unlike today's often rambling statutes, the 1449 Act is not much longer than a paragraph. Nevertheless, the 1449 Act sets out a number of key requirements that must be satisfied in order to show a lease has been made real under its terms.

Application
The 1449 Act only applies to short leases. Despite the wording of the **7.10** statute it applies to urban and rural leases, and one does not need to be "poor" to benefit from its protection. Indeed, it can apply to a lease over any piece of heritable property that can exist as a separate tenement—but note that this is different from a contract of lease. A right to shoot can be the subject of a contractual of lease, but it is not recognised as a separate tenement, and hence it is not amenable to being made real by the 1449 Act. Nonetheless, the scope of the 1449 Act's potential application to short leases is wide.

Fixed duration
In order for a short lease, which is not a "private residential tenancy" under **7.11** the PH(T)(S)A 2016, to be made real it must be of a limited duration and have a definite end date (known as an "ish"). So, while it was possible at common law to create perpetual leases, they would not have the benefit of being made real using the 1449 Act. On the other hand, a very long lease could have a definite end date—a lease that provides for a duration of one thousand years does have a definite duration, and therefore, in that sense, it would be capable of receiving protection under the 1449 Act (as we have seen the longest valid lease that can be granted in Scotland now is one for 175 years). As noted above, a private residential tenancy does not require an ish: PH(T)(S)A 2016 s.4(a).

Rent
Although there must be an agreed rent in order to constitute a contractual **7.12** lease, it is also a requirement of the 1449 Act that there is an agreed rent in order to gain real protection. The rent must not be elusory either—so there will have to be something more substantial than a mere "peppercorn rent". The concept underlying the requirement for a tangible agreed rent is that the incoming owner should receive some kind of rent to ameliorate the fact they have a sitting tenant on the land they has just obtained. As noted above, it seems that the PH(T)(S)A 2016 also requires an agreed rent at the outset of the agreement to create a private residential tenancy.

Possession

7.13 Perhaps the most important requirement is that the tenant must have taken possession of the land mentioned in the lease in order for a real right to arise as result of the 1449 Act. The tenant can have taken either natural or civil possession, and the possession must have been taken under reference to the lease itself. In *Millar v McRobbie*, 1949 S.C. 1, the tenant had taken possession of the land before the beginning of the lease, and therefore it was held not to amount to possession of a sufficient quality to provide protection by virtue of the 1449 Act: the physical actions undertaken by the tenant occurred before the lease began and hence could not be said to have constituted possession as of right under the lease. In order to create a "private residential tenancy", it is necessary for the tenancy to be one where the tenant occupies the property as their only or principal home: PH(T)(S)A 2016 s.1(1)(b). It might be that the requirement for occupation will come to serve a similar role as taking possession does for the 1449 Act, but that is far from certain. Furthermore, occupation is presumptively a different legal concept from possession. A similar provision exists for a private residential tenancy created without writing: PH(T)(S)A 2016 s.3(1)(a).

7.14 If there is a short lease whereby the tenant has taken possession of the land in question, the rent is not merely elusory, there is a fixed end date for the tenancy, and the lease is in writing if in excess of a year, then it will be protected under the 1449 Act as a real right—the significance of which is that the tenant will not be open to removal at the hand of any incoming landlord. An agreement can constitute a private residential tenancy, in accordance with the PH(T)(S)A 2016, without writing and without an ish. Similarly, a private residential tenancy does not require the tenant to take possession—while there is a requirement, at the outset, for occupation as the tenant's home, it is not clear this means actually taking occupation (which might differ from "possession") in the case of a written private written tenancy (it is necessary under s.3(1)(a) for an unwritten private residential tenancy). Notwithstanding all these things which are not requisite for an agreement to constitute a private residential tenancy, so long as an agreement constitutes a private residential tenancy according to the meaning of the PH(T)(S)A 2016, it is protected in such a way that bestows real right effect: PH(T)(S)A 2016 s.45. Any short lease which is not a private residential tenancy will be required to meet the requirements of the 1449 Act in order to achieve real effect.

Registration of Leases (Scotland) Act 1857: long leases

7.15 A long lease—that is a lease with a duration in excess of 20 years—can be made real by complying with the ROL(S)A 1857. The key requirement under ROL(S)A 1857 is that a long lease must be registered in order to gain real effect. Indeed, registration is the only way to make a long lease (which is not a private residential tenancy) a real right: ROL(S)A 1857 ss.20B–20C. Because it is possible to have a private residential tenancy in excess of 20 years, it is now possible for such tenancies to have something like real effect according to the terms of the PH(T)(S)A 2016 outlined above: see PH(T)(S)A 2016 s.45. Any lease in excess of 20 years which is not a private residential tenancy will still require registration in order to achieve real effect.

Consequences of constitution as a real right

Possession

If a lease has been made real there are a number of consequences that flow **7.16** from that real status. A tenant under a lease is (generally) most concerned with ensuring their continued possession of the subjects of the lease. The tenant will be protected in their possession against future owners of the property: if the subjects of the lease are sold to a new owner, the constitution of the lease as a real right means that it will not be possible for the new owner to remove the tenant except in accordance with the lease or general law. A similar effect is achieved for private residential tenancies: PH(T)(S)A 2016 s.45.

Inter naturalia

While the continued possession of the land by the tenant is a simple enough **7.17** proposition in itself, the details are rather more complex. When the land constituting the subject of the lease is transferred to a new owner the tenant is effectively given a new landlord. Furthermore, the terms of the lease between the tenant and their new landlord will not necessarily be the same as those with the previous landlord. The terms of the lease that will continue, and those that will not, are sometimes said to be regulated by the doctrine of *inter naturalia*: *Gyle Shopping Centre General Partners Ltd v Marks and Spencer plc* [2014] CSOH 59. This doctrine states that only the terms of the lease which are essential elements of a lease of that sort will be binding upon third parties such as the incoming landlord (the new owner). It is, unfortunately, not entirely clear what exactly is encompassed by the *inter naturalia* rule beyond this rather slippery definition. The law's modern development has been somewhat hackneyed by its limited development beyond some isolated and mutually contradictory examples regarding exclusivity clauses: *Optical Express (Gyle) Ltd v Marks and Spencer Plc*, 2000 S.L.T. 644. In the case of private residential tenancies, the statutory provision states that when "...a property let under a private residential tenancy is transferred, the landlord's interest under the tenancy transfers with it.": PH(T)(S)A 2016 s.45. The terms of s.45 suggest a totality of transfer in relation to incoming buyer landlords' rights and obligations, which appears more extensive than the common law test of *inter naturalia*. The interpretation of this section by the tribunals and courts will be interesting.

Offside goals

Real rights are ranked according to temporal priority: the oldest is first in **7.18** time, and therefore stronger by right. The rule applies to the real rights in leases as much as to any other real rights. So, in order for a tenant to have a real right to stay on a piece of land that is being sold they must make their right real before the new owner gains their title. If the new owner completes their title before the lease is made real then the tenant loses out: the ownership of the land has transferred to the new owner before the tenant's interest has been reified, and therefore the nemo plus rule prevents the tenant from obtaining a real right. There is, however, a well-known exception to this rule—the offside goals rule, which a tenant might seek to rely on: *Advice Centre for Mortgages Ltd v McNicoll*, 2006 S.L.T. 591.

RIGHTS AND DUTIES OF LANDLORD AND TENANT

Express and implied terms

7.19 Because leases are contracts they generate mutual rights and obligations that affect both the landlord and tenant. These rights and duties are generated by the express terms of the contract of lease, though sometimes the law will imply rights and duties. Therefore, a lease can be an amalgam of express and implied terms. What are the rights and duties that the law will impute between the parties to a lease? In the first place the position will be governed by the intention of the parties: remember that a lease is in fact a contract first and foremost, and therefore the rights and obligations owed by the landlord and tenant to one another will be governed by their mutual intention. Such express terms of a lease will be interpreted according to known rules of contractual interpretation: see e.g. *AWG Business Centres Ltd v Regus Caledonia Ltd* [2017] CSIH 22 at [18] et seq; *@SIPP Pension Trsv Insight Travel Services Ltd*, 2016 S.C. 243 at [17]; *L Batley Pet Products Ltd v North Lanarkshire Council*, 2014 S.C. (U.K.S.C.) 174. Yet, a lease is also a nominate contract: that is to say it is a contract which is recognised by the law by its name, and by virtue of that name the lease will have certain terms implied into it—if the parties intend to oust those terms they must make clear their intention to do so. By the same token, where the parties have reached an apparent consensus, the law might imply terms in order to augment the express terms of any agreement. The interaction between express and implied terms can be seen in *Mars Pension Trs Ltd v County Properties and Developments*, 1999 S.C. 267. An express clause in the lease purported to limit the liability of the landlord with respect to the implied term that the property would be provided in a reasonable condition for the purpose of the tenancy. The court held that the express clause had successfully altered the implied term because it evinced a clear intention by the parties to do so. In other cases, terms will be implied, such as in *Geoffrey (Tailor) Highland Crafts Ltd v GL Attractions Ltd*, 2010 G.W.D. 8-142. The landlord had previously sold clothing on the premises, but it decided to grant a lease to the tenant who proposed to conduct a similar trading operation. The lease provided that the landlord would retain access to a "control room" within the premises. There was a change of landlord and the new landlord attempted to conduct a similar trade from the "control room". The tenant sought interdict. The new landlord argued there was no generally implied term that prevented competition between landlord and tenant. The court agreed that there was no such implied term; however, the court held that in this specific case the actions of the parties meant that a term—that the control room was not to be used for retail—was to be implied. In other words, although there was no such implied term that was generally implied to all leases of this kind, in this particular case a specific term fell to be implied in the circumstances. Therefore, implied terms can be case specific or they can be more generalised implied terms that are associated with certain types of nominate lease. We turn now to consider some generalised implied terms associated with contracts of lease.

Terms implied to leases

Possession
As pointed out above, the tenant's primary focus under a lease is on the fact **7.20** that they would like to be in possession of subjects of the lease. Therefore, it is an implied term of a lease, which reflects the tenant's primary focus, that the landlord is required to allow the tenant to take natural possession of the subjects: Stair I. 15. 6; *Seaforth's Trs v Macaulay*, (1844) 7 D. 180. Furthermore, the landlord is not to undermine or interfere with that possession once it has been given: *Huber v Ross*, 1912 S.C. 898 (landlord liable for having interfered with the possession of tenant through building works); *Golden Sea Produce Ltd v Scottish Nuclear plc*, 1992 S.L.T. 942 (landlord liable for water quality); *Chevron Petroleum (UK) Ltd v Post Office*, 1986 S.C. 291. The flipside of this duty on the landlord is that the tenant is under a reciprocal obligation to actually take up the natural possession of the lease subjects, failure to do so is a breach of the contract of lease: Stair II. 9. 31; *Randifuird v Crombie*, (1623) Mor. 15256. Furthermore, the tenant may not "invert the possession" under the lease. This means the tenant must not use the subjects of the lease in a way that differs from that envisioned in the agreement. In *Cayzer v Hamilton (No.2)*, 1996 S.L.T. (Lands Tr) 21, a tenant used a piece of land that was let on an agricultural lease for the storage and sale of agricultural equipment, rather than farming the ground itself, and this amounted to an inversion of the lease.

Plenishings
The tenant is under an obligation to keep the premises that constitute the **7.21** subject of the lease sufficiently "plenished". This requirement is a direct correlative of the landlord's right to a hypothec (a non-possessory right of security) over property on the premises. In turn, the obligation to maintain a sufficient level of plenishings is probably only implied where there is a valid landlord's hypothec. The landlord's hypothec is now restricted to commercial leases. If the tenant attempts to "deplenish" the subjects it is open to the landlord to seek an interdict in order to prevent this process: *Co-operative Insurance Society Ltd v Halfords Ltd*, 1998 S.L.T. 90 at 94, per Lord Hamilton.

Rent

7.22 The tenant is under an obligation to pay any rent due under the lease, including such rent as has been adjusted by rent review clauses. If the rent is not stipulated in the lease, but a market rate has been implied as the other three cardinal features are present, there is an implied obligation to pay the market rent that was implied by the court (see above).

Reasonably fit for purposes of let

7.23 The landlord is under an obligation to ensure that the subjects of the lease are of a reasonably fit standard for the purposes of the lease as it was agreed at the tenant's entry (the start of the lease). Thus, the premises must be suitable for the type of lease that has been agreed, though the standard is a reasonable one and the fitness of the premises need not be perfect. In *Glebe Sugar Refining Co v Paterson*, (1902) 2 F. 615 the tenant leased a warehouse to store sugar, however the weight of the sugar caused the warehouse to collapse, damaging the sugar. The tenant argued that the landlord was liable for failure to make the premises reasonably fit for the purpose of sugar storage. The court rejected this view, finding that the landlord's obligation was to make the building capable of bearing an ordinary amount of weight, and the fact that the tenant had essentially overloaded the building meant that the building collapsed. In other words, the landlord's duty was to provide something reasonable for general use— it did not have to be extraordinarily strong to allow storage of sugar. The implied obligation relates to the fabric of the premises, and is not concerned with the situation of the premises and any environmental factors which might be impacting upon the habitability of the premises: *McManus v City Link Development Co Ltd* [2015] CSOH 178 at [183]–[184].

7.24 What will count as reasonably fit for its purpose will depend on the nature of the property let. If the subjects of the let are urban then the obligation on the landlord is to provide the property in a wind and watertight fashion: it must be capable of keeping out the elements. Once again this is an ordinary standard, and so it will not apply if the elements of wind or water are invading in an unusual manner: *Wolfson v Forrester*, 1910 S.C. 675. Compare the decisions in *Mearns v Glasgow City Council*, 2002 S.L.T. (Sh. Ct) 49 (pipe liable to burst was beyond reasonable fitness for purpose), and *Mechan v Watson*, 1907 S.C. 25 (extent of tenantable condition might vary according to property, rental and tenant). The requirement that the property be wind and watertight is an aspect of the more general requirement that the property is reasonably fit for habitation: *McManus v City Link Development Co Ltd* [2015] CSOH 178 at [178]. It has been observed that when "determining whether a house is in a habitable condition at entry, as a matter of fact, it is to be noted that the 'class of house' is a consideration, as are the services, such as gas, water and drainage, which are provided.": *McManus* at [179].

Continuing obligation in relation to the tenantable state of the property

7.25 The landlord is not only under an obligation to ensure that the property is in a reasonable condition at the date of entry, they are also liable for continuing repairs to the extent that they are necessary to put the property into a tenantable condition: see *McManus v City Link Development Co Ltd* [2015] CSOH 178 at [179]. In *Gunn v National Coal Board*, 1982 S.L.T. 526 the failure of the landlord to remedy a damp problem in the house was held to be a breach of the continuing obligation to maintain the property in a habitable condition. A similar decision was reached in *Mack v Glasgow City Council*, 2006 S.C. 543. However, neither the tenant nor the landlord will be liable for repairs when the damage caused to the property is a result of a *damnum fatale*, otherwise known as an act of god: *Little Cumbrae Estates Ltd v Island of Little Cumbrae Ltd*, 2007 S.C. 525 (storm damages, though note that express agreement could alter the position); *Cantors Properties (Scotland) Ltd v Swears, Wells Ltd*, 1978 S.C. 310. While the landlord is under a duty to provide reasonable and tenantable subjects, the tenant is under a concomitant duty to take reasonable care of the subjects of the lease: *Fry's Metals Ltd v Durastic Ltd*, 1991 S.L.T. 689 (tenant failed to maintain a private alarm system and the premises were broken into and vandalised: the tenants were liable to the landlord for the loss caused).

REMEDIES

Remedies available to both landlord and tenant
The general remedies available to both parties reflect the fact that a lease is **7.26** a contract, and therefore the remedies available to both the landlord and tenant are those generally available when there has been a breach of contract.

Interdict/implement
The remedies of specific implement and interdict are general contractual **7.27** remedies available to both the landlord and tenant. Specific implement is sought in order to compel someone to carry out an obligation. On one view, specific implement or an order *ad factum praestandum* is the main remedy for breach of contract, particularly non-pecuniary obligations: see *Moor Row Ltd v DWF LLP* [2017] CSOH 63 at [51]. Interdict is the remedy that can be used to stop someone doing something, including breaching an obligation. A frequently litigated issue has been the validity and efficacy of "keep open" clauses. A keep open clause requires a tenant to continue trading in a building, normally a shopping centre. Such clauses are included because certain retailers' presence contributes, so the theory goes, to the overall performance and viability of the centre. Landlords who own shopping centres are therefore keen to enforce such keep open clauses by seeking specific implement: *Highland and Universal Properties Ltd v Safeway Properties Ltd (No.2)*, 2000 S.C. 297.

Damages
Pecuniary compensation in the form of damages may be sought by either the **7.28** landlord or tenant for any loss caused by a breach of the lease. The calculation of damages has a degree of flexibility at common law, and the parties to the

lease can agree to a payment or liquidated damages clause in the lease: see e.g.
Moor Row Ltd v DWF LLP [2017] CSOH 63 at [52] et seq per Lady Wolffe.

Action for payment
7.29 An action for payment is the classic example of enforcing a contract by
seeking an order to coerce the transmission of a payment that is due to one
of the parties. The most common example is an action for payment of the
rent falling due by the tenant on the date that the rent falls due.

Rescission
7.30 It is open to either party to rescind the contract of the lease in the face of a
material breach. In the case of the landlord, however, there are some
limitations on their ability to rescind the contract. If the obligation breached
is a monetary obligation (i.e. failure to pay rent) the landlord must give the
tenant 14 days written notice to allow the tenant to pay off the outstanding
monetary obligation: Law Reform (Miscellaneous Provisions) (Scotland) Act
1985 (LR(MP)(S)Act 1985) s.4. The notice must be sent by recorded delivery
(*Kodak Processing Companies Ltd v Shoredale Ltd*, 2010 S.C. 313 (Royal
Mail)) and be clearly capable of being understood by a reasonable recipient.
The period of notice begins with the date of service of the notice: *Wing v
Henry Tse and Co Ltd*, 2009 G.W.D. 11-175. The key requirement in
connection with irritancy (see below) is that the landlord's notice must make
clear to the tenant "what he has to do and within what period": *Inverclyde
Council v McCloskey (t/a Prince of Wales Bar)*, 2015 S.L.T. (Sh Ct) 57 at
[63]. There is conflicting authority on the question of the extent to which the
notice must detail the basis of an alleged irritancy: compare *McCloskey* at
[62]–[77], with *Scott v Muir*, 2012 S.L.T. (Sh Ct) 179 at [41] et seq.
7.31   If the obligation that has been breached is not a monetary obligation the
landlord may only rescind in response to such a material breach if it is fair
and reasonable to do so: LR(MP)(S)Act 1985 s.5. What if the tenant
breached an obligation, but subsequently put the matter right: would it be
fair and reasonable to rescind? Yes: the material time is the time of the
breach, the fact that repairs were conducted afterwards does not prevent
rescission: *Maris v Banchory Squash Racquets Club Ltd*, 2007 S.C. 501
(failure of tenant to keep subjects in good order); though it might be
relevant in deciding if, at the time of rescission, it was fair and reasonable
that the tenant was given time to remedy or not. Recent authority affirms
that a trivial breach of the contact of lease will be insufficient to pursue
irritancy, though it is perhaps less clear if the breach must be material or if
a merely non-trivial breach will be sufficient: see *Lewis v Hunter*, 2017
G.W.D. 19-308, particularly at [53]–[57].

Retention
7.32 The mutuality principle, which permeates all contracts in Scotland, dictates
that if one party fails to perform their obligation under a contract the other
party may withhold their performance: *Renfrew District Council v Gray*,
1987 S.L.T. (Sh. Ct) 70 (retention of rent by tenant). One should note,

however, that the doctrine of retention is equitable in nature, and it will be for the court to decide if retention is being exercised in an equitable manner: *EDI Central Ltd v National Car Parks Ltd* [2010] CSOH 141; *Inveresk Plc v Tullis Russell Papermakers Ltd* [2010] UKSC 19.

Remedies available to the landlord only

There are a number of remedies available to the landlord which are peculiarly available in relation to leases, and are available in addition to the general contractual remedies discussed above. **7.33**

Hypothec

The landlord's hypothec is a legal hypothec, which means that it arises by operation of law. The landlord's hypothec has changed a great deal in recent years and it is now confined to commercial leases: it no longer applies to leases of private dwelling houses, agricultural leases or crofts: Bankruptcy and Diligence etc (Scotland) Act 2007 s.208. Furthermore, the landlord's hypothec is only security for unpaid rent—it cannot be used in connection with any other form of debt. The security is held over all the corporeal moveables that the commercial tenant brings onto the property. The security right will allow the landlord to rank as a secured creditor in any insolvency of a commercial tenant. **7.34**

Irritancy

Irritancy is in many respects similar to rescission in that allows the landlord to terminate the lease in response to a breach on the part of the tenant. There are two types of irritancy: conventional and legal. A legal irritancy is one that is implied by law, and there is only one type available for non-payment of rent. In most leases, the non-payment must have lasted for two years, but the period is only six months in relation to agricultural leases. The legal irritancy for non-payment of rent can be purged: the tenant can pay before the full two years of non-payment has passed and prevent the landlord from irritating the lease. Conventional irritancy is where there is a clause in the lease stating that a certain event will constitute irritancy. Thus, a lease might state that failure to maintain the subjects of the lease to a certain standard will constitute an irritancy, thereby allowing the landlord to irritate the lease. However, the landlord's ability to irritate the lease is subject to the same controls that relate to rescission under the LR(MP)(S)A 1985 that were noted above. **7.35**

Removal of the tenant

The landlord can seek judicial permission to remove the tenant from the property if the tenant fails to leave when the tenancy ends and the tenant's right to occupy or possess the premises has come to an end: Sheriff Courts (Scotland) Act 1971 s.35(1)(c). The various statutory tenancies tend to have controls about how and at whose instance a tenant can be evicted, and so removal will only occur after the tenant's rights under those statutes have come to an end. **7.36**

ASSIGNATION AND SUBLETTING

7.37 Two types of juristic acts relating to leases are of particular importance: assignation and subletting. Assignation of a lease is the name given to the way that the landlord, or indeed the tenant, transfers their interest in the lease to another person. The second form of juristic act that is of some importance is when the tenant utilises their interest in the tenancy to grant a right to another person to use the property. When a tenant grants another person a lease that is known as subletting.

Assignation

7.38 As is the case with many types of incorporeal property it is possible to assign a lease, and it is open to both landlord and tenant to assign their respective interests in a lease to another person. In the case of the landlord the process is a fairly simple one: generally, a landlord can assign the lease without seeking the consent of the tenant. The landlord can act unilaterally due to the lack of *delectus personae* relating to the landlord: the identity of the person to whom the tenant is paying rent will rarely make any difference to the tenant. If the tenant wishes to assign their interest in the property matters are more complicated. There are two potential restrictions upon the tenant's right to assign their interest in a lease, both of which relate to the question of *delectus personae* and whether the tenant will need to seek permission to assign their interest. It is common for a lease to contain an express prohibition against assignment, or a clause requiring the tenant to seek the landlord's permission to assign their interest. There are number of cases dealing with the reasonableness of a landlord's decision to refuse permission to assign. In *Renfrew District Council v AB Leisure (Renfrew) Ltd (In Liquidation)*, 1988 S.L.T. 635 the landlord's refusal to give consent was unreasonable because the landlord sought to have new elements written into the lease; whereas in *Lousada and Co v JE Lesser (Properties) Ltd*, 1990 S.L.T. 823 it was held reasonable to await the outcome of a rent review. In *Scotmore Developments Ltd v Anderton*, 1996 S.C. 368 the court formulated a test to analyse whether a landlord is unreasonably withholding consent: would failure to give consent on the part of the landlord amount to acting in a way that no reasonable landlord would have acted? If so, then the refusal of consent is unreasonable. Sometimes clauses in leases will provide that a tenant must not withhold consent to similar matters, and the applicable test is similar: *Aviva Investors Pensions Ltd v McDonald's Restaurants Ltd*, 2014 G.W.D. 7-146. If the lease has no express provisions that require the tenant to seek permission to assign their interest, the tenant may still need to seek permission to assign. The requirement to seek permission to assign might be implied where there is a degree of *delectus personae*, such as when a tenant possesses characteristics that cannot easily be replaced. Furthermore, in some cases *delectus personae* will be presumed. Thus, there are presumptions of *delectus personae* in relation to agricultural leases with a duration of less than 21 years and leases of furnished houses. Yet, these are only presumptions and they can be rebutted. In *Scottish Ministers v Trustees of the Drummond Trust*, 2001 S.L.T.

665 it was noted that rural and agricultural leases can, in some circumstances, be assigned without the landlord's consent. In commercial leases the norm will be that assignation will be possible without seeking consent where the lease is silent on the matter. Finally, the assignation of the tenant's interest under the lease must be perfected according to the type of lease. Thus, unregistered (and hence short) leases must be completed by taking possession: *Inglis and Co v Paul* (1829) 7 S. 469. An assignation of the tenant's interest under a registered (and hence long) lease must be registered in order to complete the assignation and give it real effect: ROL(S)A 1857 ss.20B–20C. A private residential tenancy cannot be assigned without the landlord's written agreement: Private Residential Tenancies (Statutory Terms) (Scotland) Regulations 2017 (SSI 2017/408) reg 3(c), PH(T)(S)A 2016 ss.7, 8, Sch.2 para.5(c).

Subletting

Subletting occurs within the context of a chain of interests. At the top of the chain is the original landlord and the first link in the chain, the original lease, connects the original landlord and the original tenant. When subletting occurs, a new link is added to the chain in the form of a sub-lease. There are two ways in which this situation can be brought about: (1) by the actions of the tenant; or (2) by the actions of the landlord. In both cases the structure illustrated below is created. The sub-lease connects the original tenant with the sub-tenant. There is not normally any direct contractual relationship between the original landlord and the sub-tenant, and hence they cannot sue one another. The original tenant is the sub-tenant's landlord. In that structure, the sub-tenant normally pays the original tenant rent under the sub-lease, and, in turn, the original tenant will pay the original landlord a rent under the original lease. **7.39**

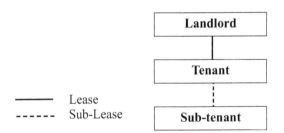

The most common way to create a sub-lease is for the tenant in a lease to grant a lease to another person. The lease granted by the tenant is a sub-lease in favour of their own tenant. The tenant can grant no greater right than he himself has, and therefore the terms and nature of the sub-lease will reflect this. Furthermore, if the original or head lease is brought to an end, then so too is the sub-lease. The sub-lease cannot be stronger than the interest from which it was granted. Finally, the grant of a sub-lease is like the grant of any other lease, and so in order to make the lease a real one it **7.40**

will be necessary to register the lease or take possession of the subjects. It was noted earlier that there are two routes to creating the sub-lease structure. The most common is where the tenant grants a sub-lease in favour of another person. The same result can, however, be achieved by the landlord as well. Instead of the tenant granting a lease to someone, the landlord can grant a lease to another person that will interpose in the chain of interests: Land Tenure Reform (Scotland) Act 1974 s.17. The person that the landlord grants the second lease to becomes the main tenant, and the original tenant becomes a sub-tenant. The tangible effect of having interposed the new lessee makes little practical difference to the original tenant—they have a new landlord to pay, but they cannot be prejudiced in their rights as the effect of the interposition is the same as if there had been an assignation of the original landlord's interest in the land to the new tenant. Furthermore, if the newly interposed lease comes to an end before the sub-lease, then the sub-lease simply reverts back to being a "normal" lease. A private residential tenancy cannot be sublet without the landlord's written agreement: Private Residential Tenancies (Statutory Terms) (Scotland) Regulations (SSI 2017/408) reg 3(a), PH(T)(S)A 2016 ss.7, 8, Sch.2 para.5(a).

TERMINATION

Termination at the end date of the lease

7.41 Almost all leases will contain an agreed date on which the lease is due to expire: that date is known as the "ish". However, without something else, the lease will not in fact come to an end on this nominated day: one of the parties to the lease must also give notice that they intend the lease to come to an end on that day. This may seem strange, but it is necessary. Different notice periods apply to different types of lease. For example, in the case of a lease of a dwelling-house a notice period of not less than four weeks is required when giving notice of the intention to end the tenancy: Rent (Scotland) Act 1984 s.112. If notice of the intention to end the tenancy on the ish is not given within the requisite notice period the lease will be renewed by virtue of a rule known as "tacit relocation".

Tacit relocation

7.42 Where a lease has come to its natural end the doctrine of tacit relocation renews the lease by operation of law because no valid notice of its end has been given. When tacit relocation occurs a new lease of similar terms is created in place of the expired lease. The duration of the newly created lease depends on the duration of the old lease that has just come to an end. If the expired lease had a duration of one year or more the new lease will have a duration of one year. If the expired lease had a duration of less than one year, then the new lease has the same duration as the expired lease. Thus, if tacit relocation does occur the longest possible duration for a newly created lease is one year. Because the effect of tacit relocation is akin to renewing a lease the new lease continues on the same terms as the expired lease: *Neilson v Mossend Iron Co* (1886) 13 R. (HL) 50 at 54. However, if the lease contains a term which is not consistent with the new lease, then that term will not form a component of the new lease. In *Commercial Union Assurance Co v Watt and Cumine*, 1964 S.C. 84 a lease for 20 years contained an option to renew the lease for a further 20 years. The tenant did not exercise the option and the lease came to an end, and was renewed for a year by the operation of tacit relocation. One year into the tenancy the tenant wished to exercise the original option to renew the lease for a further 20 years, arguing that the renewal element of tacit relocation meant that the new lease contained all the terms of the expired lease, including an option to renew for a further 20 years. The court held that the option was not a part of the new lease, because any terms which were inconsistent with the new lease of a year were not a part of the implied lease created by tacit relocation. See further: *Sea Breeze Properties Ltd v Bio-medical Systems Ltd*, 1998 S.L.T. 319 (similar result where an option was killed off by tacit relocation); *Smith v Grayton Estates Ltd*, 1960 S.C. 349 (if joint tenants, notice by one tenant sufficient to prevent tacit relocation—tacit relocation concerned with the implication of mutual intention); *Cinema Bingo Club v Ward*, 1976 S.L.T. (Sh. Ct) 90 (if the lease is silent as to duration, then one year duration implied, and tacit relocation will be for one year); *Signet Group Plc v C and J Clark Retail Properties Ltd*, 1996 S.C. 444 (some form of notice required, and mere actions on the part of the parties that may infer intention not to continue not enough); *O'Donnell v McDonald*, 2008 S.C. 189 (notice to quit by landlord gave wrong date, but was sufficiently clear notice that lease was not to be renewed and hence tacit relocation could not operate).

8. TENEM

INTRODUCTION

Not required

About 25% of all housing i~ ~ , chapter **8.01**
is concerned with the law ~ the law
relating to separate teneme. ~ ~ement
building are conventional separate ~ w the
different ownership interests which subs~ ~ vith
each other. This subject has been much ~ ~nt
of the Tenements (Scotland) Act 2004 (T(~ ~n ~~~~ of
the law relating to tenement buildings in S~ , however, important to
bear in mind that the rules set out in the ~. ~4 are default rules. That
means that the T(S)A 2004 rules only ap~ ~ne extent that there are no
express provisions in the title deeds that might regulate the situation. For
example, if the title deeds state that the back garden of a tenement building is
to be owned by the ground floor proprietor then that ground floor proprietor
is the owner of the back garden, regardless of what default rule might be set
out in the T(S)A 2004. The T(S)A 2004 operates where there is silence or there
are gaps in the deeds. Furthermore, the statute codifies many elements of the
common law relating to tenements, and so pre-T(S)A 2004 cases might still be
relevant when considering the law of the tenement.

WHAT IS A TENEMENT?

Before considering the terms of the T(S)A 2004 it is necessary to identify **8.02**
what sort of building the T(S)A 2004 applies to. A tenement building for the
purposes of the T(S)A 2004 is a building in which there are two or more flats
that are related to each other: T(S)A 2004 s.26(1). Furthermore, those related
flats must be in, or be designed to be in, separate ownership (T(S)A 2004
s.26(1)(a)), and they must be horizontally separated: T(S)A 2004 s.26(1)(b).
It is important to distinguish between a horizontal boundary line and a vertical
boundary line. In the diagram below, the building on the right-hand side is not
a tenement building—it is a terrace because the properties are vertically
separated. The building on the left is a tenement building because it is
horizontally divided: see *Humphreys v Crabbe* [2016] CSIH 82 at [27].

The definition of a tenement talks about "flats". It might be thought that a flat means a residence, however, for the purposes of the T(S)A 2004, a flat can mean residential or commercial property, and a flat can extend across more than one floor: T(S)A 2004 s.29(1).

BOUNDARIES AND OWNERSHIP

8.03 The starting point for any examination of the ownership of a tenement building must be the title deeds relating to it. Many titles have specific provisions regulating the position: see, for example, *Rafique v Amin*, 1997 S.L.T. 1385, where significant parts of the building were deemed common property by the title deeds. If there are no provisions in the title deeds, or if they do not regulate all parts of the tenement building, then the T(S)A 2004 plugs any gaps. Ownership is arranged into separate sections or sectors by the T(S)A 2004, and each sector constitutes an independent entity for the purposes of ownership. The different sectors are the flats, close, lift, or any other three-dimensional space that is not part of a flat, close or lift: T(S)A 2004 s.29(1). The tenement building is entirely divided into such sectors. Examples of a three-dimensional space would be storage cupboards, recycling areas, cellars etc. Once the tenement building has been divided into different sectors it is possible to consider the ownership of those sectors. The general rule is that where two sectors are next to each other the mid-point of the structure that separates them is the extent of the ownership of that sector: T(S)A 2004 s.2(1)(a). Thus, if there is a wall separating two flats the owner of each flat owns the wall up to the mid-point. If a structure wholly or mainly serves one of the adjacent sectors then it is owned solely by that sector: T(S)A 2004 s.2(2). An example would be a door or window of a flat that opens onto the close of the building. If the wall is an external wall there is no adjacent sector on the outside, and so the full width of the external wall is owned by the owner of the adjacent internal sector: T(S)A 2004 s.2(1)(b)(i). Likewise, if there is no boundary between a sector and the solum (the land below the building) then ownership of that sector extends to and includes the solum: T(S)A 2004 s.2(1)(b)(i). More specifically, the bottom flat extends to and includes the solum under that flat: T(S)A 2004 s.2(4). Similarly, the close extends to the solum beneath it and the roof above it: T(S)A s.2(5). A sector which includes the solum also includes the airspace above the tenement and that part of the solum: T(S)A 2004 s.2(6). There is a minor exception to this if the tenement has a sloping roof—in that case, the airspace above the slope of the roof up to the level of the highest point of the roof is part of the sector that includes the roof: T(S)A 2004 s.2(7). We can see these boundaries and sectors illustrated by the two diagrams below. The diagram on the left shows the boundaries between adjacent sectors and for external walls. The diagram on the right shows the boundaries and sectors of the whole tenement, including the solum and airspace.

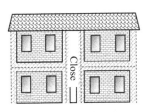 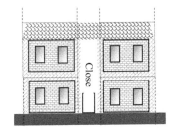

PERTINENTS AND THE CLOSE

The close of the tenement building is really a pertinent of the flats that make **8.04** up the tenement. It will be owned in common by the owners of the flats that utilise the common stair for entrance: T(S)A 2004 s.3(1)–(2). There is a similar rule for lifts. Land which is adjacent to the tenement building itself is owned by the bottom flat that is nearest to the piece of adjacent land: T(S)A 2004 s.3(3). However, if any part of that land constitutes a path, outside stair, or other way to access a sector, other than the bottom flat, then it will not constitute a pertinent of the bottom flat by virtue of T(S)A 2004 s.3(3). The ownership of any part of the tenement that is not covered by the rules contained in s.3(1) and (3) is determined by a service test: T(S)A 2004 s.3(4). In other words, the question that determines ownership is: which flats are served by that part of the tenement? If only one flat is served by that part, then it is owned by the proprietor of that flat alone: T(S)A 2004 s.3(4)(a). If more than one flat is served by that part of the tenement, then it is owned as common property by the owners of those flats that are served by it: T(S)A 2004 s.3(4)(b). A non-exhaustive list of the parts of a tenement that might be owned in accordance with this service test includes: paths, outside stairs, fire escapes, rhones, pipes, flues, conduits, cables, tanks or chimney stacks (T(S)A 2004 s.3(4)). Therefore, a fire escape that serves two of the six flats that make up the tenement building is owned in common by the owners of those two flats. Where a piece of property is owned in common as a pertinent the owners are deemed to have equal shares in that pertinent: T(S)A 2004 s.3(5). An exception is made for a chimney stack, which is owned in common: the shares of the co-proprietors are determined in accordance with the ratio of the number of flues serving the respective flats and the total number of flues in the stack. Say there is a chimney stack serving two flats: one flat has three flues, while the other flat has only one flue. There are four flues in total. The flat with three flues has a 75% share in the common ownership of the chimney stack, while the flat with only one flue has a 25% share.

SUPPORT

The owners of parts of the tenement must provide support and shelter to **8.05** their fellow owners. Thus, a flat must provide shelter for the flat below it, and, in turn, the flat below must provide support to the flat above it. The statutory scheme ensures that these duties are met by requiring owners to take both positive action and refrain from other actions. Owners are prohibited from doing anything which would, or would be reasonably likely to, impair to a material extent the support, shelter or natural light enjoyed by any part of the building: T(S)A 2004 s.9(1). In terms of positive actions, owners are obliged to maintain any part of a tenement which provides support or shelter to another part of the tenement: T(S)A 2004 s.8(1). However, an owner will not be obliged to carry out such maintenance if it would not be reasonable to do so in all the circumstances, taking into particular account the age and condition of the building, and the likely cost of such maintenance: T(S)A 2004 s.8(2). If the part of the tenement providing the support or shelter is owned in common any one of the co-owners may take steps to comply with the obligation without the approval of the other co-owners: T(S)A 2004 s.8(4).

MAINTENANCE AND MANAGEMENT

Scheme property

8.06   It is important to distinguish between the ownership of a tenement building on the one hand, and the management of the maintenance of the building on the other. The two do not always cohere exactly, and proprietors can be liable for maintenance of parts of the tenement that they do not own (solely or in common). One of the most important reforms of the law to be introduced by the T(S)A 2004 was the Tenement Management Scheme (TMS). The TMS sets out a default set of rules for running a tenement: T(S)A 2004 s.4(1) and Sch.1. As with the rules concerning the allocation of ownership, it is important to remember that these are default rules: if there are real burdens governing the management of the tenement building, then the TMS will apply subject to the terms of those burdens: *Humphreys v Crabbe* [2016] CSIH 82 at [29]. The rules set out in the TMS for the management and maintenance of the tenement are only applicable to "scheme property": T(S)A 2004 Sch.1 r.1.1. Scheme property is: (1) any part of the tenement that is the common property of two or more owners (T(S)A 2004 Sch.1 r.1.2(a)); (2) any part of the tenement which two or more owners are liable to maintain as a result of a real burden, and which does not fall within the definition of (1) above (T(S)A 2004 Sch.1 r.1.2(b)); and (3) the following specifically identified parts of a tenement building: the ground upon which the tenement is built (T(S)A 2004 Sch.1 r.1.2(c)(i)), the foundations of the tenement (T(S)A 2004 Sch.1 r.1.2(c)(ii)), the external walls of the tenement (T(S)A 2004 Sch.1 r.1.2(c)(iii)), the roof of the tenement (T(S)A 2004 Sch.1 r.1.2(c)(iv)), the gable wall of the tenement (T(S)A 2004 Sch.1 r.1.2(c)(v)), and any wall, beam or column which is load bearing (T(S)A 2004 Sch.1 r.1.2(c)(vi)). However, certain parts of the tenement are specifically excluded from r.1.2(c), with the result that they do not form scheme property: T(S)A 2004 Sch.1 r.1.3. The parts of the tenement so excluded are: extensions which form part of only one flat (T(S)A 2004 Sch.1 r.1.3(a)); any door, window, skylight, vent or other opening which serves only one flat (T(S)A 2004 Sch.1 r.1.3(b), though see *Waelde v Ulloa*, 2016 G.W.D. 11-221); and any chimney stack or chimney flue: T(S)A 2004 Sch.1 r.1.3(c). It will be apparent that the identification of scheme property is a process that is separate from identifying who owns the property: see *Hunter v Tindale*, 2012 S.L.T. (Sh Ct) 2 at [29], per Sheriff Principal Stephen. In some cases, the location of ownership will be important: when a part of the tenement is in common ownership it is scheme property. But at other times ownership will not be determinative. Thus, even though only one person owns some parts of a tenement those parts in sole ownership might still form scheme property if they are on the list set out in r.1.2(c). Likewise, the parts of the tenement that are excluded from r.1.2(c) (by r.1.3) can still constitute scheme property if they are owned in common, or are the subject of a real burden which affects two or more owners: see *Humphreys v Crabbe* at [29].

Scheme decisions

Voting and procedure
Part of the rationale behind the introduction of the TMS regime was to **8.07** allow better decision-making in relation to the maintenance of tenement buildings. The traditional common law rules on common property, which used to effectively govern the maintenance of many tenements, required the unanimous consent of all owners to a course of action. Trying to get people to agree to carry out useful repairs to buildings was a matter of great difficulty. The introduction of the TMS is supposed to facilitate the decision-making process by regulating the way that "scheme decisions" can be reached in relation to the maintenance and management of scheme property. A scheme decision is a decision taken in accordance with r.2 of the TMS, or in accordance with any real burdens regulating decision making by owners: T(S)A 2004 Sch.1 r.1.4. Once again, the provisions of real burdens will take precedence over the default rules: T(S)A 2004 s.4(4); *Boatland Properties v Abdul*, 2014 S.C.L.R 792; *Garvie v Wallace*, 2013 G.W.D. 38-734 at [200]. However, it is worth recalling that the Lands Tribunal for Scotland can alter real burdens: *Patterson v Drouet*, 2013 G.W.D. 3-99; *Gilfin Property Holdings Ltd v Beech*, 2013 S.L.T. (Lands Tr) 17. If there are no real burdens, then the rules for scheme decisions are contained in r.2 of the TMS: T(S)A 2004 Sch.1 r.2.1. Decisions are taken by voting. The owner of each flat in a tenement is given a single vote to exercise: T(S)A 2004 Sch.1, r.2.2. If the proposed decision relates to the maintenance of a piece of scheme property then only those owners who are liable to maintain it are given a vote: T(S)A 2004 Sch.1, r.2.3. Once the number of votes has been determined a decision is taken by a simple majority of all the votes allocated: T(S)A 2004 Sch.1 r.2.5. The need for a majority to be of all the votes allocated is important: see *PS Properties (2) Ltd v Callaway Homes Ltd* [2007] CSOH 162. Say, for example, a tenement

is made up of eight flats and each flat has a vote. If four owners attend a meeting and vote 3:1 in favour of a decision that will not be a valid decision, because it is not a majority of the (eight) allocated votes. Indeed, had the four owners present at the meeting voted 4:0 in favour of the decision it would not have been a valid decision for the same reason. There are few formalities about the way a vote is to be conducted. If an owner wishes to call a meeting in order to make a scheme decision they must give the other owners 48 hours' notice of the purpose, location, date, time and place of the meeting: T(S)A 2004 Sch.1 r.2.6. Alternatively, a vote can be held by consulting all the owners and counting their votes: T(S)A 2004 Sch.1 r.2.7. Not only are formalities kept to a minimum, but the TMS provides that procedural irregularities do not undermine the validity of scheme decisions (T(S)A 2004 Sch.1 r.6.1), and it has been judicially determined that this applies to scheme decisions reached under the express terms of a title deed, albeit the procedure was irregular: *Garvie v Wallace*, 2013 G.W.D. 38-734 at [202]–[210]. Once a scheme decision has been taken it must be communicated to the other owners: T(S)A 2004 Sch.1 r.2.9. Although a scheme decision might have been reached to take some form of action, the decision cannot be acted upon for a period of 28 days: T(S)A 2004 s.5(10)(a). This moratorium on action allows an owner to appeal to a sheriff to have the scheme decision annulled: T(S)A 2004 s.5(1).

Substance of scheme decisions

8.08 Having determined the mechanisms that regulate the taking of scheme decisions we can now consider the sort of matters that can be the subject of a scheme decision. Once again, the TMS provides default rules: T(S)A 2004 s.4(5). A scheme decision can be taken to carry out maintenance on the scheme property (T(S)A 2004 Sch.1 r.3.1(a)), or to arrange for an inspection of scheme property to determine if maintenance is necessary: T(S)A 2004 Sch.1 r.3.1(b). A scheme decision can also be taken to appoint someone to manage the tenement (T(S)A 2004 Sch.1 r.3.1(c)(i)), or to dismiss such a manager (T(S)A 2004 Sch.1 r.3.1(c)(ii)). It will not, however, be possible to appoint such a person if there is a manager burden (see the Title Conditions (Scotland) Act 2003 s.63) in place: T(S)A 2004 Sch.1 r.3.1(c). Managers might be appointed so that the maintenance and management of the building can be properly monitored and professionally handled, especially if there is a very large tenement building. Owners can delegate powers to such a manager, including the power to actually carry out and instruct maintenance work: T(S)A 2004 Sch.1 r.3.1(d). More specifically, scheme decisions can also be taken to arrange common insurance cover and to install an entry system for the tenement. Scheme decisions can be taken to approve maintenance already undertaken (T(S)A 2004 Sch.1 r.3.1(h)), and can be used to revoke or modify a previous scheme decision: T(S)A 2004 Sch.1 r.3.1(i). "Maintenance" is defined for the purposes of the TMS to include: repairs and replacement, the installation of insulation, cleaning, painting and other routine works, gardening, the day to day running of a tenement and reinstatement of a part (but not most) of the tenement building; however it does not include demolition, alteration or improvement unless reasonably incidental to the maintenance: T(S)A 2004 Sch.1 r.1.5. If a scheme decision is taken to carry out maintenance, then further types of scheme decisions can be taken in order to make the decision to maintain effectual. Scheme decisions can be taken to (1) actually instruct or arrange the work needed to carry out the maintenance (T(S)A 2004 Sch.1 r.3.2(b)); (2) appoint someone (who can be an owner) to manage the maintenance process (T(S)A 2004 Sch.1 r. 3.2(a)); and (3) take such other steps as are necessary to ensure the maintenance is carried out to a satisfactory standard and completed in good time (T(S)A 2004 Sch. 1 r.3.2(d)). Furthermore, if a scheme decision is made to carry out maintenance, a further decision can be made to require each owner to deposit a sum of money no greater than their share of the liability in a maintenance account: T(S)A 2004 Sch.1 rr.3.2(c) and 3.3–4.

Liability for scheme costs
Perhaps the most important matter relating to the law of the tenement is **8.09** the allocation of liability to pay for costs associated with the tenement. A default scheme for the allocation of costs is set out in the TMS, but it can be displaced by real burdens if they regulate the liability for the entire costs: T(S)A 2004 s.4(6). The costs which are recoverable are those which fall within the definition of "scheme costs": T(S)A 2004 Sch.1 r.4.1. Scheme costs include any costs arising from maintenance of scheme property in accordance with a scheme decision (T(S)A 2004 Sch.1 r.4.1(a)), the remuneration payable to someone managing such maintenance activity (T(S)A 2004 Sch.1 r.4.1(b)), the running costs relating to any scheme property (T(S)A 2004 Sch.1 r.4.1(c)), any costs recoverable by a local authority with respect to statutory works undertaken in relation to scheme property (T(S)A 2004 Sch.1 r.4.1(d)), any remuneration payable to a manager (T(S)A 2004 Sch.1 r.4.1(e)), the cost of common insurance to cover a tenement (T(S)A 2004 Sch.1 r.4.1(f)), the cost of installing an entry system (T(S)A 2004 Sch.1 r.4.1(g)), the costs of determining the floor area of flats in order to determine liability for costs (T(S)A 2004 Sch.1 r.4.1(h)), and any other costs relating to the management of scheme property (T(S)A 2004 Sch.1 r.4.1(i)). The allocation of liability for maintenance costs (i.e. scheme costs mentioned in r.4.1(a)–(d)) under the TMS's default scheme depends on the type of scheme property involved. If property is scheme property by virtue of its common ownership (T(S)A 2004 Sch.1 r.1.2(a)), then liability for costs relating to it will be equally divided between those co-owners only: T(S)A 2004 Sch.1 r.4.2(a). If, however, the property is scheme property by virtue of a real burden (T(S)A 2004 Sch.1 r.1.2(b)), or by specific identification on a list (T(S)A 2004 Sch.1 r.1.2(c)), then liability for costs relating to it are shared equally between all the owners in the tenement: T(S)A 2004 Sch.1 r.4.2(b)(ii). There is an exception to the rule of equal liability among all the owners if one of the flats is much larger than the others: T(S)A 2004 Sch.1 r.4.2(b)(i). Let us take an example. If there is a television aerial that serves three flats in a tenement made up of

10 flats, then, under the service rule, the aerial is commonly owned by those three flats and is therefore scheme property. Only those three flats are liable for the maintenance costs associated with it. On the other hand, the external walls of those three flats are scheme property (though owned by each flat only) by virtue of r.1.2(c), and therefore any maintenance costs associated with them will be shared between the owners of all 10 flats. Maintenance costs associated with a commonly owned roof over the close of the tenement are regulated specifically (to avoid r.4.2(a)) so that liability is equally divided between all owners: T(S)A 2004 Sch.1 r.4.3. Liability for maintenance costs associated with the rest of the roof will (normally) also be split between all the owners under the TMS, but that is because the roof is scheme property by virtue of r.1.2(c)(iv): T(S)A 2004 Sch.1 r.4.2(b)(ii). It is important to note that if maintenance is carried out by a single owner on a piece of scheme property, by virtue of their duty to provide support or shelter (T(S)A 2004 s.8(1)), the single owner may recover costs from the other owners as if the maintenance had been carried out pursuant to a scheme decision: T(S)A 2004 s.10. Similarly, a single owner can order emergency work—work that prevents damage to the tenement or is in the interests of health and safety—and recover costs as if they were costs associated with the maintenance of scheme property in accordance with a scheme decision: T(S)A 2004 Sch.1 r.7. The idea is that such key maintenance should be undertaken efficiently and quickly, and so a single owner can take action and recover costs. Liability for the costs associated with insurance is to be determined by scheme decision or by virtue of a real burden governing the position: T(S)A 2004 Sch.1 r.4.4. Liability for the scheme costs associated with remunerating a "non-maintenance project" manager, installing an entry system, determining floor area, and any other costs associated with the management of scheme property, are divided equally among all the owners: T(S)A 2004 Sch.1 r.4.5. If a scheme decision has been taken to absolve an owner of liability to pay their share, or, if for some reason (such as insolvency or disappearance) an owner is unable to pay their share, then the missing share must be paid by the other owners who are liable to pay: T(S)A 2004 Sch.1 r.5(a)–(b). It is possible for the local authority to pay an owner's share of scheme costs if the owner is unable or unwilling to pay their share, or cannot be identified or found: T(S)A 2004 s.4A(1)(a)–(b). The local authority cannot make such a contribution where the scheme costs concerned are related to a common insurance policy: T(S)A 2004 s.4A(2) and Sch.1 r.3(e). When the owner is unable to pay their share, that owner remains liable to the owners who do pay: T(S)A 2004 Sch.1 r.5.

Enforcement

8.10 Once a scheme decision has been reached it is binding on the owners and their singular successors: T(S)A 2004 Sch.1 r.8.2. In turn, any obligations which arise by virtue of the TMS, or a scheme decision reached in accordance with the TMS, can be enforced by any of the owners: T(S)A 2004 Sch.1 r.8.3. Any owner may apply to the sheriff for an order relating to the operation of the T(S)A 2004 or the TMS: T(S)A 2004 s.6(1). An appeal against the sheriff's determination of such an application lies (on a point of law) to the Court of Session to make a final determination: T(S)A 2004 s.6(3)–(4). An owner who was not in favour of a scheme decision when it was made, or a new owner who was not privy to the making of the decision, may apply to a sheriff for an order annulling the decision: T(S)A 2004 s.5(1)–(2). The sheriff has discretion to annul the decision (in whole or in part) if it is not in the best interests of all the owners taken as a group, or is unfairly prejudicial to one or more of the owners: T(S)A 2004 s.5(5). Furthermore, a sheriff considering whether to exercise this discretion with respect to a scheme decision concerned with maintenance, improvements, or alterations, must have regard to (1) the age and condition of the property in question; (2) the likely cost of such maintenance; and (3) whether that cost is reasonable: T(S)A 2004 s.5(6). A final appeal on a point of law lies to the Court of Session against a sheriff's determination of an application to annul a scheme decision: T(S)A 2004 s.5(8).

9. LAND OWNERSHIP

The concept of ownership has already been considered in this book, as were **9.01** the constitution, transfer, and extent of ownership of land. The focus now moves to the use that is made of land. Owners, holders of subordinate real rights, and members of the public can use land for various purposes and in different ways. In this chapter the regulation of such uses of land are considered, as are the actions of different actors in relation to the use of land.

SUPPORT

Owners of land owe a duty to those around them to provide support to their **9.02** land. The specific duties of support in relation to tenement buildings were considered earlier, this chapter is concerned with the manner in which support is offered by one piece of land to another. The owner of a piece of land must not use it in such a way that imperils the support their land is obliged to provide. The content of the duty to support extends to land beside and above the owner's land. For example, if Amy owns a plot of land, she is not allowed to remove so much soil from her land that Bob's neighbouring land begins to fall apart. The duty to support is most commonly encountered in relation to land above the supporting land. Thus, if Andy is the owner of a separate tenement of minerals one of the key uses he will have in mind is mining or extraction of the minerals; however, he must not undermine Belinda's land situated above the minerals when carrying out any mining or extraction operations. A key facet of the duty to provide support is that the duty to provide support is one of strict liability: the only question is whether the land has been undermined. There is no need to show that the neighbouring proprietor intended to withdraw the support or was negligent in doing so: *Angus v National Coal Board*, 1955 S.C. 175.

ENCROACHMENT AND TRESPASS

Boundaries
Before considering encroachment and trespass, something must be said **9.03** about the boundaries of land, as it is often at the boundaries of land that any transgressions most commonly occur. In the distant past the boundaries of land were mapped out by "march stones", but the significant disadvantage of that method was that the march stones might move. The law of Scotland had a gruesome solution to the problem: "when march-stones are solemnly set, boys used sometimes to be laid upon them and sharply whipt, whereby they will be able to remember, and be good witnesses as to those marches when they are old, that impression on their fancy lasting long." Stair, IV. 43. 7. Thankfully, the current practice for discerning boundaries has

moved on, so that walls, hedges, and fences have taken over as the boundary markers for land. The ownership of the boundary marker itself depends on where it is situated.

Boundary marker wholly on one side of a boundary

9.04 If the boundary marker (i.e. a wall, fence, hedge etc.) is wholly on one side of a boundary then it is owned entirely by the owner of the land on which the boundary marker is erected or growing. There is no need to obtain consent to the construction of such a wall, and it appears that construction can be rather lacking in consideration for others. In *Dunlop v Robertson* (1803) Hume 515, a solicitor erected a wall around his house that was 16ft tall. His neighbour protested that the wall blocked the light to his lower windows, and brought an action for spite (*aemulationem vicini*, see below). The neighbour was unsuccessful on the basis the wall was built to protect the solicitor's privacy.

Boundary marker wholly on the boundary

9.05 Where the boundary marker is placed on the boundary itself, the consent of each of the adjacent owners to the erection of the marker is required. Often there are provisions in the title deeds of the properties that govern the erection of such boundary walls. If there is no consent to the erection of such a marker then any part of it which crosses the boundary line constitutes an encroachment. The boundary marker will be owned up to the boundary point by the owners of the adjacent pieces of land as a result of accession. Thus, most markers that are built precisely on a boundary line are owned up to the midpoint of the marker by the adjacent proprietors. Any proprietor who has such an ownership interest in a boundary marker that is owned by more than one proprietor has common interest rights in the parts of the marker that they do not own.

Encroachment

Nature of encroachment

9.06 Encroachments often occur at the boundaries of a person's land: see *Smith v Crombie* [2012] CSOH 52. An encroachment is "a permanent or quasi-permanent intrusion onto land that is owned, or otherwise lawfully possessed, by another person": K.G.C. Reid, *The Law of Property in Scotland*, para.175. A person cannot encroach upon another person's land: only things can constitute an encroachment. Encroachment is treated in a literal and strict fashion: there is no real suggestion of a *de minimis* element in the rules: "a proprietor is not entitled to encroach upon his neighbour's property even to the extent of driving a nail into it" *Leonard v Lindsay and Benzie* (1886) 13 R. 958 at 964, per Lord Young. Indeed, an encroachment is committed even if there is no discernible harm, though this will affect the remedy available in terms of the choice between damages and the equitable decision to remove an encroachment. The potential examples that might be given of encroachment are legion: *Miln v Mudie* (1828) 6 S. 967: a cornice that was inches over a boundary between the boundary at the gable of tenement buildings; *Brown v Baty*, 1957 S.C. 351: wall over mutual boundary; *Anderson v Brattissani's*, 1978 S.L.T. (Notes) 42: a ventilation shaft attached to another's property; *Halkerston v Wedderburn* (1781) Mor. 10495: branches of a tree hanging over boundary.

Defences

If an encroachment has occurred the encroacher may have a valid defence **9.07** to having encroached upon another's land. It is a defence if the owner of the land encroached upon consented to the encroachment. Consent can be express, or it might be implied by acquiescence so that the owner is personally barred from objecting to the encroachment. In *Duke of Buccleuch v Edinburgh Mags* (1865) 3 M. 528 the owner's failure to object to the construction of encroaching pillars constituted acquiescence. Certain statutes create powers to install things on land that would ordinarily amount to an encroachment: see e.g. *William Tracey Ltd v SP Transmission Plc*, 2016 S.L.T 678. Finally, it would be a valid defence to demonstrate that the encroacher did, in fact, own the land encroached upon.

Remedies

A number of remedies are available to deal with an encroachment. It is **9.08** possible to seek an interdict to prevent the encroachment, but the nature of an interdict is preventative. In order to obtain an interdict, the owner must be fast to act; indeed, if an encroaching building has been substantially completed, there is little left to interdict. If an encroachment has occurred then it is possible to seek removal of the encroachment, but this remedy is subject to the court's equitable discretion to refuse to order removal in exceptional circumstances: *Munro v Finlayson*, 2015 S.L.T. (Sh. Ct) 123. The court will only exercise its discretion to not enforce the encroached upon proprietor's right to removal if removal would be impossible or would cause unreasonable loss or expense: *Anderson v Brattissani's*, 1978 S.L.T. (Notes) 42 at 43. If the encroachment is very slight, or if there is a suggestion that the encroachment is unobjectionable, the court is unlikely to order removal. Whether the encroachment was made in good or bad faith can also be relevant: see *McLellan v J & D Pierce (Contracts) Ltd* [2015] CSIH 80. Thus, although the tacks used to attach a chip shop's ventilation flue to a wall constituted encroachments, they were minor encroachments, and so the removal of the flue would have been disproportionate: *Anderson v Brattissani's*; see also *Smith v Crombie* [2012] CSOH 52 at [59]. Nevertheless, even if the court will not order the removal of the encroachment on equitable grounds, the encroacher will be liable for damages, though the seriousness of the encroachment may be relevant when quantifying the amount of damage. Finally, a so-called "self-help" remedy might be available whereby the owner takes action herself in response to the encroachment. The nature of the self-help remedy depends, to some extent at least, on the ownership of the thing constituting the encroachment. If the thing is entirely owned by the person encroached upon—as will often happen as a result of accession—then the matters are fairly straightforward:

they are the owner and can do what they want with the encroaching item. If the encroachment straddles a boundary then the encroaching parts may be removed so far as they cross the boundary, though there are some other rules. If the encroachment is a building, any removal of encroaching things across the boundary must not demolish or undermine the parts of the building on the other side of the boundary. The trunk of a tree that is on a boundary is owned in common. Branches overhanging the boundary may be severed by self-help, but where a building overhangs a boundary a court order must be sought to remove the encroachment.

Trespass

Nature of trespass

9.09 Trespass is a temporary or transient intrusion into land owned, or lawfully possessed by another: K.G.C. Reid, *The Law of Property in Scotland*, para.180. There is a widespread misconception that there is no law of trespass in Scotland: see the rejection of this argument in the "Indy Camp Protest" case, *Scottish Parliamentary Corporate Body v Sovereign Indigenous People of Scotland*, 2016 S.L.T 761 at [31] et seq per the Lord Ordinary (Turnbull). The myth might have evolved from the fact that trespass is not a nominate crime at common law, though statutory interventions have created crimes of trespass in specific situations and locations: Railway Regulation Act 1840 s.16 (trespassing on the railway, stations or associated premises: see *Caledonian Railway Co v Walmsley*, 1907 S.C. 1047); Trespass (Scotland) Act 1865 s.3 (encamping on or occupying land in a manner inconsistent with access rights under the Land Reform (Scotland) Act 2003); Regulation of Railways Act 1868 s.23 (trespassing on the railway line itself: *Thomson v Great North of Scotland Railway Co* (1899) 2 F. (J) 22); Public Order Act 1986 s.14B (20 or more persons trespassing might constitute a trespassory assembly); Criminal Justice and Public Order Act 1994 s.61 (two or more persons trespassing with the common purpose of residing on that land for any period) and s.68 (trespass with the purpose of disrupting lawful activity constitutes the offence of aggravated trespass, see *McAdam v Urquhart*, 2005 1 J.C. 28). Unlike encroachment, a trespass can be constituted by the intrusion of animals, persons, and things: trespass occurs where a person, thing, or animal enters land owned by another in a transitory manner. Thus, the distinction between encroachment and trespass rests upon the temporal quality of the intrusion: the law of encroachment suggests a degree of permanence; the law of trespass is concerned with transitory intrusions.

Defences

9.10 Perhaps the most commonsense defence to an action for trespass is that of consent. If someone consents to another person being on their land, then there is no trespass. Consent can be either express or implied. If Albert invites Bella to his house for dinner he expressly consents to her visit. The owner of a coffee bar gives implied consent to her patrons to enter the premises in order to select and consume refreshments. If the intrusion is authorised by law, then the intruder has a defence to an action for trespass. For example, we have already seen that an aeroplane's intrusion into the airspace of a proprietor is lawfully authorised to the extent that there is a statutory defence: Civil Aviation Act 1982 s.76. Likewise, there are all manner of persons who are authorised by law to enter premises in order to carry out defined activities. Generally speaking these lawful authorisations will relate to a defined activity or mode of activity—lawful authorisations do not tend to permit people to go onto the land of another person to conduct any type of activity they like, as to do so would undermine the owner's rights of exclusive use of their property. The most generalised rights to enter another's land are the rights of access created by the Land Reform (Scotland) Act 2003; but these are rights granted to the public at large, rather than rights granted to nominated persons or officers.

Remedies

There are a number of potential remedies available to a landowner who is **9.11** the victim of trespass, though the circumstances of the particular case might mean that not all of those remedies are necessarily useful or easy to obtain. A trespasser who causes damage will be liable in damages, but only to the extent that actual damage can be proven: *Lord Advocate v Glengarnock Iron and Steel Co Ltd* (1909) 1 S.L.T. 15. An interdict is another possible remedy available to the owner of a piece of land, but it might be difficult to obtain one. By its nature an interdict is a remedy with prospective effect—its purpose it to prevent something happening—which, in turn, can mean that satisfying the criteria necessary to obtain one can be problematic. In the first place, it is necessary for the landowner to know the identities of those trespassing individuals that any prospective interdicts are to apply to. Even if the identity of the trespasser is known, the grant of an interdict lies within the discretion of the court. The court may evaluate the seriousness of the threatened trespass when deciding whether to grant the interdict or not. Thus, a landowner failed in his attempt to obtain an interdict preventing a single lamb from straying onto his large estate: *Winans v Macrae*, (1885) 12 R. 1051 at 1063, per Lord Young. The interdict must also be necessary in the sense that the trespass is likely to be repeated at some point: *Hay's Trs v Young* (1877) 4 R. 398. Finally, there is shrieval authority suggesting that it is necessary to warn someone to leave your land before seeking some form of interdict: *Paterson v McPherson* (1916) 33 Sh. Ct. Rep. 237. Self-help remedies might also be available to an owner, but there is some uncertainty about the scope of the owner's power in this regard: W.M. Gordon and S. Wortley, *Scottish Land Law*, 3rd edn (2009), para.13-09. It seems the safest approach would be to use the absolute minimum force necessary, though that might vary according to the location and nature of the trespass or trespasser.

Animals

Animals are capable of trespassing, but it is their owners and keepers that **9.12** will be liable for those acts of trespass. In addition to the common law remedies relating to trespass, statute imposes strict liability on the keeper (the owner or possessor) of certain types of animal with respect to any damage caused by those animals: Animals (Scotland) Act 1987 s.1. Furthermore, it will be open to a landowner to detain or kill a straying animal depending on the circumstances: Animals (Scotland) Act 1987 ss.3 and 4, respectively.

LAND REFORM (SCOTLAND) ACT 2003

Public rights of access

9.13 Section 1 of the Land Reform (Scotland) Act 2003 (LR(S)A 2003) confers on all members of the public the right to access land in a number of different ways. These access rights can be exercised over inshore waters as well as over land. Two different types of access right are conferred on the public: (1) the right to cross land: the public can go onto land to reach one place from another (LR(S)A 2003 s.1(2)(b)); and (2) the right to be on land (LR(S)A 2003 s.1(2)(a)). In order to exercise the second type of access right, the right to be on land, a person must be on the land for at least one of a defined list of specified purposes. These specified purposes are (1) recreational purposes (LR(S)A 2003 s.1(3)(a)); (2) relevant educational activities (LR(S)A 2003 s.1(3)(b)); and (3) the purposes of carrying on, commercially or for profit, an activity which the person could carry on otherwise than for profit (LR(S)A 2003 s.1(3)(c)). The content and nature of these defined purposes are to be gleaned from reading the LR(S)A in conjunction with the Scottish Outdoor Access Code (SOAC): see *http://www.outdooraccess-scotland.com*.

Recreational purposes

9.14 The LR(S)A 2003 does not define the expression "recreational purposes", but, according to para.2.7 of the SOAC, it is taken to include: (1) "pastimes", such as watching wildlife, sightseeing, painting, photography and enjoying historic sites; (2) "family and social activities", such as short walks, dog walking, picnics, playing, sledging, paddling or flying a kite; (3) "active pursuits", such as walking, cycling, horse riding and carriage driving, rock climbing, hill-walking, running, orienteering, ski touring, ski mountaineering, caving, canoeing, swimming, rowing, windsurfing, sailing, diving, air sports and wild camping; (4) "participation in events", such as walking or cycling festivals, hill running races, mountain marathons, mountain biking competitions, long-distance riding events, orienteering events and canoeing competitions. Therefore, the SOAC provides many of the details required to flesh out the terms of the LR(S)A 2003. But the SOAC is not a formal source of law, rather, it is a piece of "soft law" a bit like The Highway Code. In other words, although the courts will take the SOAC very seriously when interpreting the legislation, they are not bound to follow it.

Educational activity

9.15 An educational activity is an activity which furthers a person's understanding of natural or cultural heritage or one that involves one person assisting another's understanding of the same: LR(S)A 2003 s.1(5)(a)–(b). Paragraph 2.8 of the SOAC explains that the effect of these definitions is that teachers, guides, support staff and students or learners can be carrying out an educational activity. Furthermore, a person conducting field surveys on their own is also to be taken to be conducting educational activity. There is some overlap between the elements of educational activities and recreational purposes, and both expressions might be applicable when justifying the existence of access rights.

Commercial or profit purposes
A person can exercise their access rights to undertake an activity **9.16** commercially or for profit if they could carry on that activity otherwise than commercially or for profit. The nub of this provision is that individuals should not have to pay to exercise their access rights; but, at the same time, individuals offering services that might relate to access rights can continue to charge for those activities so long as those charges do not relate to the exercise of the access right itself. Similarly, someone who is paying for such a service can benefit from their access rights while doing so. Let us take an example. Arnold offers walking tours in the Pentland Hills, and he charges £50 for a two-hour tour. Barbara opts to take the tour and pays Arnold. Arnold is not charging Barbara to exercise her access rights; he is charging her for the service he is providing. Barbara could walk the same route without paying Arnold. Both Arnold and Barbara can exercise their access rights on the tour, even though they are there for a commercial venture: see SOAC para.2.9.

Limitations on access rights

Nature of the land
The access rights created by the LR(S)A 2003 are not absolute and are subject **9.17** to limitations. The first type of limitation on access rights relates to the land over which those access rights may be exercised. Certain types of land, and the structures located on them, are designated as land over which access rights cannot be exercised. Access rights cannot be exercised in relation to buildings, structures, plant or fixed machinery located on land: LR(S)A 2003 s.6(1)(a)(i). Furthermore, access rights are not exercisable in relation to any land which forms a compound or enclosure containing such structures or machinery: LR(S)A 2003 s.6(1)(b)(ii). The term "structure" does not include bridges, tunnels, causeways, launching sites, groynes, weirs, boulder weirs, embankments of canalised waterways, fences, walls or anything designed to facilitate passage: LR(S)A 2003 s.6(2). Similarly, access rights cannot be exercised in relation to caravans, tents or any other place affording a person privacy or shelter: LR(S)A 2003 s.6(1)(a)(ii). Access rights are exercisable over land which forms the curtilage of a building which is not a house (for houses, see below): (LR(S)A 2003 s.6(1)(b)(i)). Curtilage is not a term of art in Scots law (*Caledonian Railway Co v Turcan* (1898) 25 R. (HL) 7 at 16, per Lord Watson), but it has been judicially observed that "ground which is used for the comfortable enjoyment of a house or other building may be regarded in law as being within the curtilage of that house or building and thereby as an integral part of the same, although it has not been marked off or enclosed

in any way. It is enough that it serves the purposes of the house or building in some necessary or reasonably useful way." *Sinclair Lockhart's Trs v Central Land Board*, 1950 S.L.T. 283 at 286, per Lord Mackintosh. Schools and the land surrounding them are also exempt from access rights: LR(S)A 2003 s.6(1)(b)(iii).

9.18   The land itself can be designated as land over which access rights cannot be exercised. If land was only accessible for a charge for at least 90 days in the year ending 31 January 2001, and a charge has continued to be levied for at least 90 days a year since that date, access rights cannot be exercised over it: LR(S)A 2003 s.6(1)(f). So, for example, access rights cannot be exercised over a safari park's land. The purpose of the provision is to ensure such organisations are able to continue operating—nobody would pay if they could exercise their access rights for free. Land which has been developed for a particular recreational purpose (LR(S)A 2003 s.6(1)(e)(ii)), or as a sports or playing field (LR(S)A 2003 s.6(1)(e)(i)), is not subject to access rights if the land is being used for those purposes, or, in the case of land which is not a sports or playing field, if the exercise of those rights would interfere with the recreational use to which the land is being put: LR(S)A 2003 s.7(7)(a). Furthermore, access rights will not apply at all (there is no need to show interference) to golf greens, bowling greens, cricket squares, lawn tennis courts or other similar areas on which grass is grown and prepared for a particular recreational purpose (LR(S)A 2003 s.7(7)(b)), or in the case of synthetic sports or playing fields: LR(S)A 2003 s.7(7)(c). The construction of groynes, deepening of pools, and any other works relating to fishing do not constitute development for a recreational purpose in terms of s.6 of the LR(S)A 2003: LR(S)A 2003 s.7(8). Quarries (LR(S)A 2003 s.6(1)(h)) and land in which crops have been sown or are growing (LR(S)A 2003 s.6(1)(i)) are not subject to access rights. Land on which crops are growing does not include grassland unless the grass is being grown for hay and silage and is likely to be damaged by the exercise of access rights (LR(S)A 2003 s.7(10)(a)); nor does it include headrigs, endrigs or other margins of a field in which crops are growing: LR(S)A 2003 s.7(10)(b). Woodlands, planted forests and orchards are not considered to be land on which crops are growing unless it is land used wholly for the cultivation of tree seedlings in beds: LR(S)A 2003 s.7(10)(c). For these purposes "crops" are plants cultivated for agricultural or commercial purposes: LR(S)A 2003 s.7(10). Finally, if public access to land has been restricted by statute then access rights are not exercisable over that land (LR(S)A 2003 s.6(1)(d)), but only to the extent of statutory restriction: LR(S)A 2003 s.7(6).

Privacy

9.19 Access rights are not exercisable over "sufficient" land adjacent to a house, or other place of shelter and privacy, that is needed to enable the people living there to enjoy a reasonable measure of privacy and to ensure that their enjoyment of that house is not unreasonably disturbed: LR(S)A 2003 s.6(1)(b)(iv). In determining how much land is sufficient to meet these objectives the characteristics and location of the house or shelter will, among other things, be taken into account: LR(S)A 2003 s.7(5). The garden of an average house will be "sufficient" land needed to ensure privacy, and therefore access rights will not be exercisable over it. Matters can be more complex with large country estates. The Stagecoach tycoon Anne Gloag successfully argued that access rights should not be exercised over 11 acres of her estate on the basis of the privacy provision: *Gloag v Perth and Kinross Council*, 2007 S.C.L.R. 530. The court stated that it had to decide what a reasonable person in a house of the sort in the immediate case would require, and, because Anne Gloag was high profile individual, a large area of land would need to be identified as sufficient land to protect her privacy. Subsequent decisions have not followed the approach taken in *Gloag* in its entirety. In *Snowie v Stirling Council*, 2008 S.L.T. (Sh. Ct) 61 the owners of a large estate sought to rely on the privacy provision in order to restrict access rights. The court took an objective approach that considered the characteristics and location of the house but did not subjectively consider the owners' characteristics; in turn the privacy-based restrictions on access rights were confined to fairly small areas of the front and back gardens. Similarly, there appear to be some variations in judicial approaches to cases dealing with smaller properties as well. In *Creelman v Argyll and Bute Council*, 2009 S.L.T. (Sh. Ct) 165 the court decided that access rights could not be exercised over a track separating fairly small rural properties in order to protect the privacy of the homeowners; whereas in *Forbes v Fife Council*, 2009 S.L.T. (Sh. Ct) 71 the court decided that access rights could be exercised over a path in a housing development because the property's garden and six foot fence was a sufficient amount land to protect the owner's privacy. Many of the decisions in this area are highly fact specific, and the law on privacy and access rights is still developing.

Responsible exercise of access rights
In a sense the requirement that access rights are exercised responsibly is as **9.20** much an inherent characteristic of those rights as it is a restriction upon them. Access rights are only given to those who exercise them responsibly: LR(S)A 2003 s.2(1). Responsible exercise means access rights are exercised in a lawful and reasonable manner that takes proper account of the interests of others and the features of the land that is being accessed: LR(S)A 2003 s.2(3). Responsible exercise is presumed if access rights are exercised so as not to cause unreasonable interference with any of the rights of any other person: LR(S)A 2003 s.2(2). Furthermore, responsible conduct will be construed in accordance with the guidance provided by the SOAC: LR(S)A 2003 s.2(2)(b)(i); see *Loch Lomond and Trossachs National Park Authority v Anstalt*, 2017 S.L.T. (Sh Ct) 138 at [31]–[32]. So, for example, there is detailed guidance in the code about how and when to keep dogs under control; if the owner of a dog is acting in a way that disregards that guidance they will probably be considered to be exercising their access rights irresponsibly, and, in turn, they will not be able to rely on those access rights (i.e. they will be trespassing). Local authorities are also empowered to make bylaws, which, if breached, will constitute an irresponsible exercise of access rights: LR(S)A 2003 s.2(2)(a)(i). Therefore, the requirement that access rights must be exercised responsibly is an important principle that permeates the entire scheme of access rights. In turn, the

responsible exercise of access rights by the public is matched by a reciprocal principle that landowners will act responsibly in the management and use of their land so as to not frustrate access rights: LR(S)A 2003 s.3.

Specific restrictions

9.21 In addition to the broader restrictions upon the exercise of access rights there is a list that specifies types of conduct that are excluded from access rights: LR(S)A 2003 s.9. Therefore, being on or crossing land for the purpose of doing anything which is an offence or in breach of an interdict or other order of a court is excluded: LR(S)A 2003 s.9(a)–(b). Hunting, shooting or fishing are activities which cannot be undertaken as access rights: LR(S)A 2003 s.9(c). A person who is on or crossing land while responsible for an animal which is not under proper control is engaged in conduct that falls outwith the access rights scheme: LR(S)A 2003 s.9(d). Someone who is on or crossing land for the purpose of taking away anything in or on that land, for a commercial purpose or profit, is not exercising access rights: LR(S)A 2003 s.9(e). If a person is on or crossing land in a motorised vehicle they are not exercising access rights, unless the vehicle is one that is adapted for, and is being used by, a disabled person: LR(S)A 2003 s.9(f). Finally, if a person is on a golf course they are not exercising access rights unless they are simply crossing the golf course: LR(S)A 2003 s.9(g). Any person who is engaged in any of these forms of conduct is not engaged in responsible exercise of access rights: LR(S)A 2003 s.2(2)(a)(i).

Enforcement of access rights

9.22 A landowner is under an obligation to use his land responsibly in relation to the public's potential access rights: LR(S)A 2003 s.3. Enforcement mechanisms for this provision are located in LR(S)A 2003 s.14, which provides that a landowner cannot undertake certain activities if they are undertaken for the purpose of preventing the public accessing land. Among the actions prohibited is the erection of a sign to discourage the public from accessing land: LR(S)A 2003 s.14(1)(a). Similarly, putting up a fence, wall or hedge (LR(S)A 2003 s.14(1)(b)) and using animals (LR(S)A 2003 s.14(1)(c)) to prevent access is prohibited. One should note that the prohibition against these actions only applies where the purpose behind the action in question was to prevent the exercise of access rights. The importance of that can be seen in reported decisions. In *Tuley v Highland Council*, 2009 S.C. 456 a landowner was asked to broaden paths and to remove barriers and gates to allow the passage of people on horseback on the basis of LR(S)A 2003 s.14. The court held that there was no breach of s.14 because the landowner's actions were concerned with protecting pedestrians and the land from damage by horses—they were not undertaken to frustrate the exercise of access rights, and, in fact, they were examples of responsible management. Similarly, the need to demonstrate an intention to frustrate access meant that a fence constructed before the LR(S)A 2003 was brought into force could not fall foul of LR(S)A 2003 s.14: *Aviemore Highland Resort Ltd v Cairngorms National Park Authority*, 2009 S.L.T. (Sh Ct) 97. The erection of the fence could not have been undertaken with the intention of frustrating access rights which were not then in existence; furthermore, the effect of the Act was not retrospective, and it made no difference if the fence did in fact interfere with access rights. Compare the *Aviemore Highland Resort Ltd* decision with that reached in *Loch Lomond and Trossachs National Park Authority v Anstalt*, 2017 S.L.T. (Sh Ct) 138, where the Sheriff Appeal Court held that the s.14 test was a mix of the subjective and objective. The landowner's "purpose" in carrying out an action is to be assessed subjectively, but whether their actions constitute acting "responsibly" is an objective assessment which will have regard to guidance from the SOAC: *Anstalt* at [34]. The court decided that although gates with a sign bearing the words "Danger Wild Boar" had been installed prior to the LR(S)A 2003 coming into force, the landowner's continued opening and locking of the gates, with a purpose to frustrate access rights without responsible grounds, distinguished the case from the decision in *Aviemore Highland Resort Ltd* and its singular temporal event of installing a fence. The landowner was therefore in breach of LR(S)A 2003 s.14.

It is the responsibility of local authorities to enforce access rights and **9.23** ensure that the legislation is complied with: LR(S)A 2003 s.13. If the local authority considers that a landowner has attempted to frustrate the exercise of access rights, by breaching LR(S)A 2003 s.14(1), it can issue a notice to the landowner requiring them to take remedial action within a reasonable time period: LR(S)A 2003 s.14(2). If the landowner fails to take action then the local authority can take action itself, and it can recover the reasonable costs of taking such action from the landowner: LR(S)A 2003 s.14(3). A landowner can appeal to the sheriff against such a notice: LR(S)A 2003 s.14(4). Local authorities are also responsible for developing a "core paths" network in their area to facilitate the use made of access rights: LR(S)A 2003 s.17. These core paths are supposed to provide routes that the public can follow in order to encourage people to use their access rights.

WATER RIGHTS

We come now to consider the rights of use and incidents of landownership **9.24** in relation to water. The best way to approach rights in relation to water is to split water rights into those relating to tidal waters and those relating to non-tidal waters.

Tidal waters

Nature of tidal waters
The sea extending up to 12 nautical miles away from the coastline of any **9.25** part of Scotland is tidal water, as are sea lochs and tidal rivers. A river is tidal if its level changes with the spring tides. Although we sometimes talk informally about the ownership of water, what we really need to focus on is the land beneath the water. The land beneath a body of water is called the *alveus*. In the case of tidal waters, the *alveus* is owned by the Crown.

Foreshore

9.26 The foreshore is what a layman would call a beach. More technically, the foreshore is the part of the beach that is covered by water at high tide but is uncovered at low tide, which is not necessarily what a layperson would think of as the full extent of a beach. The Crown owns the foreshore, though it is possible for the foreshore to be in private ownership if the Crown has granted ownership to someone else, or where positive prescription has vested ownership in the possessor of the land after 20 years possession: Prescription and Limitation (Scotland) Act 1973 s.1(1) and (5).

Public right of navigation

9.27 The public at large have a right to navigate tidal waters, though there are some complications. In relation to the sea, the public are allowed a right of navigation in waters which are capable of navigation. Navigation means travelling in a boat or equivalent vessel, but probably does not include wading on the river bed and dragging a canoe along the river bed—that is not navigation, that is a man/woman dragging a canoe through water. In most tidal waters the ability to navigate will be obvious, it is a more problematic concept in relation in non-tidal waters. Furthermore, it is not an incident of the right of navigation to attach fixed moorings to the sea-bed: *Crown Estate Commissioners v Fairlie Yacht Slip Ltd*, 1979 S.C. 156; *Crown Estate Commissioners Petrs*, 2010 S.L.T. 741.

Public right to fish

9.28 The public at large have a right to fish for any fish other than salmon (somewhat confusingly the right is said to be the right to fish for "white fish"), and the right to collect all shellfish other than mussels and oysters. The reason that the right does not extend to these specific exceptions is that they are legal separate tenements. This is only the property law dimension of the right to fish: there is currently a large body of European and domestic legislation that regulates fishing in and around Scotland, which is likely to change in some respects if (as seems likely) the United Kingdom leaves the European Union.

Non-tidal waters

Rivers

9.29 As with tidal waters the ownership focus with non-tidal waters is on the land beneath the water. The ownership of the alveus beneath a river normally depends on the ownership of the surrounding land. The owners of the land surrounding a river are known as riparian proprietors because their ownership extends to the medium filum (mid-point) of the alveus. In other words, the owners of land beside a river will normally own the riverbed adjacent to that land up to the middle of the river. Although a riparian proprietor owns a section of the river, the right is not absolute in the sense that they must tolerate certain uses of the river. Access rights under the LR(S)A 2003 can be exercised over water. Likewise, there is a common law public right to navigation that can be vested in the public after 40 years of prescriptive use: *Crown Estate Commissioners v Fairlie Yacht Slip Ltd*, 1979 S.C. 156. A riparian proprietor has an exclusive right to fish in their section of a river; but that right to fish does not include the right to fish for salmon, because the right to fish for salmon is a separate legal tenement (see below for further details relating to fishing). However, it is competent to cast across the medium filum of a small river when fishing for trout: *Arthur v Aird*, 1907 S.C. 1170 at 1174, per Lord Low. Riparian proprietors owe each other duties based upon the fact that they have a common interest in the river: *Morris v Bicket*, (1864) 2 M. 1082 at 1087–1088, per the Lord Justice-Clerk (Inglis). Thus, a riparian proprietor must not interfere with the flow of the river to proprietors further down the river. The prohibition on interference is quantitative and qualitative: the amount and quality of the water that flows downriver must not be interfered with. However, a riparian proprietor does have the right to extract or use water for domestic purposes.

Lochs

The ownership of the alveus of a loch is normally determined in accordance **9.30** with the ownership of the surrounding land. If a loch is entirely encircled by land owned by one person, then they are the owner of the entire alveus of the loch. If there is more than one owner of the land surrounding the loch, then the alveus will be in sectional ownership that corresponds to the ownership of the surrounding land. All owners of any part of the alveus of a loch have the right to fish or sail across all parts of the loch: no owner is restricted to the water above his particular section of the alveus. Restrictions based upon common interest are applicable to the owners of a loch as they apply to the owners of rivers.

GAME AND FISHING

Game

General introduction

As a general rule, the right to shoot and hunt for game is an incident of **9.31** landownership and is not (normally) a separate tenement. In other words, a landowner has the right to shoot for game on their land. The landowner is normally the only person who may (lawfully) shoot or hunt game on their land, though they can give permission to others to shoot game. Although the game are wild animals, and as such they are not owned by the landowner unless they are detained by them, the landowner can regulate who has access to their land in order to shoot or capture animals on that land. The feudal system allowed a superior to reserve the right to hunt for game on land held by vassals. Despite the demise of the feudal system, it was felt that these superiors should be able to retain their hunting rights and so superiors were allowed to convert feudal hunting rights into separate tenements: Abolition of Feudal Tenure etc (Scotland) Act 2000 s.65A. However, very few of those converted game tenements were in fact created. Somewhat unhelpfully there is no generally agreed definition of what constitutes "game", and a number of different statutes regulate hunting. Only the briefest of treatments can be given here.

Pursuit of game

9.32 A landowner may only shoot for game on their own land: if their target crosses onto another's land they may not pursue the animal across the land of someone else. The Protection of Wild Mammals (Scotland) Act 2002 makes it illegal to hunt any wild mammal, including foxes, with dogs. It remains lawful to "flush out" wild mammals to be shot, so long as the killing is humane and is carried out as quickly as possible.

Leasing the interest

9.33 The right to hunt for game is not (normally) capable of being separated from ownership of land as a separate tenement. It is, however, possible to temporarily separate the right to take game from the ownership of land by creating a lease to hunt for game. For a long time, it was doubted whether it was possible to grant a lease of rights to game, but it is now clearly established that an owner can grant such a lease or other occupancy right. The landowner can grant a lease to a person to take or hunt for game on the landowner's land: *Stewart v Bulloch* (1881) 8 R. 381 at 383, per Lord President Inglis. However, there are a number of specialities relating to leases to hunt for game. A lease is a technical form of contract and there are a number of requirements required in order to constitute a valid lease. Not all contracts between a landowner and a potential hunting tenant will satisfy the requirements of a lease—it might be a mere license, permission, or other form of occupancy right. Only leases, and then only certain types of lease, can be made into real rights. In many cases a lease to hunt for game will be merely a contractual arrangement, and not a real right, because the lease is over a right to hunt and not over the land itself. However, a lease of the land itself, which also carries an implicit right to hunt, will be capable of being made a real right. If Arthur grants Boris a lease that says Boris can shoot pheasants on Arthur's farm, and then Arthur subsequently sells the farm to Colin, Boris will probably not be able to enforce his right to shoot pheasants against Colin. If, however, Arthur granted a lease of the farm itself to Boris which stated that Boris could shoot pheasants then Boris's lease could give him a real right to possess the farm, and, in turn, allow him to shoot pheasants even if Colin purchased the farm from Arthur. It may seem an odd way to draw a distinction, but that seems to be the law.

Fishing

9.34 While the right to fish is classically an incident of landownership, it is important to be aware of the statutory regulation of fishing. A riparian proprietor has a common law right to fish in their part of a non-tidal river, and in any part of a loch of which they own a part. This common law right to fish is dependent on ownership. A person cannot obtain a right to fish that is distinct from ownership by prescription, and nor can they fish in a river if they are lawfully (or unlawfully) on the bank of a river: demonstrated clearly in the *Arthur v Aird*, 1907 S.C. 1170 at 1172, per the Lord Justice-Clerk (Macdonald). Likewise, it is important to bear in mind that there can be separate tenements for fishing for salmon and the collection of certain shellfish. The right to fish for salmon also carries the lesser right to fish for trout as well—someone who holds a separate tenement of salmon fishing can also fish for trout. However, someone with the right to fish as an incident of landownership, which includes trout as well as other fish, will not be able to fish for salmon—the right to fish for trout is the lesser right. In the case of the separate tenement of the right to fish for salmon it has long been recognised that a lease may be granted over that right because it is a separate tenement. However, at common law it was less clear whether a lease of a mere right to fish for trout and other fish was competent, and, if it was, whether such a lease could give a real right. These uncertainties have been cleared up by statutory intervention. The Salmon and Freshwater Fisheries (Consolidation) (Scotland) Act 2003 governs much of the regulation of fishing in non-tidal waters in Scotland by stipulating how fishing should be conducted, the different ways that fishing rights are regulated, and the offences for fishing unlawfully. The statute makes clear that a lease of the right to fish is competent, and such a lease is capable of being made real under the Leases Act 1449, so long as it is in writing and is for a duration of one year or more: Salmon and Freshwater Fisheries (Consolidation) (Scotland) Act 2003 s.66.

WILDLIFE CONSERVATION

Historically, the only protection at common law for wildlife was the right **9.35** of a landowner to exclude trespassers from coming onto land to kill animals—of course, that meant that wildlife had no protection at all when it came to the actions of the landowner herself! In the modern law there are many statutory rules concerned with wildlife conservation and protection, which apply to landowners and the public at large: see the leading text: C.T. Reid, *Nature Conservation Law*, 3rd edn (2009). The main statute dealing with this area is the Wildlife and Countryside Act 1981, which is a statute that applies across the United Kingdom, though it has been amended by legislation of the Scottish Parliament. Parts I, II and IV apply to Scotland, and it is in Parts I and II that most of the substantive measures are found. Part I deals mainly with protection for certain birds, animals and plants. Part II, which in its application to Scotland was heavily amended by the Nature Conservation (Scotland) Act 2004, is concerned with habitats for animals and the need to ensure that there are special measures taken to facilitate flora and fauna. Furthermore, the Conservation (Natural Habitats, etc) Regulations 1994 implement a European Directive aimed at protecting animals and habitats that are of European significance. So, for example, in Scotland the Scottish Wild Cat is so rare that it is considered an endangered European species. All of these statutory rules relating to conservation will limit landowners' right to fish or hunt for game by placing a layer of criminal or public law across the property law.

RESTRICTIONS ON OWNERSHIP AT COMMON LAW

General

9.36 Ownership of land is not absolute in the sense that it once was. There are a number of burdens and restrictions that condition and qualify an individual's ownership of land; some arise at common law, while others are statutory. Some restrictions are the result of voluntary grant of a right by an owner, or one of their predecessors in title, while others are imposed by the law. All of these restrictions ultimately give other landowners, or the public at large, rights and protections against a landowner.

Aemulatio vicini

9.37 *Aemulatio vicini* is the name given to a situation where someone demonstrates malice or malevolence towards his neighbour. The importance of the concept is that it applies to actions undertaken by an owner that would be lawful but for the malicious motive underlying them. There is a tension between allowing a landowner to use their land as they wish and restricting their lawful activity. The law's insistence that there should be some form of malice partially addresses that problem, but what constitutes the requisite degree of malice necessary to trigger a restriction is not easy to define. There are, however, some cases that suggest some doubt about the extent of the rule. The dicta contained in a speech of a Scottish judge in a nineteenth century English appeal to the House of Lords seem to suggest that the principle of *aemulatio vicini* is severely limited in Scotland, and perhaps does not exist at all: *Bradford v Pickles* [1895] A.C. 587 at 597–598, per Lord Watson; see also *Canmore Housing Association Ltd v Bairnsfather (t/a BR Autos)*, 2004 S.L.T. 673 at [13], per Lord Brodie. Nevertheless, subsequent cases have accepted that the principle is part of Scots law. Thus, when an owner of salmon-fishings cast his line in a lawful manner but did so out of malice and simply to frustrate the efforts of another fisherman, he had acted in *aemulationem vicini*: *Campbell v Muir*, 1908 S.C. 387 at 393, per Lord President Dunedin. Likewise, a landowner who shut off a water pipe running through his property had clearly acted with actionable malice: *More v Boyle*, 1967 S.L.T. (Sh Ct) 38. If someone is found to have acted with actionable malice, then interdict can be sought or damages awarded.

Nuisance

9.38 The doctrine of nuisance is often taught as part of a property law course, though in many respects it is concerned with personal obligations generated by the law of delict. The law of nuisance occupies an awkward and sometimes confused space between delict and property law. The idea underlying nuisance is that those in lawful possession of land should not have their enjoyment of that land interfered with by the actions of another landowner. A classic example of a nuisance is where a neighbouring proprietor is conducting operations in a manner that causes excessive noise or pollution that prejudices a neighbour's enjoyment of their property: *Webster v Lord Advocate*, 1985 S.C. 173; *King v Advocate General for Scotland*, 2010 G.W.D. 1-15. In order to demonstrate an actionable nuisance, an aggrieved landowner must show that the acts constituting the nuisance are more than would be reasonably tolerable in that particular situation. A court will take all the circumstances into account when assessing if something is more than reasonably tolerable or not. The test of reasonable tolerability is an objective one, but it is contextualised by the specific facts of the case: *Chalmers v Diageo Scotland Ltd* [2017] CSOH 36. It is also necessary that the person who is causing the nuisance must in some way be at fault: *RHM Bakeries (Scotland) Ltd v Strathclyde Regional Council*, 1985 S.C. (HL) 17. The interaction between nuisance and negligence has been historically unstable, but a distinction may be drawn between intentional and unintentional acts here: see G.D.L. Cameron, "Making Sense of Nuisance in Scots Law" (2005) 56 NILQ 236 at 262. If the landowner's actions are intentional in the sense that their actions are taken with the knowledge that damage will or is likely to occur then the law of nuisance is applicable: *Kennedy v Glenbelle*, 1996 S.C. 95. If the landowner's actions are unintentional in the sense that they are taken against a background of ignorance about the damage that may occur or demonstrate some kind of recklessness or lack of care, then the law of negligence is applicable. One recent case that considered what degree of fault is necessary to ground an action in nuisance or negligence does not appear to draw such a distinction: *Black Loch Angling Club v Tarmac Ltd*, 2012 S.C.L.R. 501. However, a later case does seem to distinguish between an unintentional failure to take care that amounted to negligence and an intentional and positive act which invaded the aggrieved owner's interest to an extent which exceeded what was reasonably tolerable: *Cunningham v Cameron*, 2014 G.W.D. 3-69 at [41], per Lord Tyre. If an action for nuisance is raised it is a defence for the person causing the alleged nuisance if they had lawful authorisation to undertake the actions complained of, as it is to show acquiescence on the part of the aggrieved proprietor. It seems that a person loses their right to object to a nuisance by negative prescription after 20 years (Prescription and Limitation (Scotland) Act 1973 ss.7 and 8); however, there is a question whether the obligation to make reparation for a nuisance negatively prescribes after five or 20 years: Prescription and Limitation (Scotland) Act 1973 ss.6 and 7; see further G.D.L. Cameron et al, *Delict* (2007), para.14.68; *Chalmers v Diageo Scotland Ltd* [2017] CSOH 36. It is not clear if it is possible in Scotland to acquire a right to commit what would otherwise be a nuisance by positive prescription; but a recent decision of the United Kingdom Supreme Court has confirmed that it is possible in England: *Coventry (t/a RDC Promotions) v Lawrence* [2014] A.C. 822.

STATUTORY RESTRICTIONS ON OWNERSHIP

9.39 There are many different statutory restrictions affecting landownership, indeed there are far too many to consider in detail here. These legislative restrictions encompass domestic legislation and European measures. Some areas where there has been significant statutory intervention include town and country planning law, compulsory purchase, building control, housing law, public health law, environmental law and health and safety law. For a detailed, if somewhat dated, list of statutory restrictions affecting landownership see D.A. Brand, A.J.M. Steven and S. Wortley, *Professor McDonald's Conveyancing Manual*, 7th edn (2004), Ch.20.

LAND REFORM LEGISLATION

9.40 A major development in recent years has been the enactment of statutory provisions concerning land reform, particularly with regard to communities' right to buy schemes. The relevant legislation is the Land Reform (Scotland) Act 2003 (LR(S)A 2003), as amended by the Community Empowerment (Scotland) Act 2015 (CE(S)A 2015) and the Land Reform (Scotland) Act 2016 (LR(S)A 2016). If it is brought fully into force the CE(S)A 2015 will govern some significant areas of property law itself, as well as amending the LR(S)A 2003. The LR(S)A 2016 created the Scottish Land Commission and will, amongst other things, further regulate elements of right to buy schemes and agricultural property law. A conventional introductory book on property for students taking property law courses cannot do much more than highlight these developments, but they are important as well as politically and culturally sensitive. Those looking to read more on the subject should consult the following articles for excellent analysis and an overview of the subject: M.M. Combe, "The Land Reform (Scotland) Act 2016: another answer to the Scottish land question" [2016] Jur. Rev. 291; M.M. Combe, "The environmental implications of redistributive land reform" (2016) 18 *Environmental Law Review* 104; M.M. Combe, "Parts 2 and 3 of the Land Reform (Scotland) Act 2003: A Definitive Answer to the Scottish Land Question?" [2006] Jur. Rev. 195.

BIBLIOGRAPHY AND FURTHER READING

Anderson, C., *Possession of Corporeal Moveables* (Edinburgh: Edinburgh Legal Education Trust, 2015)

Anderson, C., *Property Law: A Guide to Scots Law* (Edinburgh: W. Green, 2016)

Anderson, R.G., *Assignation* (Edinburgh: Edinburgh Legal Education Trust, 2008)

Brand, D., "Property" in Ashton, C. et al., *Understanding Scots Law*, 2nd edn (Edinburgh: W. Green, 2012)

Carey Miller, D. and Irvine, D., *Corporeal Moveables in Scots Law*, 2nd edn (Edinburgh: W. Green, 2005)

Cusine, D.J. (ed.), *The Conveyancing Opinions of JM Halliday* (Edinburgh: W. Green, 1992)

Cusine, D.J. and Paisley, R., *Servitudes and Rights of Way* (Edinburgh: W. Green 1998)

Cusine, D.J. and Rennie, R., *Missives*, 2nd edn (Edinburgh: Butterworths, 1999)

Lord Eassie and MacQueen, H.L. (eds), *Gloag and Henderson's The Law of Scotland*, 14th edn (Edinburgh: W. Green, 2017)

Gordon, W.M., *Scottish Land Law*, 2nd edn (Edinburgh: W. Green, 1999)

Gordon, W.M. and Wortley, S., *Scottish Land Law*, 3rd edn (Edinburgh: W. Green, 2009)

Gretton, G.L. and Steven, A.J.M., *Property Trusts and Succession*, 3rd edn (Haywards Heath: Bloomsbury Professional, 2017)

Guthrie, T. *Scottish Property Law*, 2nd edn (Edinburgh: Tottel, 2005)

Halliday, J.M. and Talman, IJS, *Conveyancing Law and Practice*, 2nd edn (Edinburgh: W. Green, 1996–97)

Higgins, M., *Enforcement of Heritable Securities* (Edinburgh: W. Green, 2016)

Johnston, D., *Prescription and Limitation*, 2nd edn (Edinburgh: W. Green, 2012)

McAllister, A., *Scottish Law of Leases*, 4th edn (Haywards Heath: Bloomsbury, 2013)

McDonald, A.J. et al., *Professor McDonald's Conveyancing Manual*, 7th edn (Edinburgh: Tottel, 2004)

Paisley, R., *Land Law* (Edinburgh: W. Green, 2000)

Rankine, J., *The Law of Land-ownership in Scotland*, 4th edn (Edinburgh: W. Green, 1909)

Reid, K.G.C., *The Abolition of Feudal Tenure in Scotland* (Edinburgh: Butterworths, 2003)

Reid, K.G.C., *The Law of Property in Scotland* (Edinburgh: Butterworths, 1996)

Reid, K.G.C. and Gretton, G.L., *Conveyancing*, 4th edn (Edinburgh: W. Green, 2011)

Reid, K.G.C. and Gretton, G.L., *Land Registration* (Edinburgh: Avizandum Publishing Ltd, 2017)

Reid, K.G.C. and Zimmermann, R. (eds), *A History of Private Law in Scotland* (Oxford: OUP, 2000)

Rennie, R. (ed.), *The Promised Land: Property Law Reform* (Edinburgh: W. Green, 2008)

Rennie, R., *Land Tenure in Scotland* (Edinburgh: W. Green, 2004)

Rennie, R., *Land Tenure Reform* (Edinburgh: W. Green, 2003)

Rennie, R. et al., *Leases* (Edinburgh: W. Green/SULI, 2015)
Robbie, J., *Private Water Rights* (Edinburgh: Edinburgh Legal Education Trust, 2015)
Robson P. and McCowan, A., *Property Law*, 2nd edn (Edinburgh: W. Green, 1998)
Sinclair, E.F.F. and Stewart, A.E.A., *Conveyancing Practice in Scotland*, 6th edn (Haywards Heath: Bloomsbury Professional, 2011)

INDEX

Abandoned property
  acquisition of corporeal moveable
      property, 3.06
  Civic Government (Scotland) Act
      1982, 3.08
  meaning, 3.06
Access rights to land
  be on land, right to, 9.13
  commercial or profit purposes, 9.16
  core paths, 9.23
  cross land, right to, 9.13
  educational activity, 9.15
  enforcement, 9.22–9.23
  inshore waters, 9.13
  Land Reform (Scotland) Act 2003,
      9.13–9.16
  landownership, 9.13–9.23
  limitations
      curtilage, 9.17
      designated land, 9.17–9.18
      nature of the land, 9.17
      privacy, 9.19
      responsible exercise of rights,
          9.20
      specific restrictions, 9.21
      structures, 9.17
  local authority enforcement, 9.23
  nature of the land, 9.17
  notice to landowner, 9.23
  privacy, 9.19
  public rights of access, 9.13–9.16
  recreational purposes, 9.14
  responsible exercise of rights, 9.20
  Scottish Outdoor Access Code,
      9.13–9.16
  specified purposes, 9.13–9.16
  types of right, 9.13
Accession
  accessory becomes part of the
      principal, 3.16
  adornment test, 3.22
  alluvion, 3.23
  avulsion, 3.23
  buildings, 3.10, 3.21
  ceasing to exist test, 3.22
  compensation, 3.20
  consequences
      accessory becomes part of the
          principal, 3.16
      compensation, 3.20
      conversion, 3.17
      loss of title by owner of
          accessory, 3.18
      mechanical process, 3.15

  severance, 3.19
  conversion, 3.17
  corporeal moveable property, 3.09
  crops, trees and plants, 3.25
  customs, 3.21
  decorative items, 3.22
  degree of attachment, 3.21
  example, 3.10
  fittings, 3.21
  fixtures, 3.21
  fruits
      crops, trees and plants, 3.25
      meaning, 3.24
      natural products, 3.27
      young animals, 3.26
  functional subordination, 3.13, 3.21
  general factors, 3.11–3.14
  heritable property to heritable
      property, 3.23
  identification of principal thing, 3.22
  loss of title by owner of accessory,
      3.18
  mechanical process, 3.15
  moveable property to heritable
      property, 3.21
  mutual adaptation, 3.21
  natural products, 3.27
  permanency, 3.14, 3.21
  physical attachment, 3.12
  severance, 3.19
  types
      fruits, 3.24–3.27
      heritable property to heritable
          property, 3.23
      moveable property to heritable
          property, 3.21
      moveable property to moveable
          property, 3.22
  young animals, 3.26
Accretion
  derivative acquisition, 4.10
  exception to *nemo plus* rule, 4.10
  heritable property, 4.10
  links in title, 4.10
  meaning, 4.10
  midcouples, 4.10
Acquiescence
  encroachments, 9.07
  extinction of servitudes, 6.18
  real burdens, 5.3
Acquisition
  see also **Accession; Derivative
      acquisition; Specification**
  commixtion, 3.31

confusion, 3.31
corporeal moveable property, 3.09
Aemulatio vicini
landownership, 9.37
Affirmative burdens
real burdens, 5.03–5.08
Airspace
boundaries, 2.08
trespass, 2.08, 9.10
Alluvion
accession, 3.23
Alterations
common ownership, 2.22
Animals
accession, 3.23
poaching, 3.04
trespass, 9.09, 9.12
wild animals, 3.03, 3.04
Animus transferendi dominii
derivative acquisition, 4.01
Application record
Land Register, 4.32
Archive record
Land Register, 4.32
Assignation
deeds, 4.18
derivative acquisition, 4.16–4.19
effect, 4.20
incorporeal moveable property,
4.16–4.19
intimation, 4.19
leases, 7.37, 7.38
meaning, 4.18, 7.37
prohibition, 4.16
transfer process, 4.17–4.19
Avulsion
accession, 3.23
Bills of lading
delivery, 4.12
Boundaries
see also **Encroachments; Trespass**
airspace, 2.08
horizontal boundaries, 2.05–2.06
land Register, 2.05–2.09
landownership
discernment of boundaries, 9.03
encroachments, 9.06–9.08
horizontal boundaries, 2.05–
2.06
march stones, 9.03
markers, 9.04, 9.05
vertical boundaries, 2.07–2.09
march stones, 9.03
pipelines, 2.09
tenements, 8.02, 8.03
vertical boundaries, 2.07–2.09

Cadastral map
Land Register, 4.32
Ordnance Survey maps, 4.32
Capacity
natural persons, 1.03
Chimney stacks
tenements, 8.04
Co-ownership
see also **Ownership**
common ownership
examples, 2.19
generally, 2.18
meaning, 2.17
rationale, 2.17
types, 2.18
Coelo usque ad centrum
landownership, 2.07
Commercial use
access rights to land, 9.16
real burdens, 5.02
Commixtion
acquisition, 3.31
corporeal moveable property, 3.31
meaning, 3.31
Common ownership
alterations, 2.22
characteristics, 2.20
examples, 2.19
generally, 2.18
illegal acts, 2.24
legal acts, 2.23
legal shares, 2.20
meaning, 2.18
possession, 2.21
pro indiviso shares, 2.20
repairs, 2.22
termination, 2.25
Community burdens
extinction, 5.35
types of real burdens, 5.07
Companies
legal personality, 1.03
Compensation
accession, 3.20
specification, 3.30
Compulsory purchase
extinction of servitudes, 6.18
Confusion
acquisition, 3.31
corporeal moveable property, 3.31
extinction of servitudes, 6.18
meaning, 3.31
servitudes, 6.02
Consent
derivative acquisition, 4.01
encroachments, 9.07
trespass, 9.10

Contracts
  personal rights, 1.05
Conversion
  accession, 3.17
Core paths
  access rights to land, 9.23
Corporeal moveable property
  delivery, 4.12
  derivative acquisition, 4.11–4.14
  gifts, 4.12
  meaning, 1.12, 1.13
  original acquisition
    abandoned property, 3.06
    accession, 3.09
    commixtion, 3.31
    concept, 3.01
    confusion, 3.31
    lost property, 3.05
    meaning, 3.01
    occupation, 3.02–3.04
    poaching, 3.04
    specification, 3.28–3.30
    wild animals, 3.03, 3.04
  sale, 4.13
Creation
  real burdens, 5.09–5.16
Crown
  feudalism, 1.17
  landownership
    feudalism, 1.17
    ownerless property, 1.18
  lost property, 3.07
  ownerless property, 1.18
  praediality, 5.11
  prerogative, 1.18
  regalia majora, 1.18, 1.19, 2.15
  regalia minora, 2.16
Customs
  accession, 3.21
Damages
  leases, 7.28
  trespass, 9.11
Delict
  personal rights, 1.05
Delivery
  actual delivery, 4.12
  bills of lading, 4.12
  gifts, 4.12
  meaning, 4.12
  symbolic delivery, 4.12
Derivative acquisition
  absolutely good title, 4.04
  accretion, 4.10
  animus transferendi dominii, 4.01
  assignation, 4.16
  compulsion, 4.01
  concept, 4.01–4.10

consent, 4.01
contract and conveyance
  distinguished, 4.01, 4.02
  corporeal moveable property, 4.11–
    4.14
  delivery, 4.12
  example, 4.01
  first in time, stronger by right, 4.08
  heritable property
    conveyance, 4.23
    disposition, 4.23
    general principles, 4.21
    missives, 4.22
    public act, 4.24
    registration, 4.24
    registration of land, 4.25–4.26
    stages of transfer, 4.22–4.24
  incorporeal moveable property
    assignation, 4.16–4.19
    concept, 4.15
    delegation, 4.16
    process of transfer, 4.17–4.19
    transferability, 4.16
  intention of parties, 4.01
  intimation, 4.03
  meaning, 3.01
  missives, 4.22
  moveable property
    corporeal moveables, 4.11–4.14
    delivery, 4.12
    exceptions to the *nemo plus*
      rule, 4.14
    gifts, 4.12
    incorporeal moveables, 4.15–
      4.20
    sale, 4.13
  nemo plus juris ad alium transferre
    potest quam ipse haberet, 4.07
  offside goals rule, 4.09
  principles, 4.01–4.10
  prior tempore est potior jure, 4.08
  public acts, 4.03
  publicity principle, 4.03
  quality of title, 4.07–4.08
  survival of real right post-transfer,
    4.09
  title, 4.04–4.07
  transfers, 4.01
  void title, 4.04, 4.05
  voidable title, 4.04, 4.06
Destruction
  extinction of servitudes, 6.18
Discharge
  extinction of servitudes, 6.18
Disponing property
  feudalism, 1.18

Dominium directum
  landownership, 1.17
Dominium eminens
  landownership, 1.17
Dominium utile
  landownership, 1.17, 1.18
Education
  access rights to land, 9.15
Encroachments
  acquiescence, 9.07
  consent, 9.07
  defences, 9.07
  examples, 9.06
  failure to object, 9.07
  interdict, 9.08
  landownership, 9.06–9.08
  meaning, 9.06
  nature of encroachment, 9.06
  ownership, 9.07
  remedies, 9.08
  removal, 9.08
  self-help, 9.08
Enforcement
  access rights to land, 9.22–9.23
  real burdens
    community burdens, 5.07
    interest, 5.17, 5.19
    title, 5.17, 5.18
    Tenement Management Schemes,
      8.10
Express servitudes
  see **Servitudes**
Extinction
  community burdens, 5.35
  real burdens
    acquiescence, 5.3
    community burdens, 5.35
    express discharge, 5.34
    negative prescription, 5.37
    sunset rule, 5.36
    termination, 5.35
  servitudes, 6.18
Facility burdens
  identification of benefited property,
    5.30
  types of real burdens, 5.08
Feudalism
  abolition, 1.18, 1.21
  chains of interests, 1.17
  conceptual basis, 1.16, 1.17
  conversion of burdens, 1.19
  Crown, 1.17
  disponing property, 1.18
  feudal lords, 1.16
  hierarchy, 1.16–1.17
  heritable property, 1.16–1.19
  influence, 1.16–1.19

  landownership, 5.03
  law reform, 1.21
  legal history, 1.16–1.19
  perpetual lease analogy, 1.17
  real burdens, 1.19, 5.01
  reddendo, 1.17
  registration, 1.20
  subinfeudation, 1.17
  theory, 1.16
Fire escapes
  tenements, 8.04
Fishing rights
  landownership, 9.28, 9.34
  leasing the right to fish, 9.34
  non-tidal waters, 9.34
  tidal waters, 9.28
Fittings
  accession, 3.21
Fixtures
  accession, 3.21
Flats
  tenements, 8.02
Foreshore
  landownership, 9.26
  tidal waters, 9.26
Fruits
  accession
    crops, trees and plants, 3.25
    meaning, 3.24
    natural products, 3.27
    young animals, 3.26
Game
  flushing out, 9.32
  generally, 9.31
  landownership, 9.31–9.33
  leasing the interest, 9.33
  pursuit of game, 9.32
General Register of Sasines
  bounding descriptions, 2.06
  effect of recording a deed, 4.27
  evidential value, 4.27
  general descriptions, 2.06
  General Register of Sasines, 1.20
  horizontal boundaries, 2.06
  instrument of sasine, 1.20
  Keeper, 4.27
  landownership
    boundaries, 2.06
    registration, 1.20
  phasing out, 4.30
  positive prescription, 4.27
  prescription, 2.06
  purpose, 4.27
  recording of deeds, 4.27
  searches, 4.27
Good faith
  registration, 4.39

specification, 3.29, 3.30
Heritable property
see also **Moveable property**
accession, 3.23
accretion, 4.10
alluvion, 3.23
derivative acquisition
conveyance, 4.23
disposition, 4.23
general principles, 4.21
missives, 4.22
public act, 4.24
registration, 4.24
registration of land, 4.25–4.26
stages of transfer, 4.22–4.24
feudal system, 1.16–1.19
immoveable property, 1.10
inheritance, 1.10
leases
creation, 7.03
legal history, 1.15–1.19
meaning, 1.10–1.13
missives, 4.22
nature of, 1.10–1.13
Human rights
property law, 1.23
Hypothec
leases, 7.34
Illegality
real burdens, 5.13
Immoveable property
meaning, 1.10
Implied rights
enforcement of real burdens, 5.17–5.18
Implied servitudes
see also **Servitudes**
Incorporeal moveable property
see also **Corporeal moveable property**
assignation, 4.16–4.19
derivative acquisition
assignation, 4.16–4.19
concept, 4.15
delegation, 4.16
process of transfer, 4.17–4.19
transferability, 4.16
meaning, 1.12, 1.13, 4.15
transferability, 4.16
Inshore waters
access rights to land, 9.13
Insolvency
real rights, 1.07
Intention
corporeal moveable property, 4.11–4.15
derivative acquisition, 4.01, 4.11–

4.15
leases, 7.19
possession, 2.30
Inter naturalia
leases, 7.17
Interdict
encroachments, 9.08
leases, 7.27
trespass, 9.11
Intimation
derivative acquisition, 4.03
Irreversible process
specification, 3.29
Irritancy
leases, 7.35
Joint ownership
meaning, 2.18
types of joint property, 2.26
unincorporated associations, 2.26
Juristic persons
meaning, 1.03
Jus commune
Roman law, 1.14
Jus utendi, freundi and abudendi
ownership, 2.02
Land Register
see also **Registration**
administration, 4.32
application record, 4.32
archive record, 4.32
boundaries, 2.05–2.09
cadastral map, 4.32
components, 4.32
coverage, 4.29
electronic registration, 4.29
inaccuracy, 4.36
increased use, 4.29
landownership
boundaries, 2.05–2.09
registration, 4.28
manifest inaccuracy, 4.37
rectification, 4.37
reduction, 4.41
registration, 4.28, 4.29, 4.30
sections, 4.32
title sheet, 4.32
Landownership
see also **Land Register;**
   Ownership; Registration;
   Trespass; Water rights
access rights to land, 9.13–9.23
aemulatio vicini, 9.37
boundaries
discernment of boundaries, 9.03
encroachments, 9.06–9.08
horizontal boundaries, 2.05–2.06

march stones, 9.03
markers, 9.04, 9.05
vertical boundaries, 2.07–2.09
coelo usque ad centrum, 2.07
Crown, 1.18, 2.14–2.16
disponing property, 1.18
dominium directum, 1.17
dominium eminens, 1.17
dominium utile, 1.17, 1.18
encroachments, 9.06–9.08
extent
  Crown rights, 2.14–2.16
  horizontal boundaries, 2.05–
    2.06
  vertical boundaries, 2.07–2.09
fishing rights, 9.28, 9.34
foreshore, 9.26
game, 9.31–9.33
law reform, 9.40
legal separate tenements, 2.13
lochs, 9.30
nuisance, 9.38
ownerless property, 1.18
pertinents, 2.10
reddendo, 1.17
register of Sasines
  registration, 1.20
registration
  concept, 1.20
  feudalism, 1.20
  importance of registration, 1.20
  taking infeftment, 1.20
restrictions at common law
  aemulatio vicini, 9.37
  generally, 9.36
  nuisance, 9.38
restrictions, statutory, 9.39
separate tenements
  conventional separate
    tenements, 2.12
  legal separate tenements, 2.13
  meaning, 2.11
statutory restrictions, 9.39
support, 9.02
wildlife conservation, 8.35
Law reform
feudalism, 1.21
land reform, 9.40
registration, 4.26, 4.28, 4.29
right to buy, 9.40
Scottish Law Commission, 1.21
Leases
action for payment, 7.29
agreement to create lease, 7.04
assignation, 7.37, 7.38
concept, 7.01
continuing obligations, 7.26

contractual basis, 7.01
creation
  agreement to create lease, 7.04
  consensus, 7.04
  contractual agreement, 7.04
  duration of lease, 7.05–7.06
  elements, 7.02
  general rules, 7.02
  heritable property, 7.03
  identification of subject matter,
    7.03
  rent, 7.07
  writing requirement, 7.02
damages, 7.28
duration of lease, 7.05–7.06
heritable property
  creation, 7.03
hypothec, 7.34
identification of subject matter, 7.03
implement, 7.27
implied terms
  intention of parties, 7.19
  nominate contract, lease as, 7.19
  possession, 7.20
incorporeal heritable rights, 7.03
inter naturalia, 7.17
interdict, 7.27
irritancy, 7.35
Leases Act 1449, 7.09–7.12
long leases, 7.15
meaning, 7.01
offside goals rule, 7.18
plenishings, 7.21
possession, 7.13–7.14, 7.16, 7.20
purpose, 7.01
real rights
  consequences, 7.16–7.18
  generally, 7.08
  inter naturalia, 7.17
  Leases Act 1449, 7.09–7.12
  long leases, 7.15
  offside goals rule, 7.18
  possession, 7.13–7.14, 7.16
  Registration of Leases
    (Scotland) Act 1857, 7.15
  short leases, 7.09–7.12
  statutory regulation, 7.08–7.15
reasonably fit for purposes of let,
  7.23–7.24
registration, 4.31
Registration of Leases (Scotland)
  Act 1857, 7.15
remedies
  action for payment, 7.29
  available to tenant and landlord,
    7.26–7.32
  damages, 7.28

hypothec, 7.34
implement, 7.27
interdict, 7.27
irritancy, 7.35
landlord only, 7.33–7.36
removal of the tenant, 7.36
rescission, 7.30–7.31
retention, 7.32
removal of the tenant, 7.36
rent
    creation, 7.07
    meaning, 7.01
    terms of lease, 7.22
rescission, 7.30–7.31
retention, 7.32
rights and duties of landlord and
    tenant
    continuing obligations, 7.25
    express terms, 7.19
    implied terms, 7.19, 7.20–7.25
    plenishings, 7.21
    possession, 7.20
    reasonably fit for purposes of
        let, 7.23–7.24
    rent, 7.22
short leases, 7.09–7.12
subletting, 7.37, 7.39–7.40
tacit relocation, 7.42
termination
    end date of lease, 7.41
    notice, 7.41
    tacit relocation, 7.42
terms of lease
    continuing obligations, 7.26
    contractual basis, 7.19
    express terms, 7.19
    implied terms, 7.19
    intention of parties, 7.19
    interaction between express and
        implied terms, 7.19
    plenishings, 7.21
    possession, 7.20
    reasonably fit for purposes of
        let, 7.23–7.25
    rent, 7.22
types, 7.01
use, 7.01
Legal history
    common law, 1.14
    feudalism, 1.16–1.19
    heritable property, 1.15–1.19
    Latin maxims, 1.14
    law of property, 1.14
    law reform, 1.21
    overview, 1.14
    registration, 1.20
    Roman law, 1.14

Legal personality
    companies, 1.03
    examples, 1.03
    meaning, 1.03
    partnerships, 1.03
Legal philosophy
    justification for property, 1.01
Legal separate tenements
    landownership, 2.13
Letters of obligation
    registration, 4.33
Lifts
    tenements, 8.04
Livestock
    real burdens, 5.02
Loans
    personal rights, 1.05
Lochs
    landownership, 9.30
    water rights, 9.30
Long leases
    Registration of Leases (Scotland)
        Act 1857, 7.15
Lost property
    abandonment, 3.07
    Civic Government (Scotland) Act
        1982, 3.08
    Crown, 3.07
    meaning, 3.06, 3.07
Maintenance
    real burdens, 5.02
March stones
    boundaries, 9.03
Missives
    heritable property, 4.22
Moveable property
    see also **Heritable property**
    accession, 3.22
    corporeal moveable property
        accession, 3.33
        commixtion, 3.31
        confusion, 3.31
        original acquisition, 3.02–3.04
        specification, 3.28–3.30
    derivative acquisition
        corporeal moveables, 4.11–4.14
        delivery, 4.12
        gifts, 4.12
    meaning, 1.10–1.13
    nature of, 1.10–1.13
Natural persons
    capacity, 1.03
    meaning, 1.03
Navigation rights
    tidal waters, 9.27
Negative burdens
    real burdens, 5.04

Negative servitudes
 meaning, 6.03
Nemo plus juris ad alium transferre potest quam ipse haberet
 exceptions to the rule, 4.14
 title, 4.07
Notice
 termination of lease, 7.41
Nuisance
 landownership, 9.38
Numerus clausus **principle**
 real rights, 1.08
Occupation
 original acquisition, 3.02–3.04
Offside goals rule
 derivative acquisition, 4.09
 leases, 7.18
Ordnance Survey maps
 cadastral map, 4.32
 registration, 4.28
Ownerless things
 Crown, 1.18
 possession, 2.35
Ownership
 ancient origins of concept, 2.02
 co-ownership
  common ownership, 2.18, 2.19–2.25
  meaning, 2.17
  types, 2.18
 common ownership
  alterations, 2.22
  characteristics, 2.20
  generally, 2.18
  illegal acts, 2.24
  legal acts, 2.23
  legal shares, 2.20
  meaning, 2.18
  possession, 2.21
  pro indiviso shares, 2.20
  repairs, 2.22
  termination, 2.25
 concept of ownership, 2.01–2.03
 horizontal boundaries, 2.05–2.06
 joint ownership
  meaning, 2.18
  types of joint property, 2.26
  unincorporated associations, 2.26
 jus utendi, freundi and abudendi, 2.02
 key elements, 2.01–2.02
 limitations, 2.03
 modern concept, 2.03
 physical extent
  generally, 2.04
  horizontal boundaries, 2.05–2.06

 vertical boundaries, 2.07–2.09
 real rights, 2.01, 2.02
 tenements, 8.03
 vertical boundaries, 2.07–2.09
Partnerships
 legal personality, 1.03
Paths
 tenements, 8.04
Personal burdens
 types of real burdens, 5.06
Personal rights
 contracts, 1.05
 creation, 1.05
 delict, 1.05
 enforceability, 1.05
 generally, 1.04
 loans, 1.05
 meaning, 1.05
 unjustified enrichment, 1.05
Persons
 legal persons, 1.03
 meaning, 1.03
 natural persons, 1.03
Pertinents
 meaning, 2.10
 tenements, 2.10
Plenishings
 leases, 7.21
Poaching
 original acquisition, 3.04
Positive prescription
 registration, 4.40
Positive servitudes
 meaning, 6.03
Possession
 acquisition
  animus, 2.30
  civil possession, 2.31
  corpus, 2.29
  intention, 2.30
  mental element, 2.30
  natural possession, 2.31
  physical detention, 2.29
  recognition, 2.28
 civil possession, 2.31
 common ownership, 2.21
 concept, 2.27
 continued possession, 2.33
 importance, 2.35
 intention, 2.30
 leases, 7.13–7.14, 7.16, 7.20
 linguistics, 2.27
 loss of possession, 2.33
 maintaining possession, 2.32
 meaning, 2.27
 mental element, 2.30
 natural possession, 2.31

occupancy, 2.35
ownerless things, 2.35
physical control, 2.29
prescription, 2.35
right to possess, 2.34
rights to possession, 2.27
role, 2.35
security, 2.35
spuilzie, 2.35
things, 2.27
Praedial
real burdens, 5.06, 5.11
Prescription
possession, 2.35
servitudes
creation, 6.12
extinction, 6.18
Prior tempore est potior jure
derivative acquisition, 4.08
Privacy
access rights to land, 9.19
trespass in airspace, 2.08
Property
classification
corporeal property, 1.12, 1.13
heritable, 1.10–1.13
incorporeal, 1.12, 1.13
moveable property, 1.10–1.13
concept, 1.02
philosophical justifications, 1.01
terminology, 1.02
use of term, 1.02
Property law
human rights, 1.23
law reform, 1.21
nature, 1.01
sources, 1.22
Public access to land
see **Access rights to land**
Public policy
real burdens, 5.12
Publicity principle
derivative acquisition, 4.03
Railways
trespass, 9.09
Real burdens
abolition of feudal tenure, 1.19
acquiescence, 5.37
affirmative burdens, 5.04
ancillary burdens, 5.05
benefited property, 5.02, 5.20–5.33
building obligation, 5.02
burdened property, 5.02
codification, 5.01
commercial use, 5.02
community burdens, 5.07, 5.35
converted feudal burdens, 5.31

creation, 5.09–5.16
definition, 5.02
discharge, 5.34
enforcement, 5.17–5.18
Equality Act 2010, 5.13
examples, 5.02
express discharge, 5.33
express identification, 5.23
extinction
acquiescence, 5.37
community burdens, 5.35
express discharge, 5.34
negative prescription, 5.37
sunset rule, 5.36
termination, 5.35
facility burdens, 5.29
feudal burdens, 5.03
feudalism, 1.19, 5.01
fixed list, 5.10
formalities
dual registered deed, 5.14
four corners of the deed, 5.16
real burden, 5.15
generally, 5.03
good condition, property to be kept
in, 5.02
identification of benefited property
burdens created after November
28, 2004, 5.21
burdens created before
November 28, 2004,
5.22–5.33
converted feudal burdens, 5.31
express identification, 5.23
facility burdens, 5.29
non-feudal burdens not part of a
common scheme, 5.32,
5.33
related property in a common
scheme, 5.24–5.25
requirements, 5.20
service burdens, 5.30
subdivision, 5.27
unrelated properties in a
common scheme, 5.26–
5.28
illegality, 5.13
livestock, 5.02
maintenance, 5.02
meaning, 5.02
negative burdens, 5.04
negative prescription, 5.37
non-feudal burdens, 5.03
obligations, 5.02
permissible content, 5.10–5.13
prohibitions, 5.02
related property in a common

scheme, 5.24–5.25
repugnancy with ownership, 5.13
service burdens, 5.08, 5.30
statutory developments, 5.01
subdivision, 5.27
sunset rule, 5.36
termination, 5.35
types
    affirmative burdens, 5.04
    ancillary burdens, 5.05
    community burdens, 5.07
    facility burdens, 5.08
    feudal burdens, 5.03
    negative burdens, 5.04
    non-feudal burdens, 5.03
    personal burdens, 5.03, 5.06
    praedial burdens, 5.06
    service burdens, 5.08
unrelated properties in a common
    scheme, 5.26–5.28

Real rights
see also **Ownership**
creation, 1.08
effect, 1.06, 1.07, 1.08
example, 1.07
fixed list, 1.08
generally, 1.04
insolvency, 1.07
meaning, 1.06
numerus clausus principle, 1.08
primary real rights, 1.06
rules governing use of a thing, 1.06
subordinate real rights, 1.06
things, 1.06
types, 1.06

Recreation
access rights to land, 9.14

Rectification
Land Register, 4.37
registration, 4.28, 4.37, 4.41

Reddendo
feudalism, 1.17
landownership, 1.17

Reduction
registration, 4.41

Regalia majora
Crown, 1.18, 1.19, 2.15

Regalia minora
Crown, 2.16

Registrable deeds
registration, 4.30

Registration
see also **General Register of**
    Sasines
advance notice, 4.33
application to register, 4.31
conditions for registration, 4.31

creation of system, 4.26
disposition, 4.30
effect, 4.28
effect of application, 4.32–4.35
electronic registration, 4.29
example, 4.35
gaps in stages of transfer of
    ownership, 4.34
generally, 4.25
good faith, 4.39
historical development, 4.26
inaccuracy, 4.36
introduction of registration of title,
    4.26, 4.28
Keeper's warranty, 4.38
Land Register, 4.28, 4.29, 4.30
Land Registration etc. (Scotland)
    Act 2012, 4.29
Land Registration (Scotland) Act
    1979, 4.28, 4.29
landownership
    concept, 1.20
    feudalism, 1.20
    importance of registration, 1.20
    taking infeftment, 1.20
law reform, 4.26, 4.28, 4.29
leases, 4.31
legal effects of application, 4.33–
    4.35
legal history, 1.20
letters of obligation, 4.33
nature of deed to be registered, 4.31
non-protected deeds, 4.33
obtaining registration, 4.30–4.31
Ordnance Survey maps, 4.28
positive prescription, 4.40
protected period, 4.33
ranking of applications, 4.33
rectification, 4.28, 4.37, 4.41
reduction, 4.41
registrable deeds, 4.30
standard securities, 4.31
timing of application, 4.33
transfer of ownership, 4.30–4.31
transferors in possession, 4.39
unregistered land, 4.31

Remedies
damages, 7.28, 9.11
encroachments, 9.08
interdict
    encroachment, 9.08
    leases, 7.27
    trespass, 9.11
leases
    action for payment, 7.29
    available to tenant and landlord,
        7.26–7.32

damages, 7.28
hypothec, 7.34
implement, 7.27
interdict, 7.27
irritancy, 7.35
landlord only, 7.33–7.36
removal of the tenant, 7.36
rescission, 7.30–7.31
retention, 7.32
self-help, 9.08, 9.11
trespass, 9.11
Rent
leases
creation, 7.07
rights and duties of landlord and
tenant, 7.22
meaning, 7.01
short leases, 7.12
Repairs
common ownership, 2.22
Rescission
leases, 7.30–7.31
Retention
leases, 7.32
Rights
meaning, 1.04
personal rights, 1.04, 1.05
real rights, 1.04, 1.06
Rivers
landownership, 9.29
water rights, 9.29
Roman law
influence, 1.14
jus commune, 1.14
specification, 3.28
Scottish Law Commission
law reform, 1.21
Scottish Outdoor Access Code
access rights to land, 9.13–9.16
Security
possession, 2.35
Self-help
encroachments, 9.08
trespass, 9.11
Service burdens
identification of benefited property,
5.30
meaning, 5.30
real burdens, 5.08, 5.30
types of real burdens, 5.08
Servitudes
acquiescence, 6.18
benefited property
duties, 6.15
exercise of servitude, 6.14–6.15
requirement, 6.01
rights, 6.14

burdened property
duties, 6.17
exercise, 6.16–6.17
requirement, 6.01
rights, 6.16
compulsory purchase, 6.18
confusion, 6.02
creation
express creation, 6.07–6.08
express grant, 6.07
express reservation, 6.08
implied creation, 6.09–6.11
implied grant, 6.10
implied reservation, 6.11
prescription, 6.12
destruction, 6.18
duties
benefited property, 6.15
burdened property, 6.17
elements
known to the law, 6.06
praediality, 6.04
repugnancy with ownership, 6.05
exercise
benefited property, 6.14–6.15
burdened property, 6.16–6.17
duties of owner of benefited
property, 6.14
general rules, 6.13
rights of owner of benefited
property, 6.14
express discharge, 6.18
express grant, 6.07
express reservation, 6.08
extinction, 6.18
grant
express grant, 6.07
implied grant, 6.10
implied creation, 6.09–6.11
implied grant, 6.10
known to the law, 6.06
meaning, 6.01
negative prescription, 6.18
negative servitudes, 6.03
parking, 6.05
positive servitudes, 6.03
prescription, 6.12
repugnancy with ownership, 6.05
reservation
express reservation, 6.08
implied reservation, 6.11
rights
benefited property, 6.14
burdened property, 6.16
use for other purposes, 6.15
Severance
accession, 3.19

Short leases
    duration, 7.11
    Leases Act 1449, 7.09–7.12
    rent, 7.12
Sources of law
    legislation, 1.22
    property law, 1.22
Specification
    advance agreement, 3.28
    compensation, 3.30
    concept, 3.28
    corporeal moveable property, 3.28–
        3.30
    examples, 3.28
    good faith, 3.29, 3.30
    irreversible process, 3.29
    meaning, 3.28
    new thing, creation of, 3.28
    requirements, 3.29
    Roman law, 3.28
    unjustified enrichment, 3.30
    workmanship, 3.29
Spuilzie
    possession, 2.35
Standard securities
    registration, 4.31
Subletting
    creation of sublease, 7.40
    leases, 7.37, 7.39–7.40
    meaning, 7.37, 7.39
Support
    duty to support, 9.02
    landownership, 9.02
Tacit relocation
    leases, 7.42
Tangible property
    corporeal moveable property
    accession, 3.09
    commixtion, 3.31
    confusion, 3.31
    original acquisition, 3.02–3.04
    specification, 3.28–3.30
Tenements
    background, 8.01
    boundaries, 8.02, 8.03
    chimney stacks, 8.04
    close, the, 8.04
    common stairs, 8.04
    costs of scheme, 8.09
    definition, 8.02
    divisions, 8.02, 8.03
    fire escapes, 8.04
    flats, 8.02
    horizontal boundaries, 8.02
    lifts, 8.04
    maintenance, 8.06–8.10
    management, 8.06–8.10

    meaning, 8.02
    ownership, 8.03
    paths, 8.04
    pertinents, 8.04
    requirements, 8.02
    service test, 8.04
    support, 8.05
    Tenement Management Schemes
        costs of scheme, 8.09
        decisions, 8.07–8.10
        default rules, 8.06, 8.08
        enforcement, 8.10
        insurance cover, 8.08
        introduction of, 8.06
        maintenance, 8.08
        ownership of parts, 8.06
        procedure, 8.07
        rationale, 8.07
        scheme decisions, 8.07–8.10
        scheme property, 8.06
        substance of scheme decisions,
            8.08
        voting, 8.07
    title deeds, 8.03
    vertical boundaries, 8.02
Things
    classification, 1.09
    examples, 1.02
    meaning, 1.02
    possession, 2.27
    real rights, 1.06
Tidal waters
    fishing rights, 9.28
    foreshore, 9.26
    nature of tidal waters, 9.25
    navigation rights, 9.27
Title
    absolutely good title, 4.04
    derivative acquisition, 4.04–4.07
    *nemo plus juris ad alium transferre
        potest quam ipse haberet*, 4.07
    quality of title, 4.07–4.08
    void title, 4.04, 4.05
    voidable title, 4.04–4.06
Trespass
    access rights, 9.10
    aggravated trespass, 9.09
    airspace, 2.08, 9.10
    animals, 9.09, 9.12
    assembly, trespassory, 9.09
    authorised entry, 9.10
    consent, 9.10
    damages, 9.11
    defences, 9.10
    interdict, 9.11
    landownership, 9.09–9.12
    lawful authorisations, 9.10

meaning, 9.09
nature of trespass, 9.09
pipelines, 2.09
railways, 9.09
remedies, 9.11
self-help, 9.11
use of force, 9.11
warnings to leave, 9.11
Unincorporated associations
joint ownership, 2.26
Unjustified enrichment
personal rights, 1.05
specification, 3.30
Unregistered land
registration, 4.31
Use of force
trespass, 9.11
Water rights
fishing rights, 9.28
foreshore, 9.26
generally, 9.24
lochs, 9.30
non-tidal waters
fishing, 9.34
lochs, 9.30
rivers, 9.29
rivers, 9.29
tidal waters
fishing rights, 9.28
foreshore, 9.26
nature of tidal waters, 9.25
navigation rights, 9.27
Wild animals
original acquisition, 3.03–3.04
poaching, 3.04
Wildlife conservation
landownership, 8.35